STRESS, CULTURE, & AGGRESSION

STRESS, CULTURE, & AGGRESSION

Arnold S. Linsky

Ronet Bachman

Murray A. Straus

YALE UNIVERSITY PRESS / NEW HAVEN & LONDON

Designed by Deborah Dutton

Set in Ehrhardt type by Keystone Typesetting, Inc.

Printed in the United States of America by BookCrafters, Inc., Chelsea, Michigan.

Library of Congress Cataloging-in-Publication Data

Linsky, Arnold S. (Arnold Stanley)

    Stress, culture, and aggression / Arnold S. Linsky, Ronet Bachman, Murray A. Straus.

      p. cm.

    Includes bibliographical references and index.

    ISBN 0-300-05706-7 (alk. paper)

    1. Violence—United States.   2. Self-destructive behavior—United States.   3. Stress (Psychology)—United States.   4. Quality of life—United States.   i. Bachman, Ronet.   II. Straus, Murray A. (Murray Arnold), 1926– . III. Title.

HN90.V5L55   1995

303.6—dc20   94-48643

                                                CIP

A catalogue record for this book is available from the British Library.

The paper in this book meets the guidelines for permanence and durability of the Committee on Production Guidelines for Book Longevity of the Council on Library Resources.

10 9 8 7 6 5 4 3 2 1

CONTENTS

ACKNOWLEDGMENTS

We are indebted to many colleagues who provided important help and sugges-
tions, even though we were not always able to follow their advice. They include
Robert Flewelling, Lawrence Hamilton, Colin Loftin, Michael Radelet, Heather
Turner, Sally K. Ward, Kirk R. Williams, Elizabeth Linsky, and the members of
the Family Violence Research Program seminar. Preliminary versions of most of
the chapters were presented at meetings of the American Sociological Association, the American Society of Criminology, the Eastern Sociological Society, the
Midwest Sociological Society, the Society for the Study of Social Problems, and
the Third and Fourth International Conferences on Social Stress. We also want
to express appreciation to the discussants at these conferences.

This project could not have been completed without the contributions of
the support staff of the Family Research Laboratory, especially Sieglinde Fizz,
the program administrator, who kept the Lab running smoothly by the creative
resolution of innumerable problems and thus allowed us more time to work on
this research. Doreen Roy managed the revisions of the manuscript and spotted
what would otherwise have been embarrassing errors.

This research is part of a program of macro-sociological research on stress of
the Family Research Laboratory at University of New Hampshire. Requests for a
program description and publications list ("SRP") should be addressed to the
Family Research Laboratory, University of New Hampshire, Durham, N.H.
03824. This program has been supported by the following organizations: the
National Institute of Mental Health (grant T32 MH15161, to Ronet Bachman
for a postdoctoral research fellowship) and the University of New Hampshire;
the National Institute of Mental Health (grant R01MH40027, to Richard J.
Gelles and Murray A. Straus, co-investigators, for funding of the National Fam-

ily Violence Resurvey, from which the subjective-stress and suicidal-ideation data were derived); and the National Institute of Justice (grant 851JCX0030, to Kirk R. Williams and Murray A. Straus for research on "Justifiable and Criminal Homicide of Family Members, Acquaintances and Strangers," which supported the analyses of homicide in this book).

Three of the chapters are revisions of previously published papers and are reprinted with permission of the journals listed below:

Chapter 2: Murray A. Straus, Arnold S. Linsky, and Ronet Bachman-Prehn. 1988. "Change in the Stressfulness of Life in American States and Regions from 1976 to 1982." *Social Indicators Research,* 19:27–47.

Chapter 3: John P. Colby, Jr., Arnold S. Linsky, and Murray A. Straus. 1994. "Social Stress and State-to-State Differences in Smoking and Smoking-Related Mortality in the United States." *Social Science and Medicine,* 38:373–381.

Chapter 4: Arnold S. Linsky, John P. Colby, and Murray A. Straus. 1987. "Social Stress, Normative Constraints, and Alcohol Problems in American States." *Social Science and Medicine,* 24:875–883; and Arnold S. Linsky, Murray A. Straus, and John P. Colby. 1985. "Stressful Events, Stressful Conditions, and Alcohol Problems: A Partial Test of Bales' Theory of Alcoholism." *Journal of Studies on Alcohol,* 46:72–80.

PART 1

The Stressfulness of Life in the United States

CHAPTER 1

The Concepts of Stress and Aggression

Our large towns swarm with idle, vicious lads and young men who have no visible means of support. Our rural districts are infested with tramps. Divorces have multiplied until they have become so common as to be a stock jest in the facetious column of our newspapers.

So observed Richard Grant White, writing in the *North American Review* in 1880. It is perhaps the fate of every society, including our own, to view its own times as uniquely and increasingly stressful. To our knowledge, this hypothesis has never been formally tested. The belief probably stems from a combination of cultural ethnocentrism regarding time and place, the immediacy of our own stressful experiences in comparison with those of others occupying more remote locations in time and place, and the persistence of a "golden age" mythology that makes us view earlier periods in a more idyllic light. It seems as though people have yearned from the beginning of recorded history for the "good old days" when life was simpler and society was not falling apart.

The reality is that every generation has experienced stressful events. The 1930s had the Great Depression; the 1960s had the Vietnam War and the counterculture. In spite of the presumed universality of social changes that are experienced as stressful, the extent and intensity of these stressful events have undoubtedly varied a great deal over historical time and from society to society. The United States has probably been a more stressful place to live at some points and less stressful at others. Our research focuses on the recent past—the period since 1976. In this context, we attempt to answer a number of related questions. Some of the most important of these are:

- Relative to 1976, has life in the United States been getting more or less stressful?
- Are there differences in the stressfulness of life among the different regions and states of the United States?
- What are the consequences of living in a society with a high level of stressful events?
- Is the effect of stress channeled in different directions depending on the other characteristics of the society and on particular social norms concerning aggression?

Among the many possible consequences of stress, its effect on health—for example, the development of coronary disease—has received the most attention (Mathews and Glass 1981). This subject was a major focus of our book *Social Stress in the United States* (Linsky and Straus 1986). The focus of this book, however, is on the extent to which stress results in aggression. The evidence we present provides a compelling case that the stressfulness of a society is associated with widespread and in some cases lethal aggression. This includes not only violence directed at others, such as homicide, intrafamily assault, and rape, but also violence and aggression directed inward, which manifests in self-destructive behavior such as suicide, smoking, and the abuse of alcohol.

We also investigated how a group's culture molds, directs, constrains, and channels the outcomes of stress in particular directions. We trace how cultures and subcultures may sometimes encourage aggression in response to stress and how they may even select the targets of that aggression.

THE THEORETICAL MODEL

Although our underlying theoretical model is implicit in the preceding remarks, it is important to enumerate its four main elements:

Stress Is Generated by the Social System

The theoretical model starts with the assumption that stress is both an individual and a social phenomenon. From an individual perspective, we know that some persons experience an unusually high number of stressful events in their lives. In part this is due to chance circumstances—a child killed in an accident, a company that goes out of business in a community where other enterprises are thriving. However, stress is also a social phenomenon. Some societies expose their members to far more stress than do others. For example, it is well established that the rates of residential mobility and business failure vary greatly from one community to another, as does the experience of such disasters as fires and floods. As will be shown in chapter 2, in the United States there are large differences among regions and among states in the extent to which residents are subjected to stressful events of this type. It will come as no surprise that the focus of our research is on social stress in the sense of community-to-community differences in the occurrence of stressful life events.

Inability to Cope Is Experienced as Stress

Problems in coping with changes in circumstance are experienced as stress. The employee whose job search is obstructed by a high unemployment rate or who becomes so demoralized by losing his job that he is hindered in searching for and adapting to a new position is likely to experience unemployment as much more stressful than others would. This is even more likely if the job loss occurs simultaneously with other stressful events, such as a child's becoming seriously ill when there is little or no income.

The Greater the Number of Stressful Events, the Higher the Proportion Who Cannot Cope

The third assumption is an adaptation of the basic premise of the "life events" theory of stress formulated by Holmes and Rahe (1967), Dohrenwend and Dohrenwend (1974), and others. The proposition states that as the number of stressful events in a community increases, the proportion of the population unable to adapt to these changes also increases. That is, the demands exceed the capacity of these individuals to make needed changes, and they are unable to cope. Of course, some people thrive when faced with change (Turner and Avison 1992). For example, although almost no one likes to lose a job, after the initial shock, some people are invigorated by the search for and adaptation to a new position and ultimately judge themselves better off for the move.

Culture Channels Behavior under Stress

Cultural principles, sometimes explicit but more often implicit, guide how individuals behave under stress. These principles produce differences in behavior among societies and subgroups of societies under stress. Some societies, such as our own, assume and provide numerous examples of responding to stress by lashing out at others; others assume and provide examples of responding through passivity and withdrawal. In many instances these culturally patterned modes of response can be helpful. Lashing out at others may insulate the victim of unemployment from self-blame and demoralization. Passivity and withdrawal may prevent one from making fruitless attempts to change the unchangeable. At the same time, we assume that there will always be a proportion of a population who push these cultural principles to the point where the principles become maladaptive. Lashing out can become physical assault or even murder, and withdrawal can become depression or even suicide.

STRESS AND AGGRESSION

One of the limitations of stress research has been its relatively narrow focus on mental and physical illness as consequences of stress, to the neglect of research linking stressful life events with various behavioral outcomes, including criminal violence as well as aggression turned against the self. In the article "Stress, Violence and Crime," Schlesinger and Revitch (1980) concluded that "most research and theory in the stress field emphasize physiological effects, such as changes in the viscera" and largely ignore violent and criminal behavior. A recent review of the relatively small literature on behavioral outcomes of stress concluded that the destructive aggressive responses to stress are a particularly fruitful avenue for further study (Keith 1990).

Reasons for the Neglect of Social Stress in Research on Violence

Our review of previous macro-level research suggests not only that students of stress have tended to ignore violence and certain other forms of aggression but also that students of violence have tended to ignore stress. In short, neither group has paid adequate attention to the links between social stress and aggression—a gap this research is intended to help fill.

The emphasis on disease and illness in stress research probably stems from the clinical origins of studies of stressful life events in psychosomatic medicine, a tradition that emphasizes disease states within individuals. Although research on life events is no longer the exclusive domain of medical researchers, most of the sociologists and social psychologists entering the field have followed in the steps of their predecessors by focusing on physical and mental health consequences of stress.

In the area of violence, researchers who have attempted to explain the homicide-rate differentials that exist in our society (for example, Blau and Blau 1982; Loftin and Hill 1974; Messner 1983a, 1983b; and Williams and Flewelling

1987) have also tended to ignore stress. This is true of macro-investigations of other forms of violence as well. Most researchers have investigated broad cultural and structural conditions such as economic deprivation, cultural support of violence, and the efficacy of social control rather than society-to-society differences in stressful events.

When stress has been studied as a determinant of aggression, it has been at the individual rather than the societal level. Yet there are strong a priori grounds and some indirect evidence for the assumption that there is a link between the stressfulness of life in a society and society-to-society differences in the rate of aggressive behavior. This neglect of *social* stress as an explanation for society-to-society differences in aggression may be due, in part, to the lack of an objective means of comparing the stressfulness of life in different societies, regions, or communities. Indeed, it was the development of such a measurement technique (described in chapter 2) that made possible the research reported in the chapters that follow.

Explaining the Relationship between Stress and Aggression

In the literature on response to stress, the "fight or flight" concept is prominent (Selye 1980). When the organism is faced with external threats, survival mechanisms prepare it for flight or fight (Cannon 1963). There is an emergency discharge of adrenalin, a quickening of the pulse, an increase in blood pressure, stimulation of the central nervous system, temporary suspension of digestion, a quickening of blood clotting, and a rise in the blood sugar. These physiological responses prepare the organism for heightened physical activity, such as aggression or flight.

Probably the most influential theory of aggression and violence from the psychological standpoint is the frustration-aggression hypothesis (Dollard et al. 1939). This hypothesis is useful for interpreting the relationship between stress and aggression as well.

According to this theory, aggression is likely to occur when external (aversive) events block or thwart some goal-related behavior; such thwarting may cause negative affect such as anger. This condition leads to aggressive behavior directed against the source of the frustration or in some cases to displaced aggression toward other targets. Later versions of the theory have emphasized the role of the relative power of the participants (Berkowitz 1962, 1993). Violence or aggression is more likely to be directed at persons less powerful than the perpetrator because they are perceived as less of a threat. Also, aggression is seen as a more likely outcome to blocked goals or opportunities when that blocking is viewed by the actor as illegitimate, such as unfair competition (Berkowitz 1993).

Stressful events, particularly negative events, affect aggression, according to the frustration-aggression theory, because they produce frustration which in turn produces negative affect as described (Mueller 1983). The theory also provides important clues as to the role of the cultural and social structure of communities in channeling the direction of that aggression. This theme will be developed further in later chapters.

Although this is primarily an individual-level theory, it has been used in correlational studies for social systems of various sizes—for example, the relationship between income inequality and homicide rates (Messner 1982, 1983; Blau and Blau 1982; Blau and Schwartz 1984) and the relation between the incidence of lynching and the price of cotton in the South (Hovland and Sears 1940; Beckem and Tolnay 1990). It has also been used as an explanation of family violence (Straus 1980a; Farrington 1980, 1986).

Our primary purpose is to explain the distribution of stress and aggression across the social structure of the United States. One of the classic theories of deviant behavior in sociology is Merton's theory of Anomie (1957), according to which strain and frustration (or perhaps stress) are assumed to intervene between structural disjunctions and individual responses. Deviant behavior is seen as a response to such a disjunction. Anomie theorists cite the disjunction between shared goals of economic success and the distribution of opportunities for that success as one of the major discrepancies in American society. Our State Stress Index (ssi), described in the next chapter, includes several items that would signify blockage of economic goals, including new cases of unemployment, business failures, work stoppages, bankruptcy cases, and mortgage foreclosures. We believe, however, that the mechanisms by which other important goals are blocked apply to noneconomic goals as well. For instance, our ssi contains many indicators relating to cultural expectations and goals in the family area, such as divorce and infant deaths, which represent important areas of blocked expectations or aspirations.

Consistent with frustration-aggression theory, such structurally predicated blocked expectations may result in higher levels of strain and frustration or stress within such populations.

Research on Stress and Aggression

Empirical evidence of a link between social stress levels and patterns of criminal aggression is indirect. Straus (1980b) used an abridged version of the Holmes and Rahe Schedule of Recent Life Events in a study of assault in a large, nationally representative sample of married couples. Straus found that rates of marital assault by both husbands and wives increased as the number of stressors experienced during the year increased.

Petrich and Hart (1980) applied the Holmes and Rahe Schedule of Recent Life Events to the study of criminal behavior and subsequent arrest among three samples drawn from the criminal justice system. (One sample was of juveniles, and the other two were of adult felons, all incarcerated.) The prisoners were asked about events during the years prior to imprisonment. The findings suggest that both juvenile and adult criminal behavior, arrest, and incarceration occur in the context of mounting life change. This finding is similar to those of Masuda et al. (1978) in an earlier study of prisoners. A limitation of the Petrich and Hart and the Masuda studies, however, is that they involve only incarcerated felons, a group that has been highly selected from the larger population of all criminal offenders.

One of the most extensive studies of the relationship between stressful life events and violence was conducted by Humphrey and Palmer (1986), whose subjects were a sample of offenders imprisoned for homicide (270) or nonviolent property offenses (194). These researchers measured stress through both recent and early life events. They found that the lives of criminal homicide offenders were significantly more stressful than those of their nonviolent (property crime) counterparts. Further, stress tended to be experienced more chronically by homicide offenders. Keith (1990, 541), in reviewing studies of survivors of fires, tornadoes, floods, and explosions, reports that common sequelae are "persistent irritability, anger, explosive outbursts, and occasional physical violence and delinquency."

INDIVIDUAL-LEVEL VERSUS SOCIAL SYSTEM–LEVEL ANALYSIS

The studies discussed above are all at the individual level of analysis and relate stressful events within the biographies of individuals (or families) to violence and other criminal acts by those same persons. There are, however, a few studies that examine the consequences rates of stressful events in social systems have on the rates of violence. Steinberg, Catalano, and Dooley (1981) employed a longitudinal analysis of the rates of reported cases of child maltreatment over a thirty-month period for three different metropolitan areas. They found that an increase in child abuse was preceded by periods of high job loss and attributed this change to increased levels of economic stress. Studies performed by Brenner (1976, 1980) document that in both the United States and cross-national comparisons, strong correlations existed between unemployment rates and the rates of homicide and other crimes, arrests, convictions, and imprisonments.

In a study of stress and violence in Israeli society over a thirty-two-year period, Landau and Raveh (1987) found a positive relationship between changes in aggregated stressful events (in this case, the rate of unemployment) and the rates of homicide and suicide.

Processes Linking Social Stress and Aggression

The ecological correlations just cited between stressor events and rates of violence may occur in several ways. First, they could arise from an aggregated individual effect. That is, the concentration of stressful life events in some communities may be cumulative in the lives of many of the residents. In turn, some of those who experience accumulated life events may suffer the consequences in the form of disabilities or deviance in the way suggested by the large body of previous literature on life events at the individual level. In this way, the concentration of such individuals in certain areas would result in correlations observed at the community level. Even if this were the only process underlying such findings, it is still an addition to what was known on the basis of previous individual-level research, because it traces the stress link from changes occurring in the community to experiences of individuals. This may have important implications for primary prevention of violent and other disordered behavior.

However, a new level of causal relationship or correlation may occur at the group level that is not simply a reflection of grouped individual effects. For example, a 10-percent rate of unemployment affects not only those who are out of work but also their families and the local businesses that serve them. Cumulatively it may have a socially and economically depressing effect on communities throughout a state.

Further, conditions leading to high unemployment and plant closings may substantially change the job conditions and security of those still employed. Remaining employees may be anxious that they will be laid off next, and employers struggling to survive may pressure remaining employees to increase their productivity (Fenwick and Tausig 1990). Such accumulated changes could affect the institutional level of communities (churches, schools, government) and thereby create additional stressors by increasing the demand for further adaptation.

Our research does not contain data that would allow us to differentiate the

aggregated-individual effect and the community-effect models of linkage between stressful events and outcomes. But it seems highly unlikely that the impact of large numbers of stressful life events occurring within communities
would be linked to only the relatively small proportion of the population directly
experiencing them; some spillover must certainly affect the community. Regardless of the connecting mechanism, however, the ecological relationship is important in its own right. If such a relationship is found, it would demonstrate that
there are increased risks to a population associated with a mounting incidence of
stressful events.

Empirical Indicators of Social Stress

Even though the Steinberg and the Brenner studies cited examine stress and
violence at the social-system level (instead of at the individual level) and are thus
highly relevant for this investigation, they share the limitation that community
stress is measured only by a single indicator: job loss. As stressful as this experience is, it seems to be a much too constricted measure of community stress levels,
and used alone, it confounds stress with economic deprivation, an alternative
explanatory variable. To avoid this problem, we constructed a multi-indicator
measure of the extent to which stressful events occur in each of the fifty states.
This measure is called the State Stress Index, or ssi, and is described in detail in
chapter 2.

Although the fifteen indicators of stressful events that make up the ssi do
include a number of economic stressors such as job loss and personal bankruptcy, the index is not restricted to these considerations. Such family and
community stressors as divorce, natural disaster, and moving to a new location
are also included. The ssi is, to our knowledge, the only broad-based multi-
indicator instrument for systematic empirical measurement of the stressfulness
of life within states and regions. The existence of the ssi makes it possible to
extend research on the connection between stress and aggression from studies of
individuals to studies of societies.

THE CULTURAL CONTEXT OF SOCIAL STRESS

We are not suggesting that social stress and the ensuing psychological or visceral
changes inevitably lead to violent aggression. In fact, findings from our earlier
study suggest the contrary—that stress may result in radically different outcomes depending on the social and cultural context in which it occurs. This idea
is further developed below. Although stress may provide the physiological and

psychological basis for violence toward self or others, our hypothesis is that the culture of a society influences how these changes are expressed.

Socially generated stress appears to be a highly useful explanatory variable, because it has been linked with a wide array of maladaptive behaviors and mental and physical disorders; immunological incompetence (Bieliauskas 1982), substance abuse (Linsky, Straus, and Colby 1985), mental illness (Thoits 1983), fatal accidents (Linsky and Straus 1986), child abuse (Straus and Kantor 1987), and wife beating (Straus 1980a) are but a few. At the same time, this strength is also a major weakness of stress theory. Because stress is empirically linked to such a variety of dependent variables, stress theory suffers from nonspecificity in regard to predicting the direction of the outcome. Why should stress be linked to self-abusing behaviors and even suicide in some situations and to aggressive behaviors directed against others in other situations? Clearly we need something beyond prevailing stress models to understand this process.

It is a major hypothesis of this study that the cultural context within which stress occurs serves to constrain, mold, and channel the outcomes of that stress in particular directions. This influence occurs both through the socialization process, during which people are trained to deal with stress, tension, and frustration in a culturally approved fashion, and through the situational norms that encourage, or at least tolerate, certain responses to stressful situations and events and disallow others.

Hutterite Depression

A good example of the role of culture in molding the outcome of stress is found in Eaton and Weil's study of mental illness and other deviant behavior among the Hutterites, a religiously orthodox communal and agricultural society (1955). A high level of social control exists within the Hutterite community. Expectations for religious piety and social conformity are very rigid; individuals are expected to subordinate their own goals in favor of the group's welfare. Hutterite children are trained to deal with the inevitable tensions of living in a highly controlling society by looking inward for signs of personal imperfections rather than by attending to sources of tension in their relationship with other members of their communities. Consequently, assaults and homicides are extremely rare. Alcohol and other such substances are strictly forbidden as forms of release from those tensions, and suicide is unthinkable because it violates powerfully held religious norms. The Hutterites experience instead extremely high rates of depressive mental illness. In this case, the culture of the Hutterites effectively cuts off several alternative avenues for the expression of stress.

Alcoholism in Ireland

In chapter 4, we discuss Bales's explanation for the presumably high rates of alcoholism in men in nineteenth- and early twentieth-century Ireland. In that case, the normative structure encouraged young men to deal with the especially strong tension created by sexual and status frustration by drinking heavily in local taverns. Irish society at that time was so accepting of heavy drinking that teetotalers were likely to be regarded with suspicion (Bales 1946).

American Subcultures of Violence

Wolfgang and Ferracuti (1967) investigated the high level of violence in certain urban areas and found that young men in these areas are socialized to respond violently to affronts to their personal or family honor. In societies with these types of norms, we anticipate finding a stronger relationship between stress and rates of homicide and other aggressive violence than in areas where there is less reliance on violence. To test this theory, we developed an multi-indicator measure called the Legitimate Violence Index (LVX), which measures the extent to which violence is used for socially legitimate purposes (such as physical punishment of children and capital punishment of criminals). The chapters on the stress-homicide link use the LVX to investigate the extent to which the relationship between stress and homicide is affected by differences in the extent to which such subcultures exist.

Stress and Drinking in the United States

Culture need not operate in the straightforward manner discussed above. In chapter 4, which examines the connection between stress and alcohol, we show how strong normative sanctions against the use of alcohol (proscriptive norms) may unintentionally create more alcohol problems of certain types than may exist in populations where attitudes are less fervent. This paradoxical finding arises because the strong antialcohol norms lead to more stringent and aggressive social control, which in turn can lead to more alcohol-related offenses being discovered.

In chapter 7, we deal with the potentially lethal mixture of stress, alcohol, and family violence. Again cultural context is employed to examine why stress leads to violent drunkenness in some places, violence not connected with drunkenness in other places, and nonviolent drinking in still others. Our strategy in this chapter is to examine the outcomes of stress within the various configurations of normative approval of alcohol and normative approval of violence. We hypothesize that violence is more often a response to drinking when both of these normative dimensions coincide.

Stress and Rape

In our attempt to account for the link between stress and the rate of aggravated rape, the cultural issues become more complex. We need to explain not only why stress leads to criminal violence (as we did in the chapter on homicide) but, in the case of sexual violence, why women become targets for that violent aggression. Consequently, the research reported in chapter 10 employs, in addition to the LVX, a measure of the status of women based on women's relative political and economic power. This enables us to test the hypothesis that the lower the status of women in a society, the more likely they are to be selected as targets of aggression under conditions of social stress. We also employ a pornography index based on "adult magazine" subscriptions as one cultural indicator of the degree to which women are viewed primarily as sexual objects, which may place them at greater risk of sexual violence under conditions of stress.

The idea that culture may direct aggression arising from stressful situations toward a particular class of victims is not new. As we noted earlier, several early studies summarized in Berkowitz (1962, 1993) have demonstrated that annual changes in the price of cotton bore an inverse relationship to changes in the number of African-Americans lynched in the South before 1930 (Hovland and Sears 1940; Mintz 1946; Roper, cited in Henry and Short 1954). The prosperity of the southern states was so dependent on "King Cotton" that the price served as a general index of well-being for the area. He suggests that bad economic times generally produced serious threats to the status and future security of the citizens of the area. Berkowitz also suggests that the lynching of African-Americans posed a relatively low-risk outlet for whites because of the perceived lack of power of the target population.

The scenario summarized by Berkowitz offers considerable parallel to the stress, culture, and aggression model we employ in our interpretation of state variations in the rates of rape. Our State Stress Index includes economic disruptions such as personal bankruptcies, plant closings, business failures, and new cases of unemployment, as well as a broader range of community and familial sources of stress. These environmentally derived stressors pose a threat to the status and security of state residents, which leads to frustrations and in some cases to culturally directed aggression toward women, particularly when they are perceived as having low power and status. This issue is pursued further in chapter 10.

METHODOLOGY

The research reported in this book occurred over several years. Consequently, some of the findings are based on stress measured as of 1976 by the State Stress Index, some are based on our 1982 measure of stress, and some use both measures. Chapter 2, which describes differences in the stressfulness of life in different parts of the United States, also uses the 1976 and 1982 measurements of stress to investigate the widely held belief that American society has become more stressful.

Chapter 4, which deals with stress and the epidemiology of smoking behavior, uses both the 1976 and 1982 versions of the State Stress Index. This allows us to replicate the relationship between the ssi and smoking and cancer of the respiratory system for both 1976 and 1982 and to determine through time series the various lags between periods of social stress, smoking, and the ensuing increase in deaths from cancer of the respiratory system. Chapter 4, which explores the connection between stress and alcohol abuse, is based on 1976 data for both stress and alcohol abuse.

Lagged Relationships

For some outcomes, the stressor events presumably precipitate behaviors, such as smoking or drinking, that may continue for several years before resulting in fatal illness. Clinical knowledge of such diseases suggests that appropriate time lags or incubation periods be included in research designs between stress and outcome. In the chapter on stress and smoking, we include both immediate and longer term (or lagged) outcomes for the stress–smoking–lung cancer link. This problem of time lags may not be as serious when looking at the connection between stress and homicide, rape, and other forms of violence, because we are dealing with the more immediate consequences of acts that may be precipitated by mounting stress levels. Likewise, suicides are more likely to be the result of precipitant actions that may not require extensive lag time.

Other Indexes

In addition to the State Stress Index, the Legitimate Violence Index, and the Status of Women Index, we developed and used certain other scales and indexes. These measures, which we regard as one of the major contributions of the study, made this research possible and will, we hope, open the way to future research in this area. To make the use of these indexes available to other researchers, the scores of each state on the following indexes are given in various tables.

The ssi, as noted above, is based on the life-events approach to stress research, which emphasizes new demands or important changes in people's life situations that require adaptation. This is the primary measure of stress employed in this volume, but there is also a second emphasis in the literature on stress involving chronic strains or "hassles." These are conditions that exact a toll over time, not because new adjustments are required but because of the persistence of noxious, threatening, or difficult factors in an individual's environment. In chapter 4, we employ such an instrument, the Measure of Status Integration (Gibbs and Martin 1964; Dodge and Martin 1970), which is based upon the concept of role conflicts built into the social structure.

Some of the later chapters move away from the exclusive use of objective stress to include measures of subjective stress, for which we developed a Perceived Stress Index. We used this measure along with the ssi to extend the analysis to a larger segment of the stress process than would be possible with ssi alone (Landau 1988).

Earlier we discussed the importance of cultural factors in channeling stress toward different outcomes. To successfully make the case that cultural factors affect stress outcomes requires the measurement of cultural factors *independent* of the measurement of those outcomes that culture is purported to influence. For example, in chapter 4 we test the hypothesis that permissive alcohol norms encourage drinking as a response to social stress. To test this hypothesis, one should not use the actual drinking behavior or prevalence of alcoholism as an indicator of norms favorable to drinking because there would be an obvious circularity in the analysis. We therefore constructed a Proscriptive Norm Index using as indicators of prohibitionist cultural norms the number of legal impediments to the use of alcoholic beverages and the religious composition of each state's population.

For chapter 9, which focuses on the relationship between stress and weapon-specific homicide rates, we created a measure of "gun culture" by using the readership rate for several gun magazines.

Multiple Indicators of Outcome Variables

Multiple indicators are used where possible for the different types of inwardly and outwardly directed aggressive behaviors on which we focus. Such an approach has certain advantages. If the results are consistent in spite of using different indicators of a variable, it demonstrates the robustness of the findings. If, on the other hand, the results differ depending on which indicator is used, those differences may provide clues to the nature of the underlying processes linking stress and aggression.

In chapter 4 we employ nine different indicators of alcohol problems to test various hypotheses about the relationship of stress, drinking culture, and alcohol problems. These measures are based upon alcohol-related death rates (deaths attributed to cirrhosis, alcoholism, and alcoholic psychosis), apparent consumption of alcohol based on state sales records, and indicators of the social disruptiveness of alcohol (arrest rates for DWI and other alcohol-related offenses). At other points, we use self-reported data on the incidence of drinking, drunkenness, and driving while intoxicated taken from two national surveys.

No measure of alcohol problems is completely free of bias, because all the indicators of alcoholism arise or are at least mediated through social-control processes that reflect social response to alcoholism. This includes arrest data, which may be as much an indicator of community, police, and law-enforcement proclivities and tolerance of drunken comportment as it is of drunkenness per se. Attribution of cause for alcohol-related deaths by physicians or medical examiners may also reflect community social structure and attitudes, because both the examiners and the deceased and their families may be members of the same normative community and may wish to protect the reputation of the deceased and his or her survivors. For some of the same reasons, respondents in community surveys may underreport their drinking behavior in predominantly "dry" areas of the country.

By employing indicators drawn from such diverse sources of data one is not protected against bias but is at least assured that the measures will not all have the same type of bias. To the extent that the tests of a hypothesis are replicated with different indicators, we can have additional confidence that the findings are not an artifact of a specific measure.

There are further advantages to the use of multiple indicators. Some indicators refer to different aspects of problems. Thus, when the correlates of stress vary according to which indicator of a concept is employed, those differences may provide important theoretical clues as to how stress is related to alcoholism, homicide, and the like.

Williams and Flewelling (1988, p. 421) suggest that some of the inconsistent findings in the comparative homicide literature are attributable to the "failure to desegregate the overall homicide rate into more refined and conceptually meaningful categories of homicide." They therefore created the Comparative Homicide File, or CHF, which includes separate homicide rates according to the relationship between victim and offender (family, acquaintance, stranger) and the weapon employed (handgun, shoulder gun, knife, and so on). This is far more specific data than are usually used for testing comparative theories of homicide rates. These different indicators of homicide allowed us to examine the more distinct processes that link such broad explanatory variables as social stress and the subculture of violence with homicide.

STATES AS UNITS FOR THE ANALYSIS

The societal units used for this research are the fifty states of the United States. In addition, we sometimes combined states into the regional divisions of the U.S. Bureau of the Census.

As units for macro-sociological research, states have both advantages and disadvantages. States were employed as the units of analysis in this book for a number of reasons, the most important of which are listed below.

There are large differences between states in the indicators of stress, aggressive behaviors, and other important economic, social, and cultural measures. Thus, although American society may be becoming more uniform over time, states continue to vary markedly on many important variables. An analysis of a broader set of data in the State and Regional Indicators Archive (SRIA), done in conjunction with another study (Baron and Straus 1989), suggests that the state-to-state differences observed in stress and homicide are typical of the differences found for most social characteristics.

States may well be the most important budgetary and political units for dealing with stress and its consequences. They are the basic unit of government and have primary or exclusive responsibility in all spheres not allocated by the Constitution to the federal government. This includes such vital functions as education, police, family, law, and welfare. It is at the state level that many medical, legal, and social problems are addressed.

Despite trends toward homogenization and population mobility, the identification of residents with the state in which they reside continues to be widespread and strong. States are a source of identity and pride. Even adjacent states are frequently perceived as sharply different in their cultural characteristics—for example, New York and New Jersey. Such differences are important in the social-psychological lives of individuals.

Data of the type most useful for measuring both stressful events and indicators of aggressive and maladaptive behaviors are all more extensively covered for states than for other geographical units. Some of the indicators of variables critical for this research are not available for units smaller than states.

There may also be disadvantages to using the state as an analytical unit. State boundaries are, to a certain extent, artificial in that they do not delineate clearly defined economic and social systems. They are not, however, necessarily meaningless in that regard. Even more than is the case with cities, Metropolitan Statistical Areas (MSAs), counties, and regions, states have distinctive social, cultural, and political identities.

In addition, the use of average figures for states masks their considerable internal heterogeneity, which is a concern whenever a single statistic is used to represent any group such as Catholics or Hispanics or any city or metropolitan area. The heterogeneity problem is even more severe with social indicators on a national level. Compared to the United States as a whole, states are clearly more homogeneous. But this has not deterred those who compile and use national social-indicator statistics. Nor has it prevented the developers of important cross-national comparative research. If researchers are willing to accept (at least for certain purposes) a single statistic to represent the entire United States and each of many other nations (some as internally heterogeneous as India), the same logic should apply to data on individual states.

Validity of State-Level Analyses

Straus (1985b) investigated the validity of using state-level data for purposes of testing macro-sociological theories. His review of the literature determined that the debate on whether the fifty states are meaningful units for macro-sociological research has been carried out mostly on the basis of deductive reasoning, bolstered by examples showing discrepancies between research using state-level data and research using other units, such as counties. To provide a more systematic and empirical basis for understanding the validity of research using the states as the units of analysis, Straus performed three sets of analyses:

a. All variables in the *County and City Data Book* were used to compute correlations across states between variables describing characteristics of the MSAs of each state with the identical variables describing the nonmetropolitan parts of the states (Bureau of the Census 1984). Of the 90 correlations, 85 were statistically significant, 41% were in the .50–.79 range, and 36% were correlations of .80 or higher. These correlations are consistent with the idea that the metropolitan and nonmetropolitan areas within each state tend to share sociocultural characteristics.

b. Three analyses were carried out to provide information on the extent to which tests of hypotheses produce different results when the units are the entire state, the MSA areas, or the non-MSA areas; or rural versus urban areas of the states. In each case, the conclusions one would reach from testing the hypothesis with state-level data were close if not exactly like those one would obtain on the basis of the more homogeneous aggregations. For example, the hypothesis that there is little or no relationship between educational achievement and the median income of the African-American population was supported, regardless of whether the hypothesis was tested with rural, urban, or state-wide data.

c. Published research on the macro-structural correlates of homicide and rape revealed parallel results using states, metropolitan areas, and cities. For example, both state-level and city-level studies find that poverty, inequality of income, divorce, and the percentage of African-Americans in the population are correlated with homicide.

These findings suggest that there is a "state effect" in spite of internal heterogeneity. For these reasons, we believe our use of states as units of analysis is justifiable. In fact, they may be the most appropriate units for macro-sociological research on social stress.

CHAPTER 2

Change in Social Stress

The development of the State Stress Index (SSI) in the early 1980s was an important advance in research technology in that it expanded the scope of empirical research on social stress beyond the individual-level measures then available. With the SSI one can test macro-level theories—that is, theories about differences between societies or major units of society such as states. An example of this type of theory is the widely held belief that American society is becoming more stressful. This chapter summarizes the methods we used to measure the stressfulness of life in the United States in 1976 and 1982 and then analyzes changes in stressfulness that occurred in the intervening six years.

MEASURING SOCIAL STRESS

The development of the State Stress Index began in 1980. The first paper, presented in 1981 (Linsky and Straus 1981), described a preliminary version of the SSI and reported our first findings on state-to-state differences in stressful events. It also provided preliminary evidence suggesting a strong link between stressful events and crime. Subsequent papers and a book described the process used to arrive at the current version of the SSI (Linsky and Straus, 1986; Linsky, Straus, and Colby, 1985; Straus, Linsky, and Bachman-Prehn 1988). Because the procedures used to create the SSI are explained in detail in these earlier publications, this chapter will only summarize them.

As indicated in chapter 1, the rationale of the State Stress Index is based on the life-events theory of stress, which holds that the more events (such as divorce or the movement to a new community) to which individuals must adapt, the greater risk they have of not being able to cope and of therefore developing illness. An accumulation of such events serves as a precipitator that determines the timing but not the type of illness (cf. Rabkin and Streuning 1976). The general strategy of life-events research has been to investigate whether increases in the number of events occurring in the lives of individuals are associated with the onset of illness and psychosocial problems.

Researchers, beginning with Holmes and Rahe (1967), have developed a number of somewhat similar checklists or inventories of stressful life events (see also Coddington 1972; Dohrenwend et al. 1978; Paykel et al. 1971). What the diverse events in these lists have in common is the presumption that important changes are required in ongoing adjustment. Most of the inventories include both events that are positively valued in American society, such as marriage, births, and significant personal achievements, and events that are negatively valued or undesirable, such as divorce or death.

The administration and scoring of life-event measures of stressors experienced by an individual are straightforward. The subjects are asked to indicate events on the list that they experienced in the recent past. The number of life events is then added, in either weighted or unweighted form, to provide a score that indicates the extent to which the subject has experienced these stressful events. A number of studies have found that the higher the score on the stressful events index, the greater the probability of subsequent physical illness, psychiatric disorders, depression, imprisonment, or pregnancy, among other variables (Holmes and Masuda 1974; Kaplan 1983; Dohrenwend and Dohrenwend 1974, 1981; Bieliauskas 1982; Elliott and Eisdorfer 1982).

THE STATE STRESS INDEX

The State Stress Index is a translation of the life-events approach from the original individual level to the macro or societal level. The basic strategy is to measure the *rate* at which these events occur in each state so that the stressfulness of living in different states can be evaluated. Many of the items in the individual-level life-event scales have direct analogs at the societal level. For example, the death of a child and the infant mortality rate; the loss of a home through fire, flood, or other disaster and disaster assistance per 100,000 families. For other events, state-level indicators may only approximate the events at the individual level, and for still others, as will be indicated below, no state-level indicator is available.

We chose to use the fifty states of the United States as the societal units for our research for a number of practical and theoretical reasons (see chapter 1). In principle, however, the procedures used to create the State Stress Index could also be used to measure the level of stressful events that occur in other social units such as cities, counties, or nations. The main limitation is the extent to which data is available for different types of societal units.

Selection of Stressor Events

The most extensive of the currently available life-events scales is the PERI scale developed by B. S. Dohrenwend et al. (1978) for use with individuals. The Dohrenwend PERI Scale was therefore used as the basis for the SSI. A number of Dohrenwend individual-scale items such as "Found out was NOT going to be promoted," "Had trouble with boss," or "Started new love affair"—probably cannot be operationalized at the macro-level because such data are unlikely to exist for each state.

Table 2–1 illustrates how we translated a sample of items from the PERI scale into macro-indicators for the SSI and the source of the data for each indicator. Table 2–2 lists the fifteen indicators that make up the SSI.

Positive and Negative Events

Critics of the original Holmes-Rahe Social Readjustment Rating Scale have suggested that negatively valued life events have more severe impact on physical and mental health than do positively evaluated events (Rabkin and Streuning 1976). This position is counter to Holmes and Rahe's contention that all events that require important adaptation exert stress on individuals in proportion to the number of events and the magnitude of the adaptation required. Evidence pro and con from individual correlations has not been conclusive, but it appears that negative events do exact a greater toll than positive ones (Gersten et al. 1974; Rabkin and Streuning 1976; Ross and Mirowski 1979; Thoits 1981). Consequently, the State Stress Index includes only negative and ambiguous events. An ambiguous event is one in which the cultural evaluation is not clearly positive or negative but dependent on circumstances.

The 1976 and 1982 Indexes

Our original or baseline study used the SSI as a social indicator for describing variations in the distribution of social stressors in different states and regions of the country for 1976. That year was selected because at the time we began the work, it was the most recent year for which data were available.

TABLE 2-1. SAMPLE ITEMS FROM THE PERI LIFE EVENTS SCALE (DOHRENWEND ET AL. 1978) AND STATE STRESS INDEX

PERI Item	State Stress Index	
	Indicator	Source*
Having children		
43. Abortion	Legal abortions per 100 K pop.	SA
44. Miscarriage or stillbirth	Fetal deaths per 1 K live births	SA
45. Found out that cannot have children	None	
46. Child died	Infant mortalities per 1 K live births	VS
Residence		
55. Moved to a better residence or neighborhood	None	—
56. Moved to worse residence or neighborhood	None	—
57. Moved to a residence or neighborhood no better or worse than the last one	% of pop. aged 14+ residing in state 5 yrs. or less	CEN
58. Unable to move after expecting to be able to move	None	—
59. Built a home or had one built	New housing units authorized per 100 K pop.	SA
60. Remodeled a home	None	
61. Lost a home through fire, flood, or other disaster	Disaster assistance to families per 100 K pop.	ARC

*VS = *Vital Statistics of the United States;* SA = *Statistical Abstract of the United States;* CEN = U.S. Census; None = No comparable item found for inclusion in the SSI; ARC = Communication from the National Red Cross.

In 1986, when our first book on this research was published, we decided to recompute the index for the most recent year possible, which, because of the delay in publishing key federal statistics, turned out to be 1982. Although we would have preferred a more recent year, the 1982 ssi nevertheless makes it possible to determine the nature and extent of change in the stressfulness of life in the United states over a six-year interval. Additionally, it allows us to investigate the extent to which these changes differ from state to state and from region to region in the United States.

HISTORICAL CONTEXT AND THE MEANING OF STRESS

The historical and cultural scope of our research is the United States during the period 1976–1982. With some difficulty, it might be possible to investigate changes in stressor events over broad sweeps of history. That is, it might be possible to estimate the likelihood of experiencing some of the more common stressful life events, such as losing a spouse, being orphaned, being geographically uprooted, or being subjected to financial stressors, technological job displacements, periodic food shortages, or physical dangers. The more difficult question, however, is the meaning of those events to the populations in these different eras.

TABLE 2-2. LIFE-EVENTS INDICATORS IN THE 1982 STATE STRESS INDEX

Variable name[a]	Variable[b]
A. *Economic Stressors*	
STR1R	Business failures per 1 million population, 1982
STR2R	Unemployment claims per 100 K adults age 18 and over, 1982
STR3R	Striking workers per 100 K adults age 18 and over, 1981
STR4R	Bankruptcy cases per 100 K population, 1982
STR5R	Mortgage foreclosures per 100 K population, 1982
B. *Family Stressors*	
STR6	Divorces per 1 K population, 1982
STR7R	Abortions per 100 K population, 1982
STR8R	Illegitimate births per 100 K population age 14 and over, 1982
STR9	Infant deaths per 1 K live births, 1982
STR10R	Fetal deaths per 1 K live births, 1982
C. *Community Stressors*	
STR11R	Disasters assistance per 100 K population, 1982
STR12	% residing in state less than 5 years, 1980
STR13R	New housing units per 1 K population, 1982
STR14R	New welfare recipients per 100 K population, 1982
ST15R	High school dropouts per 100 K population, 1982

[a] Over 15,000 variables are identified in the State and Regional Indicators Archive; those wishing to obtain further information on these data should specify variables by the abbreviations used in the table.
[b] For a complete listing of sources of these data, see appendix b. The population estimates by age for 1982, which were used as the denominators to compute these rates, are from U.S. Bureau of the Census. Current Population Reports, Series P-25, no. 951, *Estimates of the Population of States by Age, July 1, 1981–1983.*

The critical issue from the standpoint of assessing differences in stress levels across large expanses of time is the difference between the occurrence of stressful events and the psychological impact and meaning of such events. The latter would require major research by a cultural historian who might be able to describe the cultural definitions surrounding such life events during particular periods in history. Some stressful events, for example, were clearly more common in earlier periods, such as infant and childhood deaths and the loss of a spouse at a comparatively early age. It is unclear whether the greater commonness of these events made them more normative and more expected and thereby mediated their stressfulness. Also, earlier families may have had larger kinship and support systems, allowing the loss to be more widely shared and perhaps defusing the impact on those most directly related. Although we lack the training needed to investigate those questions, this research might stimulate a suitably trained person to do so.

The historical embeddedness of the meaning of life events is one of the considerations that cast doubt on the prospects for developing a precise calculus for assessing historical changes in subjectively experienced stress. But although we may not be able to accurately reconstruct the phenomenology of stressfulness in earlier periods, we can look at comparatively recent changes in stress levels. In doing this, we assume that the cultural norms and expectations that structure the subjective meaning of stressful events are not likely to have changed significantly. We therefore opted for this more modest goal of attempting to measure recent changes in the rate of stressful events for states and regions of the United States.

The specific questions to be investigated in this chapter are:

- Has the United States as a whole, become a more or less stressful place to live during the six-year interval between 1976 and 1982?
- Did subgroups of stressful events among the component indicators making up the State Stress Index change at about the same rate over this period? For example, did economic stressors or family stressors change the most?
- Did the geographic pattern of stressful events remain the same between 1976 and 1982, or did new states and regions emerge as the most stressful locales in the country?

CHANGE IN STRESS AT THE NATIONAL LEVEL

Figure 2–1 suggests that the answer to the question of whether the rate of stressful events is increasing in the United States depends on the type of events in question. As indicated, there was a large (almost 50%) increase in the rate of economic stressors between 1976 and 1982, a moderate increase in the rate of family stressors, and a moderate decrease in the stressful events in the remaining category, which we call community stressors. On average, the overall State Stress Index increased by 16% during the six-year period of this study.

Table 2–3 permits us to examine the changes in stressful events in detail. Among economic stressors, four of the five types of events showed increases. There were more unemployed workers, more business failures, more personal bankruptcies, and more mortgage foreclosures in 1982 than in 1976. Only the rate of striking workers declined. Combined, there was a mean increase in the rate of stressful economic events of 36.5%.

Family events present a mixed picture. Divorce rates showed only a slight increase or no increase, whereas abortions and illegitimate births showed substantial increases (24% and 31%, respectively). However, both infant deaths and

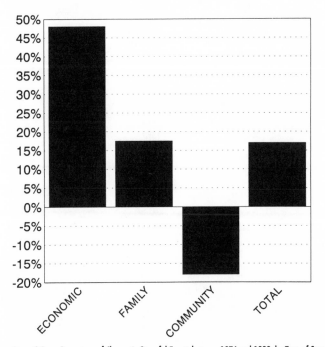

Figure 2-1.　Percentage of Change in Stressful Events between 1976 and 1982, by Type of Stress

fetal deaths declined during the period 1976–1982. Overall, stressful events in the family category increased 17.2% on average.

The category of community stressors showed an overall decline of −18.0%, with four of the components clearly declining. There were declines in the rate of geographic mobility, new housing units, persons going on welfare, and students dropping out of high school. The rate of families assisted in disasters showed a small decrease in the state mean (−11.0%), but an increase in the median (17.7%).

Considering all fifteen indicators together, there was a 16.7% increase in average state-stress scores over the six-year period. Seven stressful events increased and seven decreased, but the increases were substantially larger than the decreases on average. However, the issue is more complex than this implies. The year 1982 coincided with the peak year of a widespread economic recession. The unemployment rate was higher than in any year since the Great Depression, and inflation and interest rates were still close to their 1980–1981 peak. Hence, it is hardly surprising that economic stressors increased over the earlier period.

Although we chose 1982 because of the availability of data for that year, not

TABLE 2-3. CHANGES IN THE FIFTEEN INDICATORS OF THE STATE STRESS INDEX, 1976–1982

Stressful Event Indicator	Year	U.S. Total	State Median*
A. *Economic Stressors*			
Unemployment claims	1976	13.4	12.0
	1982	17.9	16.4
	% Change	33.6	36.6
Striking workers	1976	1.6	1.0
	1981	0.6	0.4
	% Change	−62.5	−66.5
Business failures	1976	44.8	33.6
	1982	107.4	91.8
	% Change	139.7	173.2
Personal bankruptcy cases	1976	114.8	111.0
	1982	161.6	128.6
	% Change	40.7	15.8
Mortgage foreclosures	1976	22.6	12.5
	1982	29.7	19.9
	% Change	31.4	59.2
B. *Family Stressors*			
Divorces	1976	5.0	5.2
	1982	5.1	5.3
	% Change	2.0	2.0
Abortions	1976	549.3	505.0
	1982	678.9	552.3
	% Change	23.5	9.3
Illegitimate births	1976	2.9	2.5
	1982	3.8	3.3
	% Change	31.0	32.0
Infant deaths	1976	15.2	15.0
	1982	11.5	10.9
	% Change	−24.3	−27.3
Fetal deaths	1976	10.5	9.6
	1982	8.9	8.2
	% Change	−15.2	−14.5
C. *Community Stressors*			
Disaster assistance	1976	50.5	20.9
	1982	44.9	24.6
	% Change	−11.0	17.7
% resident less than 5 years	1976	−11.7	12.7
	1982	9.7	11.0
	% Change	17.0	13.3
New housing units	1976	6.1	5.7
	1982	4.3	3.3
	% Change	−29.5	−42.1
New welfare recipients	1976	1041.0	954.0
	1982	929.0	844.0
	% Change	−10.7	−11.4
High school dropouts	1976	539.0	477.0
	1982	420.0	327.0
	% Change	−22.0	−31.4
Mean % Change for 15 Stressors, 1976–1982 = 16.7			

*Includes the District of Columbia.

because of the economic events cited, the coincidence is useful for showing the impact of the economic cycle on general stress levels. It also shows the need for replicating the measure at other time points, or if resources permit, at a systematic intervals.[1]

The changes that occurred between 1976 and 1982 also highlight the multifaceted nature of the indicators included in the ssi. Specifically, just as some stressful events have a positive aspect, a reduction in some of the presumably negative stressful events may have a problematic side. Fewer workers, for example, had to endure the stress of a strike because in the economic climate of 1982, fewer unions were willing to risk a strike. Fewer persons had to undergo the joy and turmoil of moving into a new house, because so few people could afford the prevailing prices and interest rates. There was a decrease in the trauma of identifying oneself as a welfare case, because of lack of funds and new policies shut out more persons in need of assistance.

In summary, some types of stressful events increased and some decreased, but those living in the United States in 1982 were at somewhat greater risk of experiencing stressful events than they had been in 1976.

CHANGES IN STATE AND REGIONAL DISTRIBUTION OF STRESS

The next question relates to whether some states and regions of the country were more stressful places to live than others in 1982 and whether there were important shifts in the most stressful locales during the six-year interval.

1. When we began research on stress in America, the construction of an index did not seem a major task. The first index was, of course, the most difficult to develop; deciding on the fifteen indicators, securing the data, and converting the raw data to rates took more than a year. For the current study, we believed the index would go more quickly because we already knew our sources. It took about five months, however, to construct the 1982 State Stress Index because of the following problems: some states failed to provide statistics to the federal agency collating the data, which required us to contact several state agencies directly; responsibility for collecting one of the indicators shifted from one organization to another; one series was discontinued because of decreases in funding for federal statistics work; one set of data changed publication and publisher and, in the process, ended up being labeled somewhat differently, raising the question of whether the data were indeed the same; and, contrary to our expectations, vital statistics for 1982 were not available in 1986 and had to be obtained in prepublication form through the Office of Vital Statistics. As a general point, the decreases in funding for federal statistical work have overburdened remaining staff, making it difficult for them to provide any help at all, much less on short notice. We are therefore indebted to the many people in various federal, state, and private organizations who extended themselves to provide necessary data.

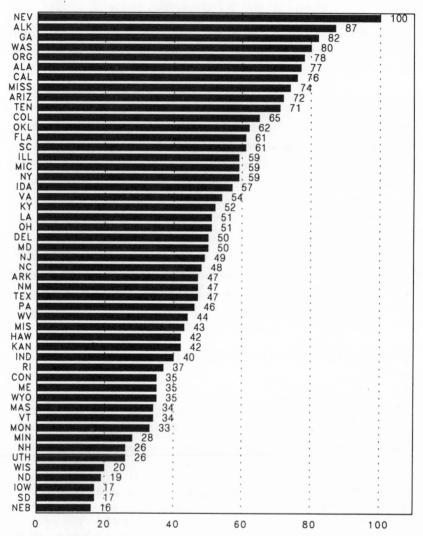

Figure 2-2. State Stress Index, 1976

Ranking of the States and Regions in 1976 and 1982

Figures 2–2 and 2–3 present states in rank order on the SSI for 1976 and 1982. Overall there was remarkable stability or continuity in the position of the states with regard to their level of stressful events between 1976 and 1982 as witnessed by the state rankings on the SSI in table 2–4. In fact, the correlation was .94 between the index scores for those two years.

In 1976, Nevada had the most stressful environment of the fifty states, with Alaska in second place. Also in the highest quintile in terms of stress were the

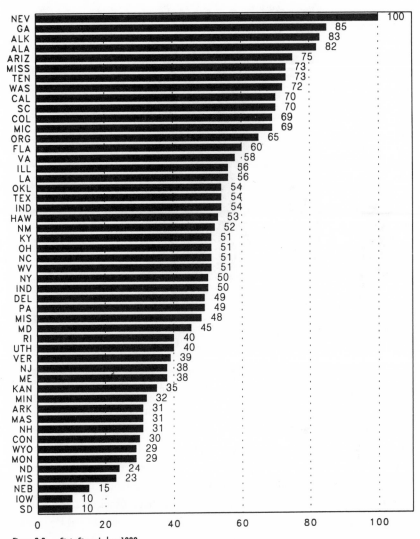

NEV 100
GA 85
ALK 83
ALA 82
ARIZ 75
MISS 73
TEN 73
WAS 72
CAL 70
SC 70
COL 69
MIC 69
ORG 65
FLA 60
VA ·58
ILL 56
LA 56
OKL 54
TEX 54
IND 54
HAW 53·
NM 52
KY 51
OH 51
NC 51
WV 51
NY 50
IND 50
DEL 49
PA 49
MIS 48
MD 45
RI 40
UTH 40
VER 39
NJ ·38
ME ·38
KAN 35
MIN 32
ARK 31
MAS 31
NH 31
CON 30
WYO 29
MON 29
ND 24
WIS 23
NEB 15
IOW 10
SD 10

0 20 40 60 80 100

Figure 2-3.   State Stress Index, 1982

states of Georgia, Washington, Oregon, Alabama, California, Mississippi, Arizona, and Tennessee, in descending order. These states vary widely in their social and economic characteristics, but all are located either in the western part of the United States or in the South.

At the opposite end of the spectrum in 1976 were the least stressful states, led by Nebraska, which had a lower incidence of stressful events than any state in the country. Also among the least stressful states were Iowa, South Dakota, North Dakota, Wisconsin, New Hampshire, Utah, Minnesota, Montana, Mas-

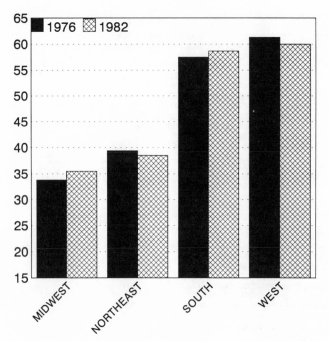

Figure 2-4.   State Stress Index for 1976 and 1982, by Region

sachusetts, and Vermont, in ascending order. The ten states in the low-stress quintile were almost all located in the Midwest or northern New England.

Although there are a number of exceptions, the states with the highest SSI scores tend to be in the Pacific and mountain regions of the country. This finding could be described as a "frontier" pattern, because several of the states are western, were among the last to be admitted to the Union, and have remained sparsely settled. Although this geographic distribution of societal stress is interesting in its own right, our focus in this book is on whether such stressor events are related to various types of aggression against others such as homicide and aggression against the self such as suicide.

Nine of the ten most stressful states in 1976 continued to be in the top ten in 1982. Of the ten least stressful states in 1976, six remained in that category in 1982. Figure 2–4 shows the average State Stress Index scores for 1976 and 1982 for the four census regions of the United States.[2] The states in the western and southern regions were highest in both years. The Midwest contains several

2. We included the District of Columbia in tables ranking states in order to make this data available to interested persons. However, the statistical analyses reported in this book are based on the fifty states and do not include the District.

farm–belt states that were experiencing depressed prices. These states showed slightly increased rates of stress relative to other states, but the rank order of the regions remained unchanged.

Percentage of Change in Stressful Events, by State

The version of the SSI in Figures 2–1, 2–2, and 2–3 was constructed using Z-scored versions of the items. This procedure was used to create an index that is useful for comparing states *with one another* within a specific year.[3] However, Z-scoring obscures changes in the absolute level of stressful events.

The Percentage of Change Index (PCI) in table 2–4 was designed to bring out changes in the rate at which stressful events occurred (as compared to changes in the rank ordering of the states). This answers the question of the degree to which the stressfulness of each state increased or decreased between 1976 and 1982. The figures represent the average percentage change from 1976 to 1982.[4]

The right-hand column of table 2–4 gives the percentage of change in the overall rate of stressful events. Almost all the percentages are positive, indicating

3. Each of the fifteen events was transformed to a "ZP score" and then combined for each state. This scoring is a method of weighting each type of stress equally, so that each type of event contributes 1 / 15 to the total score. Thus, no single type of event is allowed to dominate the SSI. See Linsky and Straus (1986) for details. This method of standardization (Straus 1980a) is designed to accomplish two things. First, as with Z scores, ZP transformation creates a variable in which the units have a known meaning (i.e., deviation from the mean). In addition, ZP scoring includes additional calculations that transform the Z score into a score with a mean of 50 and a range of from 0 to 100. Zero is assigned to cases that are 2.5 or more standard deviations below the mean, and 100 is assigned to cases with scores that are 2.5 or more standard deviations above the mean. The interpretation of ZP scores can focus either on percentages, since a change of 1 ZP score point is a change of 1% of the 0 to 100 scoring range, or on standard deviation changes, since each change of 20 ZP score points is a change of one standard deviation. Thus, statistically trained readers can interpret ZP scores in terms of standard deviation units, and other readers can interpret ZP scores as showing the percentage of the maximum score.

4. These scores were computed using the following formula:

% change in X = [(X1982 − X1976) / X1976] × 100

The Percentage Change Index shown in table 2–4 is the mean of these 15 percentages. A few states, however, experienced such extreme changes in 2 of the indicators that it was necessary to adjust these outliers to prevent the Percentage Change Index Score for those states from being dominated by those 1 or 2 indicators. To accomplish this, the value for any percentage change greater than 500% was set at 500. This limit was used in the cases of business failures (Colorado 815%, Hawaii 12,889%, New Mexico 991%, Rhode Island 1,310%, South Dakota 507%, West Virginia 1,078%) and of mortgage foreclosures (Idaho 1,645%, Montana 1,456%, North Dakota 1,424%, South Dakota 1,983%, Utah 810%, Wyoming 799%). Although there were 6 states adjusted for outliers in the case of business failures and 6 states in the case of mortgage foreclosures.

TABLE 2-4.   PERCENTAGE OF CHANGE IN STRESSFUL EVENTS, 1976–1982, BY TYPE OF STRESS

Rank	Economic State	STRPE	Family State	STRPQ	Community State	STRPO	Total State	STRPL
1	ND	278.44	VT	25.71	ALAS	70.02	ND	87.99
2	UTAH	235.82	NM	24.59	ME	29.71	WYO	74.16
3	WYO	219.27	ME	22.60	ARIZ	22.30	UTAH	69.85
4	SD	210.37	UTAH	20.21	COLO	19.93	SD	64.31
5	MONT	181.32	ND	15.18	GA	15.27	RI	56.28
6	RI	164.48	NH	13.70	SC	13.18	MONT	54.32
7	KANS	151.50	RI	13.46	WYO	11.62	COLO	46.39
8	DC	131.11	INDI	11.70	TEX	11.05	KANS	42.59
9	COLO	119.03	SC	11.41	INDI	8.53	ALAS	41.58
10	HAWA	116.97	NJ	10.83	KY	6.00	NM	40.52
11	OREG	110.43	MONT	10.77	NC	4.58	HAWA	38.68
12	IDA	108.17	NEBR	10.47	VT	2.31	DC	37.96
13	NEBR	104.24	CAL	10.11	LA	0.70	SC	35.60
14	NM	102.50	MISS	10.08	IOWA	0.62	NC	35.23
15	NC	99.98	NY	9.44	MO	0.49	NEBR	31.37
16	ALA	88.32	NEV	9.26	MICH	−0.16	ME	28.62
17	TENN	86.96	MASS	8.22	CAL	−1.04	INDI	27.26
18	MISS	86.76	MD	7.72	NH	−1.93	WVA	27.18
19	WVA	86.67	CONN	7.20	HAWA	−5.38	IDA	26.12
20	SC	82.21	WIS	6.49	NM	−5.54	NH	25.96
21	DEL	75.90	WVA	5.92	MASS	−7.85	MISS	25.81
22	KY	75.46	IDA	5.49	OHIO	−8.75	LA	24.85
23	LA	69.77	ALA	5.38	DEL	−9.09	KY	24.52
24	WASH	66.43	HAWA	4.44	RI	−9.10	OREG	24.48
25	NH	66.12	MO	4.28	OKLA	−9.13	DEL	22.81
26	NEV	61.75	LA	4.08	DC	−10.52	TEX	21.69
27	INDI	61.54	VA	3.96	CONN	−10.54	ALA	21.26
28	MINN	57.40	ARIZ	3.14	WVA	−11.04	MO	19.63
29	TEX	55.85	FLA	2.20	FLA	−11.51	ARIZ	18.87
30	ALAS	54.61	DEL	1.63	MD	−14.23	NEV	17.56
31	MO	54.11	NC	1.13	WIS	−17.87	TENN	17.15
32	OHIO	53.35	SD	0.86	SD	−18.30	IOWA	15.26
33	PA	48.95	COLO	0.21	NEV	−18.34	OHIO	14.19
34	MICH	48.10	ALAS	0.10	KANS	−18.53	MICH	13.76
35	IOWA	46.23	IOWA	−1.08	MISS	−19.43	CAL	12.98
36	WIS	45.90	ARK	−1.23	VA	−19.57	VT	12.73
37	VA	44.65	GA	−1.67	NEBR	−20.60	GA	12.04
38	ARK	44.11	TEX	−1.83	MINN	−23.50	WIS	11.51
39	MD	38.37	OHIO	−2.03	PA	−24.19	MD	10.62
40	ILL	34.76	PA	−2.18	TENN	−24.68	MINN	10.47
41	ME	33.57	MINN	−2.48	NY	−26.27	VA	9.68
42	ARIZ	31.17	OKLA	−2.92	NJ	−26.35	WASH	9.43
43	CAL	29.88	OREG	−3.41	ARK	−26.91	PA	7.52
44	GA	22.52	KANS	−5.21	ILL	−27.10	ARK	5.32
45	OKLA	18.47	WASH	−5.22	MONT	−29.15	FLA	2.51
46	FLA	16.84	MICH	−6.66	ND	−29.65	OKLA	2.14
47	VT	10.18	DC	−6.72	ALA	−29.92	ILL	0.24
48	NJ	7.52	ILL	−6.94	WASH	−32.92	NJ	−2.67
49	NY	−2.97	KY	−7.90	OREG	−33.57	NY	−6.60
50	CONN	−21.02	WYO	−8.40	IDA	−35.30	CONN	−8.12
51	MASS	−25.25	TENN	−10.83	UTAH	−46.48	MASS	−8.30

an increase in the average rate of stressful events. In fact, forty-four out of the fifty states experienced at least some increase in the average frequency of stressful events between 1976 and 1982, with only Massachusetts, Connecticut, New York, and New Jersey showing a decline. Residents of North Dakota, Wyoming, Utah, South Dakota, Rhode Island, and Montana experienced more than a 50% increase in the rate of stressful events.

CONCEPTUAL AND METHODOLOGICAL ISSUES IN THE ANALYSIS OF STRESSFUL EVENTS AS A SOCIAL INDICATOR

This section deals with what appears to be a discrepancy between the high stability in the state ranks on the one hand and the unequal changes occurring between states on the other. The correlation of .94 between the ssi scores for 1976 and 1982 indicates that despite the fact that some states experienced very large increases in stressful events, the stressfulness of life in each state *relative to other states* remained remarkably constant. The discrepancy turns out to be an issue both of theoretical interpretation and of the method of index construction.

The discovery of this inconsistency, and our attempts to explain it, revealed an ambiguity in the stressful life events theory on which the State Stress Index is built. The ambiguity concerns the relative emphasis given to the number of *different types of events* versus the *frequency of events*, regardless of type of event. The two methods therefore reflect different interpretations of the life-events theory of stress, and operationalizations based on each provide a different picture of the changing stressfulness of American society.

Because the first approach emphasizes the number of different types of events, it will be called the "events approach." The second, which emphasizes the frequency of events, will be called the "frequency approach." It is important to realize, however, that the distinction between the events approach and the frequency approach is a matter of which aspect is emphasized. Each takes into account both the number of different types of events and the frequency of events.

Events Approach

The methods used to construct the State Stress Indexes for 1976 and 1982 illustrate the events approach. Although the *frequency* with which each type of event occurs is included in the index, the scoring method is designed to limit the possible contribution of any one of the fifteen stressful events to 1/15 of the total index score. This approach implicitly assumes that in addition to the number of events that occur, the number of different spheres of life that are affected is an important aspect of stress. Using this approach, for example, the ssi implicitly assumes that it is more stressful to experience both unemployment and serious illness than it is to experience two illnesses in the same year or to be unemployed twice in the same year.

Frequency Approach

This approach was used to construct the Percent Change Index. It emphasizes the *frequency* of events, regardless of the type of event. The scoring method does not impose a restriction on the contribution that any one type of stressful event can make to the total index score. It allows each type of event to contribute to the index in proportion to its frequency of occurrence. This approach implicitly assumes that, regardless of the mix of events, it is the number of times stressful events occur that is important. The following situations are therefore implicitly assumed to be equally stressful: unemployment and a serious illness, two serious illness, or two instances of becoming unemployed.

Because equally plausible arguments can be made in favor of both approaches, we constructed an alternative version of the ssi: the Frequency Index. The Frequency Index and the ssi (events index) have a correlation of .41, and therefore, though related, are far from identical. It is evident that the State Stress Index and the Frequency Index are not comparable, because they differ in two fundamental ways. First, the ssi sums Z scores for each of the indicators, thereby comparing each state with the average of the other states, whereas the Frequency Index sums the absolute rate of events of all types. Second, the ssi weights each of the fifteen indicators equally, whereas the Frequency Index allows some indicators to make a larger contribution to the index total score than others.

We examined the "construct validity" of the two indexes by correlating each with the homicide rate and the robbery rate. The correlations using the ssi as the independent variable are .67 for 1976 and .41 for 1982. The correlations using the Frequency Index are .28 and −.03. These results clearly favor the events version (the ssi) as compared to the frequency version. However, because both stress and crime are confounded with a number of other variables, we did a multiple regression analysis, controlling for the percentage of the population that is urban, African-American, and of low income and the percentage of males aged 15–39 (the high-crime ages). The results showed that both indexes have an equally significant relationship to homicide, net of the control variables, and that neither index has a significant relationship to the robbery rate. Although further research is needed to arrive at a more definitive understanding of these two methods of measuring the stressfulness of a social environment, the balance of this book uses the SSI rather than the Frequency Index, because the evidence somewhat favors the SSI. In addition, using the SSI enables us to compare the results in this book with our previously published research on social stress, which also used the SSI.

SUMMARY AND CONCLUSIONS

This chapter described the procedures we used to measure the occurrence of stressful events in the regions and states of the United States in 1976 and 1982 and analyzed change in the stressfulness of life from 1976 to 1982. The State Stress Index enables states and regions to be *compared with* one another to determine which parts of the country are high in stress and which are low, relative to the U.S. average. The "Frequency Index enables each state and region to be *compared to itself* at an earlier time to determine which states have experienced the largest increase or decrease in levels of stress.

Because the results stemming from these two measures were somewhat different, we reexamined the conceptual basis of the life-events method of measuring stress and found that the discrepancy reflects two different theoretical interpretations, one of which is implicitly reflected in the SSI. We carried out an exploratory analysis of the effects of constructing a stress index based on the alternative formulation, which we call the frequency approach, to distinguish it from the "events approach" of the SSI. The two measures had only a moderate correlation (.41). However, a multiple regression analysis performed to provide information on the construct validity of the two approaches did not demonstrate one to be superior to the other.

The substantive analysis using the State Stress Indexes for 1976 and 1982 suggest the following conclusions:

- The United States became a more stressful society between 1976 and 1982. This was largely because of the deep economic recession in 1982. If data for the latter half of the 1980s were available, the findings might be somewhat different.
- There are differences between the three domains or subgroups of stressful events in their rates of change. Economic stresses increased sharply, family events increased moderately, and the residual category of other stressful events decreased moderately. These differences, as well as the special

circumstances of a severe economic recession, are important qualifications
of the finding that American society became more stressful between 1976
and 1982.

- The diversity of American society and the importance of state and regional
  differences is underlined by our findings. Some states and regions
  experienced much greater increases in stress than did others, largely
  because of their economic structure. The states most effected during this
  period were those that were highly dependent on agriculture.

- The increases in stressful events in some states and regions did not
  basically alter the large difference between the states and regions in the
  stressfulness of life that we found in 1976. The West remained the most
  stressful region of the United States, despite its other attractions, and the
  Midwest and Northeast remained the least stressful regions, despite their
  so-called rust-belt and frost-belt images.

PART 2

Stress and Self-Destructive Behavior

CHAPTER 3

Stress, Smoking, and Death

Aggression is a many-faceted phenomenon that takes numerous forms. The four chapters in this section are devoted to aggression directed against the self. Perhaps the most obvious example of such aggression is suicide, with its deliberate acts of extreme violence against the self.

Stressful conditions may also lead to more gradual and incremental forms of self-destruction. The abuse of alcohol and tobacco, which involves the knowing ingestion of large quantities of toxic and addictive substances, is a case in point. The use of tobacco has been implicated in a wide variety of debilitating and life-threatening illnesses. Yet in spite of this well-publicized connection, many persons continue to smoke. In this chapter, we investigate the role that stressful environments play in the use of tobacco.

Decades of research have helped establish a correlational link between stress and disease that encompasses an impressive number of physical and mental disorders (Dohrenwend and Dohrenwend 1974; Dohrenwend and Dohrenwend 1981; Elliott and Eisdorfer 1982; Kaplan 1983; Bielauskas 1982; Levi 1976; Dodge and Martin 1970), but the processes through which that link operates remain elusive. In fact, several theoretical models compete (Dohrenwend and Dohrenwend 1981; Ensel and Lin 1991). In the "direct physiological arousal" model, stressors are purported to operate directly on the viscera of the individual, resulting in disease-generating processes. These processes occur at a direct and prerational level (Holmes and Rahe 1967; Selye 1966) and therefore do not require the mediation of psychological processes. In the "cognitive" model of stress, on the other hand, psychological discomfort, anger, and perceived threats

John P. Colby, Jr., was coauthor of this chapter.

mediate the stress–disease relationship (Lazarus 1966). Still a third model of the stress–illness relationship focuses on the "patient role," in which individuals under stress are more likely to pay attention to their symptoms, to report these symptoms in interviews, to seek medical care, and to take more time off from work when sick in comparison to less stressed persons of equivalent health status (Mechanic 1976).

Although the above models are the most common, they do not exhaust the theoretical possibilities. The current study involves a less common model, in which health-related behaviors are viewed as the intervening process between stress and disease. That is, under conditions of stress some people fail to exercise normal prudence in protecting their health, or they engage in practices inimical to health.

In an earlier study we found support for the "health-behavior model" in the area of stress and alcohol problems (see chap. 4). Stressful events and ongoing stressful conditions were both linked to greater consumption of alcoholic beverages, which in turn was linked to a number of alcohol-related problems (Linsky, Straus, and Colby 1985; Linsky, Colby, and Straus 1987). We also found that fatal accidents from a variety of causes were associated with life in stressful environments, and those correlations could not be explained away by other factors, thus further supporting the stress–health behavior link (Linsky and Straus 1986).

The hypothesis that smoking is a nervous habit in response to stressful conditions is intuitively plausible, but surprisingly few empirical studies link these two variables. Smoking was found to be heavier within stressful situations by Schachter et al. (Schachter et al.1984; Schachter, Silverstein, and Perlick 1977) in a series of laboratory experiments. Lindenthal et al., in a survey, also reports heavier smoking among persons experiencing highly stressful life events (Lindenthal, Myers, and Pepper 1972). In their survey of hospital nurses, Tagliacozzo and Vaughn (1982) found smoking associated with the physical and emotional stress of the job. Similarly, Burr's survey of Navy enlisted men (Burr 1984) found that stress associated with job organization and family is related to smoking.

The surveys of Lindenthal et al., Tagliacozzo and Vaughn, and Burr were all limited by a cross-sectional design. Conway et al. (1981), on the other hand, conducted a longitudinal study in which a group of seamen assigned to a naval training center were followed over an eight-month period. Smokers were monitored during both high- and low-stress periods. In general, more cigarette smoking occurred on days in which stress (both objective and subjective) was high.

The findings from these studies are consistent with the hypothesis that stressful events or conditions lead to higher levels of smoking behavior. But the above studies involve relatively small samples, and none of them deals with stressors and smoking at the community level or for larger social systems. The current study, on the other hand, uses the fifty states as units of analysis and relates state-to-state differences in stressfulness to the rates of smoking by the populations in each state. In addition, we examine death rates attributed to lung cancer and to chronic obstructive pulmonary disease, thus allowing a partial examination of processes linking community-based stressors, smoking behavior, and mortality from smoking-related diseases.

STATE-TO-STATE DIFFERENCES IN SMOKING

Two indicators of state smoking levels were employed in this study: the number of packs of cigarettes sold per capita and the percentage of residents who reported smoking. Tobacco sales are the only indicator of smoking available on a nationwide basis, but they are based solely on location of purchase rather than on state of residence and do not include illegal sales. Sales figures may be inflated for states with low cigarette taxes because of purchases by individuals from out of state.

Because of these limitations in sales figures, we employed an additional source of data from the Behavioral Risk Factor Surveys (BRFS), conducted by the Centers for Disease Control (1984). The BRFS is an annual survey conducted in collaboration with the health departments of many states. We used data from the years 1981, 1982, and 1983. Respondents were asked if they currently smoked. The major limitations of the BRFS are that it was available for only twenty-seven of the fifty states for the period studied (it is now available for forty-four states), and residents were asked not how much they smoked but only whether they smoked. The major strength of the BRFS information in regard to the current study is that it avoids the sales bias of the packs-per-capita measure.

Table 3–1 ranks the states in order of these two measures of smoking. Examination of the state-to-state differences in smoking behavior fails to reveal clear regional patterns. Of the twenty-seven states that furnished data on smoking, North Carolina, Kentucky, and Alaska had the highest percentages of smokers. Kansas, Nebraska, and Montana had lowest. Using the criterion of cigarette packs sold per capita (reported by all fifty states), New Hampshire, Kentucky,

TABLE 3-1. SMOKING INDICATORS, RANKED BY STATE

Rank	% Smokers		Packs per Capita	
	State	SMOKE82	State	PACKS82
1	NC	37.7	NH	239.8
2	KY	36.6	KY	210.6
3	ALAS	36.0	NC	179.0
4	COLO	34.4	NEV	165.1
5	PA	34.0	VT	162.3
6	VA	33.6	WYO	157.7
7	INDI	32.8	DEL	154.1
8	FLA	32.3	ALAS	148.3
9	WVA	32.2	INDI	147.7
10	ARIZ	32.0	VA	147.4
11	NJ	31.8	OKLA	147.0
12	WYO	31.5	RI	146.3
13	MICH	31.1	LA	143.9
14	DEL	30.6	MO	139.7
15	ALA	30.5	ME	139.5
16	ND	30.2	MICH	137.3
17	TEX	29.9	SC	136.0
18	IOWA	29.6	OREG	135.3
19	NM	29.1	OHIO	134.0
20	NH	29.1	FLA	131.8
21	GA	28.6	TENN	131.4
22	CAL	28.4	MD	131.3
23	ARK	26.8	TEX	131.2
24	MONT	25.7	GA	131.2
25	NEBR	23.2	KANS	130.9
26	KANS	22.1	ILL	130.7
27	TENN	21.9	COLO	130.5
28	NEV	−999.0	NY	128.5
29	INDI	−999.0	ARK	127.4
30	WASH	−999.0	ND	126.8
31	ME	−999.0	NJ	126.3
32	OREG	−999.0	MISS	125.8
33	VT	−999.0	PA	123.3
34	OHIO	−999.0	MONT	122.4
35	MO	−999.0	MASS	122.3
36	UTAH	−999.0	WVA	119.8
37	MD	−999.0	MINN	119.4
38	OKLA	−999.0	ALA	119.1
39	RI	−999.0	NEBR	117.1
40	SC	−999.0	IOWA	116.2
41	ILL	−999.0	WIS	115.6
42	MASS	−999.0	CAL	115.4
43	SD	−999.0	CONN	114.7
44	NY	−999.0	ARIZ	113.5
45	LA	−999.0	SD	113.0
46	MISS	−999.0	INDI	111.5
47	WIS	−999.0	WASH	106.6
48	MINN	−999.0	NM	97.5
49	CONN	−999.0	HAWA	77.7
50	HAWA	−999.0	UTAH	73.6

and North Carolina were highest, and New Mexico, Hawaii, and Utah were lowest.

The correlation between the two measures of smoking (packs sold per capita and percentage of smokers) is .35 (p < .05), indicating some correspondence between the two, but they are far from isomorphic. To account for this modest correlation, one may surmise that the percentage of smokers is more of an indicator of the acceptability of smoking in a state or region, a sort of cultural measure, whereas packs per capita may be a more direct behavioral measure of tobacco consumption. The correlation may also be low because of distortions created by purchases of tobacco by out-of-staters in states with low cigarette tax. In the earlier version of the study we attempted to correct for these phenomena by eliminating the three states that were extreme outliers on cigarette consumption. The states were North Carolina, Kentucky, and New Hampshire, each of which had substantially lower cigarette taxes than their neighbors. With omission of those three states, correlations between tobacco sales and the ssi were substantially higher. The improvement in the correlations between stress and smoking with the outliers removed suggests that measurement error may be responsible for at least part of the low correspondence between the two smoking indicators.

Because the two indicators appear to be measuring different aspects of smoking behavior, both are included in the study. The use of measures that depend on different sources and have different limitations should offset the weaknesses in the use of either one alone.

SMOKING-RELATED MORTALITY

The dependent variables are two causes of death substantially attributable to smoking: malignant neoplasms of the respiratory and intrathoracic organs (that is, lung cancer) and chronic obstructive pulmonary disease (COPD). Cigarette smoking is estimated to account for more than 80% of deaths from lung cancer and COPD (Centers for Disease Control 1989a, 1989b).

Age-adjusted mortality rates for lung cancer were calculated using the direct method (Shryock and Siegel 1976) for each state population between the ages of 45 and 74 and for males and females separately. Age-adjusted COPD death rates for each state (total population) were abstracted from a recent publication of the Centers for Disease Control (1989a). The referent year for all mortality rates is 1986. The time lag between the 1982 stress and smoking measures and

TABLE 3-2. LUNG CANCER AND COPD RATES, RANKED BY STATE, 1986

| | Lung Cancer | | | | | | Obstructive Pulmonary Dis. | |
| | Male | | Female | | Total | | | |
Rank	State	LC86M	State	LC86F	State	LC86T1	State	COPD8
1	KY	404.3	ALAS	195.0	KY	268.0	WYO	49.1
2	LA	378.4	NEV	178.2	LA	241.1	NEV	48.3
3	TENN	368.4	OREG	162.3	NEV	237.3	COLO	42.6
4	ALAB	365.1	KY	144.8	TENN	236.8	MONT	41.1
5	ARK	353.6	WVA	144.7	MISS	233.6	NM	39.9
6	MISS	352.8	VT	139.8	ALAB	228.8	KY	39.6
7	SC	333.4	ME	139.1	WVA	226.6	WVA	39.4
8	GA	325.8	INDI	138.2	INDI	225.4	INDI	39.0
9	WVA	321.8	OKLA	134.5	ARK	219.3	ARIZ	37.9
10	INDI	321.3	WASH	133.6	OKLA	218.7	WASH	37.5
11	NC	317.2	MO	133.4	OREG	217.3	ME	36.6
12	OKLA	312.1	OHIO	132.5	ME	214.6	ALAS	35.4
13	DEL	311.3	MISS	132.2	OHIO	210.5	OREG	34.9
14	VA	302.2	MD	132.0	GA	209.0	INDI	34.4
15	ME	299.6	MONT	129.5	SC	209.0	VT	34.1
16	NEV	297.1	ILL	122.4	VA	205.3	OHIO	32.7
17	OHIO	296.3	CAL	122.4	MO	205.1	CAL	32.5
18	FLA	287.2	TENN	121.9	MD	203.8	TENN	32.2
19	MO	285.1	WYO	120.8	ALAS	201.8	MICH	31.5
20	RI	283.5	FLA	120.5	NC	201.4	MO	31.1
21	MD	282.9	NJ	120.4	DEL	198.6	GA	31.0
22	MICH	279.2	LA	120.0	FLA	197.5	NH	30.9
23	ILL	277.0	VA	116.6	ILL	196.5	ALAB	30.8
24	OREG	276.9	MICH	115.2	MICH	193.9	KANS	30.8
25	PA	265.1	CONN	115.0	WASH	189.0	DEL	30.7
26	IOWA	255.0	NY	114.0	RI	183.7	VA	29.9
27	TEX	252.0	MASS	113.9	VT	183.6	UTAH	29.4
28	NJ	251.9	ALAB	111.4	NJ	182.7	MD	29.2
29	WASH	247.0	NH	110.2	PA	182.7	PA	29.1
30	NH	240.0	PA	109.8	TEX	175.4	OKLA	29.0
31	VT	237.0	ARIZ	109.0	NH	171.7	RI	28.9
32	MASS	232.1	SD	107.6	MASS	169.3	IOWA	28.4
33	NY	226.4	GA	107.0	NY	166.6	FLA	27.6
34	KANS	222.9	WIS	106.0	IOWA	166.6	SC	27.5
35	NEBR	220.3	INDI	105.7	CAL	163.7	ILL	27.5
36	SD	216.1	TEX	104.7	WYO	162.9	NC	27.4
37	ALAS	212.8	ARK	101.8	SD	160.7	MASS	26.5
38	ARIZ	211.0	SC	100.9	ARIZ	157.1	ARK	25.6
39	WIS	210.8	MINN	100.9	CONN	156.4	NY	25.6
40	WYO	209.8	COLO	100.2	WIS	156.4	SD	25.6
41	CAL	208.1	NC	99.9	MONT	155.7	NJ	25.3
42	CONN	202.0	DEL	98.5	NEBR	153.1	TEX	25.3
43	MINN	189.1	RI	96.6	KANS	149.3	NEBR	25.0
44	INDI	186.1	NEBR	91.6	INDI	144.2	LA	24.9
45	MONT	184.0	ND	91.4	MINN	143.5	MISS	24.7
46	ND	183.4	IOWA	85.5	COLO	136.9	WIS	24.0
47	COLO	176.6	KANS	81.6	ND	136.4	MINN	23.7
48	HAWA	173.7	NM	81.5	NM	122.4	CONN	23.2
49	NM	166.5	HAWA	72.2	HAWA	122.0	ND	22.6
50	UTAH	117.4	UTAH	40.6	UTAH	77.7	HAWA	16.9

the 1986 mortality measures allows for at least some of the latency between exposure to stress or smoking and death from the smoking-related diseases.

Table 3–2 shows that lung cancer mortality for the total population is highest in the southeastern states, with Kentucky, Louisiana, Tennessee, Mississippi, Alabama and West Virginia exhibiting six of the seven highest rates. Nevada also ranks high on lung cancer mortality. States with low rates tend to be located in the Midwest and mountain regions of the country. With some exceptions, notably Kentucky and West Virginia, COPD death rates are highest in the mountain and western states.

BIVARIATE RELATIONSHIPS

Table 3–3 presents the zero–order correlations between the State Stress Index, smoking related dependent variables, and control variables. As seen in the first column, stress is correlated significantly with lung cancer mortality for the total population (.44), for males (.36), and for females (.43). Stress is also correlated with mortality from COPD (.34).

The next two correlations show that the SSI is correlated with the prevalence of smokers (.44) but not with per capita cigarette sales (.06). As noted earlier, the two measures are only moderately correlated with each other (.35), suggesting that they measure somewhat different aspects of smoking behavior.

The first measure of smoking, "Cigarette Sales Per Capita," is significantly correlated with all four mortality measures. As for the smoking prevalence measure, "Percent Smokers," the correlations with mortality are not quite as high and only two are significant. The results, however, generally parallel the relationships found with the cigarette-sales measure. The difference may be because the data on smoking prevalence are available only for twenty-seven states, as compared to all fifty states for cigarette sales.

MULTIVARIATE ANALYSIS

The bivariate analysis in table 3–3 shows strong support for the theory that levels of stressful events within populations are linked to rates of cigarette smoking and smoking-related mortality. However, table 3–4 also shows (as expected) significant relationships between four demographic variables and many of the independent and dependent variables. Consequently, a multivariate analysis is needed to examine the effect of stressful events and smoking-related phenomena net of these demographic variables. The four characteristics em-

TABLE 3-3. CORRELATION OF ALL VARIABLES IN THE STUDY FOR FIFTY STATES

Variable Year and Name[a]	STR82	LC86T	LC86M	LC86F	COPD86	PACKS82	SMOKE82	African-American82	POOR82	METRO82	LTHS80
State Stress Index 1982 STR82											
Lung Cancer Mortality, Total 1986 LC86T	.44***										
Lung Cancer Mortality, Male 1986 LC86M	.36**	.94***									
Lung Cancer Mortality, Female 1986 LC86F	.43***	.68***	.39**								
Chronic Obstructive Pul. D. 1986 COPD86	.34**	.16	−.01	.44***							
Cigarette Sales per Capita 1982 PACKS82	.06	.52***	.46***	.42**	.26*						
% Smokers 1981–83 SMOKE82	.44*	.44*	.31	.48**	.20	.35*					
% African-American 1982 African-American82	.44***	.55***	.68***	.04	−.31*	.11	.18				
% below Poverty 1982 POOR82	.26*	.44***	.56***	.00	−.13	.00	.11	.61***			
% of Pop. in Metro Areas 1982 METRO82	.24*	−.28*	−.29*	−.15	−.12	−.32*	−.03	−.02	−.42**		
% with less than H. S. Ed. 1980 LTHS80	.15	.62***	.79***	−.01	−.28*	.23	.23	.71***	.74***	−.36**	
Mean	50.06	185.40	262.60	116.15	31.13	133.07	30.82	9.14	9.59	66.94	32.54
Standard Deviation	19.92	37.03	63.78	25.64	6.58	27.15	3.77	9.22	2.88	14.40	7.57

Note: $*p < .05$, $**p < .01$, $***p < .001$

[a] The capitalized variable names are included to enable readers to obtain the raw data by writing to the State and Regional Indicators Archive, 126 Horton, University of New Hampshire, Durham, NH 03824. See note to table 2-2.

ployed as control variables were: the percentage of African-Americans; the percentage living in metropolitan areas; the percentage below the poverty level; and the percentage with less than a high school education. Table 3–4 presents the results of six regression analyses, each of which uses either a mortality rate or a smoking rate as the dependent variable. The independent variables are the State Stress Index and the four control variables.

Stress and Mortality

In general, multiple regression results parallel those of the bivariate correlation analysis. Section A of table 3–4 reveals that the State Stress Index is associated significantly with increased lung cancer mortality net of the four control variables. For every increase of one point in the State Stress Index, there is a corresponding average increase of .88 deaths from lung cancer per 100,000 population ($p < .01$). The regression coefficients in sections B and C of .94 and .84 indicate that this relationship applies for both males and females separately.

Similarly, a significant link of stress and mortality from chronic obstructive pulmonary disease is shown in section D—an average increase of .22 deaths from chronic obstructive pulmonary disease per 100,000 population for every one point increase in the State Stress Index.

Stress and Smoking

Multiple regression results for the smoking indicators (table 3–4, sections E and F) also parallel the zero-order correlations. Net of all other variables, the State Stress Index is significantly related to the percentage who smoke. The link, however, between stress and packs-per-capita consumption of cigarettes, although in the anticipated direction, is not significant. The fact that stress is significantly associated with one measure of smoking, the percentage reporting smoking, but not the other (the average per capita consumption of cigarettes), although unexpected, is not implausible. It should be recalled that the two indicators are based on a different set of states, since the percentage of those who smoke is available only for twenty-seven of the fifty states included within the Behavioral Risk Factor Surveillance. Second, the packs-per-capita sales figures referred to are based on state of purchase rather than state of residence and are thereby subject to various distortions already discussed.

Examination of state cigarette sales shows two outliers (states with sales over 2½ standard deviations greater than the mean), Kentucky and New Hamp-

TABLE 3-4. REGRESSION OF SMOKING-PROBLEM MEASURES ON STATE STRESS INDEX AND CONTROL VARIABLES

Independent Variables	b[a]	se	beta[b]	p <
A. *Total Lung Cancer*				
Stress	.88	.31	.47	.010**
% African-American	.38	.94	.09	.693
% Metro	−.81	.45	−.81	.087
% Poverty	−4.42	2.96	−.34	.150
% with Less than H.S. Ed.	3.09	1.25	.63	.022*
B. *Male Lung Cancer*				
Stress	.94	.44	.29	.043*
% African-American	1.16	1.32	.17	.387
% Metro	−.90	.63	−.20	.167
% Poverty	−5.94	4.14	−.27	.166
% with Less than H.S. Ed.	6.40	1.74	.76	.001***
C. *Female Lung Cancer*				
Stress	.84	.28	.65	.006**
% African-American	.24	.83	.09	.774
% Metro	−.77	.40	.43	.066
% Poverty	−2.95	2.62	.33	.272
% with Less than H.S. Ed.	.15	1.10	.05	.891
D. *Chronic Obstructive Pulmonary Disease*				
Stress	.22	.06	.68	.002**
% African-American	−.34	.19	−.48	.092
% Metro	−.17	.09	.36	.085
% Poverty	−.19	.61	−.08	.762
% with Less than H.S. Ed.	−.10	.26	.12	.699
E. *Smoking Prevalence*				
Stress	.11	.04	.59	.014*
% African-American	−.09	.12	−.23	.460
% Metro	−.04	.06	−.14	.537
% Poverty	−.44	.38	−.35	.269
% with Less than H.S. Ed.	.25	.16	.51	.141
F. *Packs per Capita*				
Stress	.36	.30	.26	.256
% African-American	.11	.92	.04	.907
% Metro	−.91	.44	−.48	.050*
% Poverty	−6.08	2.88	−.64	.047*
% with Less than H.S. Ed.	1.71	1.21	.48	.175

Note: *p < .05, **p < .01, ***p < .001.
[a]b = unstandardized regression in this and subsequent tables.
[b]beta = standardized regression in this and subsequent tables.

shire. Kentucky is one of the leading tobacco-producing states with very low cigarette taxes and thereby cheaper cigarette prices. In the second state, New Hampshire, taxes have deliberately been set substantially lower than in the large neighboring states of Massachusetts and Maine to attract sales from those states. Thus, in both situations there is the strong possibility that sales figures were substantially augmented by purchasers from out of state.

ROBUSTNESS OF FINDINGS

A number of other analyses were carried out and yielded findings that are consistent with those already described. Our first analysis of stress and smoking related the 1976 version of the State Stress Index (identical in composition, but based on 1976 data) to lung cancer mortality for 1975–1977 (Linsky, Colby, and Straus 1986b). In that study, lung cancer mortality was unstandardized, with age effects controlled through partial correlation. The demographic background variables (the percentage of African-Americans, percentage in metropolitan areas, percentage with four years of high school) were controlled through partial correlation instead of multiple regression. In spite of these differences, the findings from the earlier analysis paralleled the findings reported in this chapter—namely, that the ssi was significantly correlated with smoking and mortality from lung cancer and that those correlations that existed for both males and females became stronger with background variables controlled.

Our earlier study also included a measure of chronic stress, that is, ongoing conditions of stress as opposed to more discrete events: Gibbs and Martin's Measure of Status Integration (MSI). That measure has been previously used in epidemiological studies of suicide, alcoholism, and chronic diseases (Gibbs and Martin 1964; Colby 1985).

All the correlations between the MSI and the smoking-related outcomes were negative, as expected by the theory. The MSI correlations were lower than those reported for our measure of acute stress, the ssi, but two of the correlations reach the .01 level of significance. As in the case of the ssi, the correlations were considerably stronger once other important variables were controlled.

Thus, there appears to be considerable robustness to the relationship between the level of social stress, smoking behavior, and subsequent mortality rates from two major smoking-related diseases (cancer of the lung and chronic obstructive pulmonary disease). The relationship holds for different time periods, for different measures of social stress, for two different smoking-related diseases, and regardless of the mortality measures employed (standardized or unstandardized) or the methods utilized. This replication of the major findings lends additional confidence in the dependability of the findings, despite some of the limitations in the measurement of smoking discussed earlier.

DISCUSSION AND CONCLUSIONS

Although stress and smoking have been previously linked at the individual level and the smoking–cancer link has been established for many years, to our knowledge this is the first study that links living in stressful geographic locales with an increased risk of respiratory cancer and chronic obstructive pulmonary disease. Thus, findings are consistent with the health-related behaviors model of the mechanisms linking stress with disease. Residents of areas experiencing the highest average level of stressor events also tend to have the highest rates of engaging in a behavior that is extremely inimical to health, that is, cigarette smoking. Though consistent with the health-related behaviors model, the findings do not rule out competing hypotheses of stress and disease. One of these— the "promotional hypothesis"—has received increased attention recently and suggests the possibility of a direct effect of stress on cancer, independent of smoking and other mediators. The idea behind the promotional hypotheses is not that stress "causes" cancer per se but that it may promote already-initiated cancer cells through a stress-induced neuroendocrinological mechanism. Such a mechanism could have the consequence of shortening normal latency periods and result in at least short-run increases in mortality. A recent editorial in the *American Journal of Public Health* (Janerich 1991) commenting on a study of environmental pollution, stress, and cancer rates (Hatch et al. 1991) suggests that such an interpretation "is not a far-fetched idea."

To the degree that there may be such a direct effect of social stress on lung cancer mortality rates, one would expect that a relationship between these two variables would persist when the effects of smoking are statistically controlled. We explored this possibility by regression analyses using the available stress, smoking, and lung cancer variables. When smoking prevalence is used as the control variable with the State Stress Index, each contributes equally to variation in total lung cancer mortality (beta = .31 for both), but neither reaches an acceptable level of statistical significance. When packs per capita is used as the control variable instead of smoking prevalence, it reveals the strong independent effect of both stress and smoking on lung cancer mortality (beta = .41 and .50, respectively; p = .020 and .006). These results provide at least preliminary support for the promotional hypothesis.

Current public health efforts toward the prevention of smoking-related diseases focus almost exclusively on education about the effects of tobacco, legal restrictions, and controls on smoking behavior. The current findings suggest that primary prevention would require extending public health efforts farther upstream in the process, that is, by alleviating the stressful conditions that may be implicated in smoking behavior and associated mortality from lung cancer and COPD.

CHAPTER 4

Stress, Drinking Culture, and Drinking Problems

In a classic article on the social causes of alcoholism, Robert Bales (1946) cites repressed aggression as a common maladjustment created by social organization that may lead to high rates of inebriety. Bales's theory of alcoholism clearly focuses on causes of alcoholism that are located in the culture and social structure of societies rather than on causal factors within the motivation of the individual alcoholic. The theory also has the virtue of being well conceived and conducive to research in a field not notably crowded by well-articulated theoretical frameworks. Perhaps that is why the theory continues to occupy a central place in alcoholism literature and to be attractive to sociologically oriented researchers more than four decades after its publication. Unfortunately, despite its centrality and influence on subsequent investigations, its major propositions have rarely been the subject of systematic empirical testing (Room 1976).

BALES'S THEORY

Bales asserted that cultures or social structures influence the rate of alcoholism in three ways. First, there are social-structural factors that create stress and inner tension for members of a particular group or society. We shall refer to this factor as the "stress hypothesis." Second, there are culturally supported attitudes toward drinking and intoxication that determine whether alcohol will be used as a means for relieving that stress and tension (the "normative hypothesis"). The third factor is whether the culture provides alternative mechanisms for relief of that tension (the "functional alternative hypothesis").

John P. Colby, Jr., was coauthor of this chapter.

Bales developed his theory primarily on the basis of an analysis of drinking problems in nineteenth-century Ireland. He explained the high rates of alcoholism among men in that society as resulting from a combination of a social structure that blocked young men from attaining the respectability and status of householder and married man and at the same time permitted and encouraged heavy drinking in local taverns as a release from the tensions and frustrations produced by the denial of status and sexual fulfillment.

This chapter does not provide a full test of all of the hypotheses implied by Bales's theory. Instead, it tests the stress and the normative components of the theory by investigating whether differences in the level of stress or tension and differences in the extent of normative constraints on drinking are related to the level of alcohol problems in populations.

One reason why the stress aspect of the theory has not spawned more empirical research is that severe measurement difficulties abound, particularly for the measurement of the amount of social stress that exists within populations. The research reported in this chapter was made possible by our development of the State Stress Index described in chapter 2. The ssi provides for the first time a broad-based objective index for determining whether one population is subjected to more or fewer stressful life events than another. In this case, it allows the investigation of whether the amount of stress and tension to which a population is subjected is linked to alcohol problems.

DRINKING NORMS

Several studies emphasize the quality or content of norms governing drinking and its relationship to alcoholism (Lafferty et al. 1980; Snyder 1958; Skolnick 1958; Klein 1993). Mizruchi and Perrucci (1962) were among the first to call attention to the importance of proscriptive norms ("Thou shalt not . . . ") versus prescriptive ("Thou shalt . . . ") in the development of alcohol pathology. Based on their literature review, they conclude that predominantly restrictive norms are more likely than predominantly prescriptive norms to be tied to pathological reactions when deviation does occur (Mizruchi and Perrucci 1962, p. 398).

Some investigators have divided societies according to qualitative differences in drinking norms—for example, restrictive, prescriptive, and nonscriptive (Larsen and Abu-Laban 1968); abstinent, ambivalent, permissive, and overpermissive (Pittman 1967); and abstinent, prescribed, convivial, and utilitarian (Bales 1946). Our research follows the approach suggested by Larsen and Abu-Laban, which treats normative approval as a single, more or less continuous variable.

Although the above studies are conceptually rich, they have inspired only qualitative comparative studies or quantitative studies based on individuals as units for analysis. They have therefore not provided an empirical test of the hypothesis at the appropriate level, that is, the social level.

The few quantitative comparative studies of the impact of norm content on drinking and alcohol problems investigated preliterate societies. Whitehead and Harvey (1974), for example, used data on 139 preliterate societies. The correlation between approval of drunkenness and alcohol problems was between .32 and .43 (in socially integrated and nonintegrated societies, respectively). Both approval of drunkenness and approval of drinking were positively related to alcohol problems, but not as much as was the consumption level.

Stull (1975) has criticized this and other studies of drinking behavior that depend on a single qualitative summary estimation of the cultural characteristics of entire societies. First, this type of study assumes greater homogeneity within preliterate societies than is warranted. Second, it depends on reports of participant observers that are difficult to replicate and that fail to distinguish the normative structure from the actual behavior.

As will be explained in the section on procedure, the methods we used to investigate the relation of norm content to alcohol problems eliminates several of these problems. Our approach concentrates on a single society (the United States) but views the question of degree of internal variation as an empirical question by examining differences among the states. All indicators of both alcohol problems and other variables are quantified, and norms and behavior outcomes are separately measured.

THE RESTRICTIVE NORM INDEX

Much more extensive and complex data than are now available would be necessary to measure the entire range of normative issues surrounding alcohol. For example, the degree of normative integration or conflict between norms governing alcohol use is an important issue. More integration or consistency between norms is usually hypothesized as leading to lower rates of alcoholism (Room 1976; Ullman 1958; Chafetz 1971). Our research, however, does not deal with this issue. We focus instead on the degree to which the drinking of alcoholic beverages is disapproved of and restricted, and we develop a Restrictive Norm Index for measuring states and regions in this regard. Although it does not reflect the breadth of some discussions in the literature, it is the first normative scale of which we are aware that measures drinking sentiment according to states and regions. Our index has a further advantage of measuring normative standards independent of alcohol consumption and so avoids potential circularity from that source.

The fifty states vary on a number of measurable characteristics indicative or reflective of norms surrounding alcohol use, including the prohibitionist status of the state, the degree of legal restrictions placed on drinking behavior, and religious composition. The following indicators were used to determine each state's position on the content dimension of restrictive versus permissive sentiment.

1. Religion. The percentage of a state's population that are members of Fundamentalist and Mormon churches, both of which are known to be restrictive (cf. Linsky 1965).[1]

2. Dry Areas. The percentage of a state's population residing in legally "dry" areas (Distilled Spirits Council of the United States 1978, as reported in Hyman et al. 1980).

3. Liquor Outlets. The rate of on-premise liquor outlets per million population (Distilled Spirits Council 1978). A study by Hyman and Driver (reported in Hyman et al. 1980) concludes that dry sentiment has a greater influence on the number of on-premise liquor licenses, whereas financial considerations have a greater influence on the number of off-premise liquor licenses.

4. Sales Restrictions. The degree to which on-premise sale of alcohol was restricted in hours or prohibited on Sundays and other days of the week (calculated by the authors from Distilled Spirits Council of the United States 1983).

The Restrictive Norm Index was computed by Z-scoring each indicator and summing the four indicators. The resulting variable was then transformed to a ZP score (Straus 1981) to present scores in a more easily interpreted range of 1 to 100.

The internal-consistency reliability of the index was evaluated through the alpha coefficient of reliability. The results showed that the Restrictive Norm Index has an alpha coefficient of .76, indicating a moderately high level of reliability.

The left-hand columns of table 4–1 rank the states according to their scores on the Restrictive Norm Index. The substantial differences among states are

1. The Fundamentalist churches, in order of size, include: churches affiliated with the Southern Baptist Convention; and the Lutheran Church (Missouri Synod, Christian Churches [formerly Disciples of Christ], Churches of Christ, Church of the Nazarene, and Seventh Day Adventists). The figures are from a study of church membership, as summarized by state in Hyman et al. (1980).

TABLE 4-1. RANK OF THE FIFTY STATES ON THE SSI AND ALCOHOL-RELATED PROBLEMS

Rank	Restrictive Norms Index		Cirrhosis Deaths per 1 Million		Deaths from Alcoholism and Alcoholic Psychosis per 1 Million		Per Capita Annual Consumption of Absolute Alcohol per Pop. 15+ (U.S. gallons)[a]	
	State	Score	State	Score	State	Score	State	Score
1	MISS	99	NEV	323.91	NM	165.31	NEV	5.33
2	UTAH	95	NY	270.38	ALAS	143.24	NH	4.83
3	KY	90	CALIF	255.46	NEV	86.96	ALAS	3.49
4	GA	88	FLA	248.06	WYO	67.36	WIS	3.15
5	TENN	87	DEL	229.31	NC	66.04	CALIF	3.13
6	ALA	81	RI	227.53	RI	61.33	VT	3.07
7	SC	81	NM	218.47	DEL	59.98	MD	2.96
8	OKLA	79	MASS	214.17	GA	59.31	RI	2.94
9	ARK	76	NJ	213.40	OKLA	58.49	WYO	2.91
10	IDAHO	70	MICH	212.99	UTAH	56.84	COLO	2.86
11	TEXAS	70	ARIZ	206.12	MONT	54.01	MASS	2.85
12	NC	69	ILL	203.70	ARIZ	48.70	ILL	2.82
13	KANS	57	NH	197.87	MD	48.54	ARIZ	2.76
14	MINN	53	MAINE	194.99	CONN	47.72	DEL	2.75
15	MO	52	OREG	190.83	SC	47.46	WASH	2.74
16	VA	51	WASH	190.49	WV	43.50	HAWA	2.73
17	FLA	49	MD	190.29	WASH	41.08	NY	2.70
18	SD	46	WV	189.60	FLA	40.81	MONT	2.70
19	NM	46	ALAS	188.76	KY	39.12	FLA	2.70
20	WVA	45	CONN	186.54	VA	37.94	MICH	2.83
21	DEL	45	PENN	186.69	MAINE	36.95	NJ	2.61
22	MAINE	45	NC	171.63	TENN	35.44	CONN	2.58
23	ARIZ	45	WYO	169.57	COLO	34.81	NM	2.54
24	MICH	44	OHIO	169.15	ND	33.76	OREG	2.54
25	CONN	44	MONT	164.92	IDAHO	33.55	ND	2.48
26	ND	44	OKLA	162.02	MISS	32.85	TEX	2.45
27	IND	43	VA	158.17	SD	32.76	MINN	2.43
28	OREG	43	GA	155.75	NY	32.38	LA	2.42
29	MASS	42	VT	155.06	ALA	31.81	MAINE	2.38
30	COLO	42	SD	152.86	OREG	31.40	NEB	2.37
31	WASH	41	TEX	150.10	WIS	31.30	IDAHO	2.29
32	IOWA	41	COLO	149.52	VT	30.64	SC	2.23
33	LA	40	WIS	147.44	LA	30.49	PENN	2.21
34	NEBR	40	LA	145.20	CALIF	30.32	VA	2.20
35	CALIF	40	SC	143.49	MINN	29.63	GA	2.19
36	RI	38	MO	140.32	KANS	28.86	SD	2.13
37	NH	38	KY	135.52	NH	27.20	OHIO	2.12
38	HAWA	38	NEB	134.93	IND	26.36	IOWA	2.07
39	WYO	37	IND	134.90	MO	23.66	MO	2.07
40	MD	36	IDAHO	128.79	MICH	22.08	IND	1.98
41	OHIO	36	MINN	126.47	MASS	21.83	NC	1.96
42	ILL	36	UTAH	125.68	ILL	21.80	MISS	1.88
43	NY	35	ALA	123.37	ARK	21.23	OKLA	1.85
44	NJ	32	IOWA	123.35	PA	20.28	ALA	1.83
45	MONT	30	ND	123.07	OHIO	20.13	KANS	1.83
46	PA	28	TENN	122.55	TEX	18.57	KY	1.79
47	ALAS	28	KANS	118.31	NJ	15.85	TENN	1.79
48	VT	24	HAWA	110.76	IOWA	14.85	WV	1.73
49	WIS	24	MISS	106.86	NEB	14.52	ARK	1.51
50	NEV	17	ARK	106.17	HAWA	8.88	UTAH	1.48

[a]With adjustment for tourism (Hyman et al. 1980).

clear. The state with the highest index score (most restrictive) is Mississippi, followed by Utah, Kentucky, and Georgia. In fact, most of the highly restrictive states tend to be southern, with the exception of Utah, with its large Mormon population. At the other end of the continuum are the most permissive states with regard to drinking norms. Nevada is most permissive, followed by Wisconsin, Vermont, Alaska, and Pennsylvania.

INDICATORS OF ALCOHOL PROBLEMS

We used the following three factors as indicators of alcohol problems:

1. Deaths attributed to cirrhosis of the liver per 100,000 adult population (National Office of Vital Statistics 1975–1977). Table 4–1 shows the states in rank order on this measure.
2. The combined death rate for alcoholism and alcoholic psychosis (National Office of Vital Statistics 1975–1977).
3. Alcohol consumption, corrected for tourism: gallons per person (with corrections made by the authors following Hyman et al. 1980).[2]

No measure of alcohol problems is completely free of bias, because all the indicators of alcoholism arise or are mediated through social control processes, which in turn reflect a social response to alcoholism. This includes arrest data, attribution of cause for alcohol-related deaths, or self-reports of drinking or drunkenness in community surveys. Death due to alcohol-related problems could be underreported in order to protect the reputation of the deceased or the surviving family members. Similarly, state alcohol sales from which consumption is estimated may be distorted by sales to out-of-state residents and do not include the consumption of illicitly manufactured alcohol. By employing several indicators of alcohol problems based on different sources of data or different reporting systems, the bias associated with the dependence on any one source of data is at least minimized.

STRESS AND ALCOHOL PROBLEMS

Table 4–2 shows that the State Stress Index is correlated with the death rate from cirrhosis, the death rate for alcoholism and alcoholic psychoses, and the total rate of alcohol consumption, all in the direction expected by the theory.

2. The correction was made by multiplying the total apparent alcohol consumption by a correction factor formed by the ratio of out-of-state tourist expenditures to total personal income for

TABLE 4-2.   CORRELATION OF SSI WITH ALCOHOL-RELATED PROBLEMS IN THE FIFTY STATES

	Correlation with SSI	
Dependent Variable	Zero Order	5th-Order Partial[a]
Cirrhosis Death Rate		
Total	.37**	.45**
White Males	.33**	.37**
White Females	.41**	.47***
Nonwhite Males[b]	.02	.25
Nonwhite Females	−.03	.26
Alcoholism and Alcoholic Psychosis Death Rate		
Total	.30*	.25*
White Males	.19	.17
White Females	.32*	.35*
Nonwhite Males	.09	.20
Nonwhite Females	.06	.14
Alcohol Consumption Rate		
Corrected for Tourism	.20	.31*
Total Consumption	.22	.34*

Note: *p < .05, **p < .01, ***p < .001.
[a]Correlations are 4th order with nonwhite males and females, because % nonwhite was omitted from the controls.
[b]Nonwhite correlations are based on 38 states.

Although the overall pattern of correlations appears highly consistent with the hypothesis no matter which alcohol-problem measure is used, the zero-order correlations in table 4–2 can be misleading. One possibility worth considering is that the correlation of stress with alcoholism is partly or wholly spurious, because it is accounted for by factors such as age structure or other variables correlated with stressor events. For this reason, partial correlation was employed to control for five variables: the percentage of the population over fifty-five years of age; the percentage with more than four years of high school; the percentage of families below the poverty line; the percentage of African-Americans; and the percentage living in metropolitan areas. The right-hand columns of table 4–2 report correlations with these five variables controlled for simultaneously. If the correlations between stressful events and alcohol-related behavior were either wholly or partly spurious, we would expect those correlations either to drop out or to become significantly smaller when these variables are controlled. However, the correlations for the total death rate from alcoholism and alcoholic psychosis becomes only marginally smaller, and the correlations for the cirrhosis and the

---

states. This correction factor probably undercorrects for states that have notably lower beverage prices, because nontourist residents of neighboring states may enter the state specifically to purchase alcoholic beverages.

alcohol-consumption variable actually increase. Thus, if anything, the five control variables were partly suppressing the strength of the relationship between stressor events and the dependent variables.

This pattern of relationship between the ssi and alcohol-related mortality applies to white females and males separately, although the pattern is slightly stronger for females. For nonwhite males and females, the relationship between the ssi and alcohol-related mortality also appears to be in the same direction, but in this case it is not significant.

NORMS AND ALCOHOL PROBLEMS

The evidence presented up to this point appears to be highly compatible with Bales's first hypothesis. His theory, however, emphasizes that it is not stress alone but the combination of stressful conditions and certain types of culturally approved attitudes toward drinking that result in high rates of alcoholism. Our findings suggest that the stressfulness of life in a population accounts by itself for some of the state-to-state variations in levels of alcoholism, without reference to normative controls. We now examine the effect of normative controls on alcohol problems.

Because of the special interest in social control over alcohol in this part of the research, we expanded the set of dependent variables to include several behavioral outcomes of drinking in addition to alcohol consumption and alcohol-related disease variables considered in the investigation of the stress hypothesis. These additional variables are:

1. Driving while intoxicated arrest rate (U.S. Department of Justice 1981).
2. The combined arrest rate for other alcohol-related offenses, including violation of alcohol laws, vagrancy, drunkenness, and disorderly conduct (U.S. Department of Justice 1981).
3. The percentage of arrests for alcohol-related offenses, calculated by dividing the number of alcohol-related arrests by the number of arrests for all causes.

Correlation among Alcohol-Problem Indicators

Before looking at the impact of restrictive norms on alcohol problems, we first consider how the different types of indicators of alcohol problems relate to one another, as shown in table 4–3. As expected from other research, the death rate for cirrhosis of the liver is highly correlated with both per capita consumption of

TABLE 4-3. CORRELATION AMONG INDICATORS OF ALCOHOL-RELATED PROBLEMS IN THE FIFTY STATES

Indicators	1	2	3	4	5	6
1. Death rate from cirrhosis		.62**	.64**	−.12	.02	−.31*
2. Alcohol consumption			.99**	.03	.07	−.21
3. Alcohol consumption corrected for tourism				−.04	.00	−.25*
4. DWI arrest rate					.48**	.49**
5. Other alcohol-related arrests						.68**
6. Alcohol-related arrests as % of all arrests						

Note: *p < .05, **p < .001.

alcohol and consumption corrected for tourism. In addition, the three measures of alcohol disruptiveness (variables 4, 5, and 6 from table 4–3) are also highly intercorrelated. However, since variables 5 and 6 use a partly overlapping count of arrests, the correlations between them may be inflated.

At the same time, the rate of arrests for alcohol offenses and for DWI— both of which are measures of the extent to which alcohol-related behavior becomes socially disruptive—were uncorrelated with cirrhosis deaths and with the total rate of consumption of alcoholic beverages. The correlations in both cases approach zero. This suggests that DWI arrests and arrests for other alcohol-related offenses do not arise as a response or reaction to heavy drinking, because there is apparently no more drinking in states with high arrest rates than in states with low arrest rates. In the next section of this chapter we examine this issue in terms of what social factors are related to DWI and other alcohol arrests.

Restrictive Norms and Alcohol Problems

Table 4–4 provides data on the question of whether a relationship exists between the Restrictive Norm Index and the indicators of alcohol problems. There is a striking difference between the correlations in part A of table 4–4, which deals with the indicators of heavy drinking, and part B, which deals with disruptive alcohol-related problems.

The first three correlations in section A of the table show that the Restrictive Norm Index is strongly and inversely related to the rate of deaths from cirrhosis of the liver and also to the two measures of alcohol consumption (−.52, −.60, −.63). All three correlations are highly significant. That is, the stronger the sentiments against the use of alcohol within a population, the fewer deaths from cirrhosis of the liver. Comparison of the left and right columns of the table

TABLE 4-4. CORRELATION OF RESTRICTIVE NORM INDEX WITH INDICATORS OF HEAVY DRINKING AND DISRUPTIVE ALCOHOL-RELATED BEHAVIOR

Indicator of Alcohol-Related Problems	Correlation with Restrictive Norm Index	
	Zero Order	5th-Order Partial
A. Indicators of heavy drinking		
Death rate from cirrhosis	−.52.***	−.56***
Alcohol consumption	−.60***	−.55***
Alcohol consumption corrected for tourism	−.63***	−.58***
B. Indicators of disruptive alcohol-related behavior		
DWI arrest rate	.37**	.25*
Other alcohol-related arrests	.32**	.17
% of all alcohol-related arrests	.49***	.36**

Note: *p < .05, **p < .01, ***p < .001.

shows that there are no important changes in the relationship between restrictive norms and alcohol when controls are introduced for five variables that plausibly could affect the relationships (poverty, educational level, metropolitan population, nonwhite population, and age).

The situation changes radically, however, when alcoholism is measured by disruptive behavior related to alcohol (section B) rather than by disease-related deaths and consumption of alcohol. There is a complete turnaround in the direction of the relationship. The Restrictive Norm Index is positively and significantly correlated with the arrest rate for DWI, the arrest rates for other alcohol-related offenses, and the percentage of all arrests that are alcohol related (.37, .32, .49).

When the five control variables are partialed out, the correlations between the Restrictive Norm Index and disruptive alcoholic behavior are somewhat smaller, but two of the three (DWI and percentage of all arrests for alcohol-related offenses) remain statistically significant. Thus, the more restrictive the norms concerning alcohol consumption, the greater the incidence of behavior that is defined as socially disruptive. Moreover, as we pointed out above, arrests for DWI and arrests for other alcohol-related offenses do not seem to arise as a response to the amount of drinking, because there is apparently no correlation between level of alcohol consumption and arrests for DWI or other alcohol-related offenses. Instead, such alcohol problems appear to be a response to the strong cultural disapproval of drinking, with the restrictively oriented states experiencing the highest rates of arrests related to alcohol.

SOCIAL CONTROL VERSUS PSYCHOLOGICAL AMBIVALENCE

So far we have not explained the somewhat paradoxical finding of why DWI and other alcohol-related arrest rates are high within restrictive or dry communities. At least two possible intervening processes could account for the observed correlation: the "social control" hypothesis and the "ambivalence" or "inoculation" hypothesis. Each has plausibility based on sociological and alcoholism theory.

Social Control

The social-control approach emphasizes the fact that the observed arrest rates are a product of both true incidence of the behavior in question and society's reaction to that behavior. According to this reasoning, dry communities may be less tolerant of public drunkenness and may encourage stricter policing of that behavior. Other communities with more liberal traditions concerning alcohol may be more forgiving of the same types of public behaviors influenced by alcohol.

Ambivalence and Inoculation

The ambivalence hypothesis, in contrast, suggests that the true incidence of disruptive and dangerous drinking is actually higher in restrictive communities despite lower overall consumption of alcohol. This occurs, according to several authors (Chafetz 1971; Room 1976; Ullman 1958), because those who drink within predominantly dry cultures are especially vulnerable to alcohol problems. The normative conflict between acceptance and rejection of alcohol competes within the psyche of those who drink, and they experience anxiety and guilt in connection with drinking, which in turn leads to loss of control.

A related form of the ambivalence hypothesis is sometimes referred to as the "inoculation hypothesis." Individuals reared within normatively dry environments are not properly socialized to maintain control over their drinking and over their behavior when under the influence (Skolnick 1958; Chafetz 1971; Room 1978). For example, research by Globetti (1978) on drinking by high school students and by Straus and Bacon (1953) on drinking by college students within strongly restrictive environments found that fewer students drank than in less restrictive environments but that a disproportionate number of those who did drink did so excessively and were more disruptive when drinking. There were more reports of students getting into fights, destroying property, and driving while under the influence. Thus teaching abstinence seems to inadvertently encourage the behavior that is deplored (Skolnick 1958).

In this analysis, we group ambivalence and inoculation hypotheses together, because they both assume a higher true prevalence of unruly drinking behavior among those who drink in restrictive communities. Both hypotheses posit a loss of control, the one because of internal conflict over drinking, and the other because of lack of socialization to responsible drinking. Both lead to identical predictions. The expectation of the ambivalence/inoculation hypothesis is that there will be less drinking in restrictive environments but that when drinking occurs it will be more dangerous and disruptive. According to this hypothesis, the higher arrest rates in restrictive communities simply reflect the true prevalence of this dangerous and disruptive drinking.

Empirical Test

A critical test of the social-control versus the ambivalence/inoculation hypothesis requires additional data beyond the arrest rates for DWI and other alcohol-related offenses—namely, information on the true incidence of alcohol-related disruptive behavior independent of the police response to that behavior. Such data are partially available for the United States through the recently initiated Behavioral Risk Factors Survey conducted by the Centers for Disease Control (1984).

Approximately twenty-one thousand survey respondents in twenty-four states (selected in such a way as to represent the adult population of their state) were asked if over the last month they had driven when they might have had too much to drink. This data is of course subject to the same limitations as any self-reported survey data on crimes or misconduct. In addition, respondent reports on this subject could be influenced by community views on drinking. We use this data despite the limitations, because it is the most broadly based data set allowing state-by-state comparisons of the prevalence of drinking and driving.

In table 4–5 the 24 states are divided into three categories ranging from restrictive to permissive. The three sets of states can be compared according to their average level of consumption of alcohol per capita, DWI self-reports, and DWI arrests. This table allows a partial test of the ambivalence hypothesis through comparison of consumption of alcohol with amount of drunken driving, and a test of the social-control hypothesis through the ratios of DWI arrests per 100,000 to DWI self-reports under different normative contexts.

The first row of table 4–5 shows that the average consumption of alcohol increases markedly as one moves from restrictive to permissive states, whereas the next row shows that DWI arrest rates *decrease*. The third row shows that DWI self-reports increase from restrictive to permissive states, with the increase roughly proportional to the increase in average alcohol consumed. Thus there is

TABLE 4-5. MEAN RATES FOR DWI ARRESTS, DWI SELF-REPORTS, AND CONSUMPTION OF ALCOHOL, BY RESTRICTIVE NORM INDEX RANK[a]

	Restrictive ($N = 8$)	Moderate (8)	Permissive (8)	Total (24)
Alcohol consumption (gallons per capita)	2.06	2.66	3.26	2.66
DWI arrests per 100 K	11.15	6.41	6.19	5.46
% DWI self-report	4.51	4.95	6.91	7.92
DWI arrests per 100 K self-reports	247.20	129.50	89.60	145.10

[a]Findings are based on the 24 states for which self-reported data are available.

no indication that drinkers behave more recklessly in restrictive environments. At least as far as drinking and driving is concerned, the ambivalence hypothesis is not supported by this data. This is consistent with the correlation data reported in table 4–3.

The relationship of self-reported driving while drinking with DWI arrests reveals another pattern. As we move from permissive to restrictive states, the self-reported incidence of driving while under the influence decreases, whereas arrests for DWI increase. This results in dramatically higher ratios (bottom row) of arrest rates to prevalence rates in restrictive states (247.2) as compared to permissive (89.6) states. Higher DWI arrests in restrictive areas appear to be a reflection of the lower tolerance and tougher law enforcement with regard to drinking and driving. Thus the elevated arrest rates for DWI's within restrictive states appear to be highly consistent with the control hypothesis.

To summarize, two distinct patterns in the data are salient. First, permissive normative systems are significantly correlated with all the indicators of heavy drinking and cirrhosis deaths. Second, restrictive normative systems are significantly correlated with all of the indicators of disruptive alcohol behavior. States that have the strongest cultural biases against beverage alcohol tend to be the same states that experience the most problems, that is, the highest arrest rates associated with drinking.

The DWI rates and other arrests related to alcohol do not appear to arise as a response to the incidence of heavy drinking, because we also found that alcohol-related arrests were completely uncorrelated with the amount of alcohol consumed; nor did they correspond with self-reported incidence of driving while under the influence of alcohol. The data suggest that even with respect to behaviors that are seemingly objective and obviously dangerous, such as driving while intoxicated, norms regarding drinking may be as important as the drinking behavior itself in determining the extent to which alcoholism is defined as a social problem.

Thus, strong normative proscriptions regarding alcohol seemingly produce results opposite to their intent not so much by increasing disruptive deportment among those who drink as by increasing the law enforcement against such behavior once it occurs.

The somewhat paradoxical pattern discussed above has been observed with regard to other types of deviance. As Kai Erikson (1966, p. 22) concluded from his analysis of deviancy and societal values in the early Puritan colonies of New England, "It is not surprising that deviant behavior should seem to appear in a community at exactly those points where it is most feared. Men who fear witches soon find themselves surrounded by them; men who become jealous of private property soon encounter eager thieves." The results of the present analysis suggest a parallel conclusion, namely, that societies that fear alcohol soon encounter problems with disruptive alcoholics.

THE INTERACTION OF STRESS AND DRINKING NORMS

So far we have reported investigation of Bales's two major propositions, the stress hypothesis and the normative hypothesis, and presented evidence that stress and restrictive norms are each separately related to alcohol problems. Although these findings are consistent with Bales's theory, they fail to provide a full test of it because that theory clearly implies an interactive relationship among stress, alcohol norms, and alcohol problems rather than a simple catalog of the determinants of alcoholism. In the study of alcohol problems in Irish culture, Bales argues that it was the combination of stress produced in young men by a social system that denied them sexual and status fulfillment, in the context of a normative system that allowed and encouraged them to release their frustration by drinking in local taverns, that led to the especially high rates of alcoholism among that population. Hence, to test the theory fully, both variables must be combined within the same research design.

According to Bales's theory, the highest rates of alcohol problems should prevail in situations where high stress is coupled with norms encouraging and allowing alcohol consumption. Consequently, this final section of the chapter considers the question of whether normative differences between states influence the relationship between stress and alcohol problems. In table 4–6, states are arranged in quartiles according to permissiveness of alcohol use. If Bales's theory is correct, the State Stress Index should be linked most strongly to alcohol problems in states that are most permissive regarding alcohol use. The correlations reported in table 4–6 support Bales's theory. Stress is most strongly

TABLE 4-6. CORRELATION OF SSI WITH HEAVY DRINKING AND ALCOHOL-RELATED ARRESTS FOR RESTRICTIVE, MODERATELY RESTRICTIVE, MODERATELY PERMISSIVE, AND PERMISSIVE STATES (ZERO-ORDER CORRELATIONS)

| | Correlation of Stress with Alcohol Problems for States in Which Normative Constraints Are:[a] | | | |
Indicators of Alcohol Problems	Restrictive (N = 13)	Moderately Restrictive (N = 13)	Moderately Permissive (N = 12)	Permissive (N = 12)
Average consumption of alcohol	.26	.38	−.02	.56*
Average consumption corrected for tourism	.31	.38	−.02	.60*
Death rate from cirrhosis	.04	.69**	.40	.75**

Note: *p < .05, **p < .01, ***p < .001.
[a]The 13 highest ranking states on the Restrictive Norm Index constitute the Restrictive States, the second 13 are the Moderately Restrictive, the next 12 are Moderately Permissive, and the last 12 are the Permissive states. The exact N for the quartiles was governed by the convenience of cutting points.

linked to the amount of alcohol consumed and to cirrhosis deaths within the most permissive group of states (see right-hand column of table 4–6). For all three indicators of heavy drinking, the correlations with stress are highest, and in each case statistically significant, within the most permissive quartile of states (r = .56, .60, and .75). Stress and the indicators of heavy drinking are correlated in some of the other quartiles as well, but the correlations are not as high for the most part, and only one of the nine other correlations is statistically significant.

We shall return to the relationship of the stressfulness of a society to alcohol-related problems in chapter 7, where we examine the potentially lethal mixture of stressful events, alcohol, and violence.

SUMMARY

This research discussed in this chapter represents the first time that the links between social stress, drinking norms, and alcohol problems have been investigated using broadly based and systematic social system measurements of these concepts. The stressfulness of the social environment in the fifty states was found to be consistently correlated with heavy drinking and alcohol-related disease problems. Those correlations were, for the most part, undiminished and, when we controlled for additional variables, even enhanced in some cases. This evidence is highly compatible with the Bales's stress hypothesis of alcoholism.

With regard to Bales's normative hypothesis, the findings are more complex. States with more permissive drinking norms do experience greater problems with alcohol-related disease (cirrhosis deaths) and higher consumption levels. However, it is the restrictively oriented states that experience the most problems with regard to disruptive drinking (DWI and other alcohol-related arrests), despite the fact that disruptive alcohol problems were not correlated with consumption of alcohol. Disruptive alcohol problems apparently arise because of lower tolerance of public drunkenness and stricter policing of that behavior within restrictive communities.

Finally, we found strong support for Bales's original theory, because when both the stressfulness of life and the normative approval of alcohol are combined within the analysis, it appears that the stress is most closely linked to cirrhosis deaths and heavy drinking within the context of strong cultural support for the use of alcohol.

CHAPTER 5

The Relation of Objective and Subjective Stress to Suicide

Societal conditions have been known to be linked to suicide rates at least since the pioneering study of Emile Durkheim ([1897] 1951). It was Durkheim who first persuasively argued that as personal a decision as suicide seems to be, it is a social fact when considered in the aggregate. This aspect of suicide—that is, the rate among society as a whole—is predictable from social processes and social-structural conditions.

Following Durkheim, a research tradition developed in sociology linking objective indicators of various social conditions, such as anomie, social disorganization (Cavan 1928), status integration (Gibbs and Martin 1964), tight and loose social structures (Straus and Straus 1953), and more recently, social stress, with rates of suicide (Brenner 1977; Landau 1984; Landau and Raveh 1987; Linsky and Straus 1986). The gap between these two sets of objective social indicators (social structural conditions and suicide) is usually filled by various hypothesized but unmeasured intervening variables (Landau 1988).

Our earlier extensive study of social stress in America (Linsky and Straus 1986) found that the higher the State Stress Index, the higher the suicide rate ($r = .52$ for 1976 data, and $r = .34$ for 1982 data). The relationship of the ssi with the suicide rate persisted even when nine other variables frequently associated with suicide were controlled in the regression analysis. Thus, the link between social stress and suicide appears to be highly stable. This analysis, however, shares the design problems cited above. There is no empirical data on the intervening process, that is, no measure of how a state's stressor events insinuate themselves into the psyche of its residents, altering their mental status, creating dispositions toward various actions, and finally inducing suicide in some.

Lazarus (1966) was a pioneer in pointing out that stress is not a product of events alone. Instead it is a function of both the events and the subjectively defined demands of a situation created by those events. As noted above, however, the aspect of stress measured by our earlier work was limited to the frequency of stressor events within social systems. The untested presumption was that the level of stressful life events influenced the rate of suicide through some psychological processes. At a minimum, there should be a perception or awareness by those in high-stress states that their world is stressful or difficult to cope with. In turn the populations of such areas may have a greater disposition toward suicidal thoughts, which would therefore lead to higher suicide rates. We were previously unable to test this stress theory of suicide in the whole because our earlier research did not have available measures of subjectively defined stress. It was limited to objective statistics for both stressful events and suicide.

Psychological studies of suicide, on the other hand, focus primarily on personality attributes and psychological processes such as attitudes and world-views that may be linked to suicide, including depression, negative self-attitude, hopelessness, and lack of purpose in life (Harlow, Newcomb, and Bentler 1986; Kovaks, Beck, and Weissman 1975). These psychological studies, however, do not measure the impact of social and cultural conditions and the social nature of suicidal behavior. Thus, neither of these approaches is wholly satisfactory when it comes to understanding suicide.

The current study attempts to combine these approaches by including within a single research design the objective social conditions measured directly at the macro-level (using the State Stress Index and survey data on subjective or self-perceived stress and on suicidal thoughts of the same geographically located population) as well as state suicide rates.

STRESS AND SUICIDE

Durkheim's seminal study of European suicide rates focused on the extent to which individuals were firmly tied to others and to their society as the major explanatory variable. As part of that general theory, he argued that when social, cultural, and economic changes occurred too rapidly to be assimilated, the result was a condition of normlessness or anomie, which in turn was linked to rising suicide rates. That condition of externally induced changes in people's lives is not unlike our own focus stemming from the stressful life-events tradition that posits excessive demands for adaption to new external conditions as the central cause of stress.

At the individual level, stressful life events have been implicated in attempted suicides. For example, Paykel et al. (1975) report that those attempting suicide experienced four times as many events in the six months prior to the attempt as did a control group drawn from the general population. At the individual level, stressful life events also have been linked extensively with depression and depressive symptomatology (Warheit 1979; Thoits 1983a). Depressive disorders share some of the psychodynamic components of suicides, inasmuch as both are presumed to represent aggression turned inward upon the self, and depressed persons are at high risk of suicide (Arieti 1959).

At the aggregate level, suicide has been linked with specific stress factors such as unemployment (Brenner 1977, Boor 1980). However, the problem with using single indicators of social-system stress is that they often confound other issues. The unemployment rate, for example, may represent a chronic stressor rather than a stressful event, which is the focus of this study. Moreover, it may signify poverty rather than stress per se. (See chapter 8 for a more detailed discussion of these issues.)

METHODS

This chapter combines both state-level data on stressful events and suicide with subjective types of data obtained from individuals living within the given state.

MEASURES

The suicide rate used as the dependent variable was computed from the number of suicides in each state for the years 1982 and 1983 as given in the *Vital Statistics of the United States*. It is the mean rate per 100,000 population for these two years and is presented in the last column of table 5–1.

Our measure of subjective stress was obtained from the National Family Violence Resurvey (Straus and Gelles 1986, 1990), a survey of a national probability sample of 6,002 households that was conducted by telephone interviews in 1985. Eligible households had to include an adult eighteen years of age or older who (1) was presently married, (2) was presently living with a person of the opposite sex as a couple, (3) had been divorced or separated within the last two years, or (4) was a single parent with a child under eighteen residing in the household. When more than one eligible adult was in the household, a random procedure was used to select one respondent according to gender and marital status. Thus, approximately half the respondents are men and half women. The interviews lasted an average of thirty-five minutes. The response rate, calculated as "completed portion of eligible," was 84%. For more information on the sample, see Straus and Gelles (1990). Two measures were computed from this data:

The Perceived Stress Index was computed by summing responses to the three questions that ask how often the following problems had occurred in the previous twelve months: Felt difficulties were piling up so high that you could not overcome them; (2) Found that you could not cope with all of the things you had to do; (3) Felt nervous or stressed. The response categories used a 5-point format ranging from 0 (Never) to 5 (Very Often). The state-level variable is the percentage of respondents in each state who scored 5 or more. This index is presented in the first column of table 5–1.

This measure Suicidal Thoughts is the percentage of respondents in each state who said they had "Thought about taking your own life" one or more times in the last year. This variable is presented in the second column of table 5–1.

Three variables are included as controls in the analysis, because they are correlated with both stress and suicide and thereby could contribute to spurious results. Those variables are: the percentage living in poverty, the percentage living in urban areas, and percentage of African-Americans among respondents.

RESULTS

Zero-Order Correlations

Table 5–2 presents the zero-order correlations between the independent, control, and suicide variables. The first column of correlations in the table shows that the ssi correlates with suicide and with each of the intervening variables in the direction anticipated by the theory. Four of the six correlations are significant, with a fifth correlation almost significant. The second column indicates that the perceived or subjective stress index is significantly related to suicidal thoughts but is not significantly related to the rate of suicide. The third column shows that suicidal thoughts are significantly correlated with the suicide rate for states.

The control variables appear to be correlated with both stress and suicide but not necessarily in the same direction. For example, the percentage of African-Americans is positively related to the State Stress Index but negatively correlated with the suicide rate. Whatever the direction of the correlation, it is important to control these variables in the analysis, because they may be either masking some of the relationships between the stress and suicidal variables or contributing to a

TABLE 5-1. STATES RANKED IN ORDER OF PERCEIVED STRESS, SUICIDAL THOUGHTS, AND SUICIDE RATE

Perceived Stress Index		% Suicidal Thoughts		Suicide Rate	
State	B63YP2	State	VB3JP1	State	SD8283TR
NEV	39.1	VT	20.1	NEV	26.48
WVA	37.5	NEV	13.7	WYO	19.71
UTAH	36.2	OREG	9.4	NM	18.95
KY	35.1	MASS	9.1	COLO	17.48
NH	33.4	RI	8.3	ARIZ	17.45
ARK	31.3	NM	8.1	FLA	16.75
OREG	30.3	TENN	7.8	MONT	16.46
IDA	30.3	UTAH	7.5	IDA	15.15
MO	30.2	SD	7.1	VT	15.10
ND	30.0	NC	7.0	OREG	15.07
INDI	30.0	COLO	6.9	CAL	14.95
VT	29.9	MICH	6.8	WASH	13.89
ALA	29.9	NH	6.7	OKLA	13.79
OHIO	29.9	WVA	6.6	ME	13.51
KANS	28.9	WIS	6.4	VA	13.49
ALAS	28.6	LA	6.3	KY	13.32
TENN	28.6	MONT	6.2	UTAH	13.18
NY	28.5	SC	6.2	LA	12.94
NJ	28.0	PA	5.9	SD	12.90
VA	27.7	MINN	5.8	NC	12.86
CAL	27.3	CAL	5.7	MO	12.80
ARIZ	27.1	GA	5.7	TENN	12.75
OKLA	27.0	IDA	5.7	TEX	12.65
RI	26.5	TEX	5.6	WIS	12.64
MISS	26.4	INDI	5.4	ALAS	12.39
MD	25.4	MO	5.4	GA	12.34
SC	25.1	OHIO	5.0	WVA	12.26
PA	25.0	VA	4.9	ARK	11.99
MONT	24.9	FLA	4.9	MICH	11.97
NC	24.2	ARK	4.7	KANS	11.90
DC	24.2	MISS	4.7	DEL	11.83
MASS	24.1	ARIZ	4.7	NH	11.60
GA	24.1	CONN	4.5	INDI	11.51
ILL	23.5	ALA	4.4	OHIO	11.45
LA	23.5	KANS	4.3	PA	11.33
MICH	22.8	ME	4.1	DC	11.26
NEBR	22.7	NJ	3.8	MINN	11.06
TEX	22.5	NEBR	3.7	IOWA	10.92
COLO	22.2	MD	3.5	RI	10.86
WASH	22.1	ILL	3.1	MD	10.84
FLA	21.3	WASH	3.1	SC	10.83
MINN	21.2	KY	3.0	ALA	10.82
SD	20.1	NY	3.0	ND	10.42
WYO	19.6	DC	2.9	NEBR	9.79
WIS	19.3	OKLA	1.8	ILL	9.71
CONN	17.9	IOWA	1.6	HAWA	9.58
ME	16.5	ND	0.0	MASS	9.30
IOWA	13.7	ALAS	0.0	MISS	9.27
NM	12.9	WYO	0.0	CONN	8.05
DEL	12.4	DEL	0.0	NJ	7.69
HAWA	10.1	HAWA	0.0	NY	7.64

TABLE 5-2. CORRELATION OF INDEPENDENT, CONTROL, AND SUICIDE VARIABLES

Variable	1	2	3	4	5	6	7
1. State Stress Index	1.00						
2. Perceived Stress Index	.27**	1.00					
3. Thought about Suicide	.12	.34**	1.00				
4. % Poor	.25*	.08	.01	1.00			
5. % Metro	.24	−.16	−.13	−.41**	1.00		
6. % African-American	.44**	.03	−.07	.60**	−.01	1.00	
7. Suicide Rate	.34**	.14	.36**	−.09	.02	−.27**	1.00

Note: $*p < .05$, $**p < .01$ (one-tailed tests). The labels needed to locate these variables in the State and Regional Indicators Archive are: (1) EVNTINDX = State Stress Index; (2) VB63YP2 = Perceived Stress Index; (3) VB63JP1 = Thought about Suicide; (4) PBPTOT = % Poor; (5) PCTURB = % Urban; (6) PCTBLCK = % African-American; (7) = SD8283TR = Mean Suicide Rate per 100 *K* Population, 1982 and 1983.

spurious relationship. The next part of the analysis therefore controls for race and other demographic variables.

PATH ANALYSIS

We decided to use path analysis because it most closely models our theoretical argument. We hypothesize (1) that the level of objective stress (the State Stress Index) leads to the subjective experience of stress within a state population (the Perceived Stress Index, or PSI); (2) that populations perceiving stress are more likely to experience more frequent suicidal thoughts; and (3) that such state populations are in turn likely to experience higher rates of suicide. The path analysis presented in figure 5–1 reveals several interesting findings.

Objective and Subjective Stress

There is a highly significant association (beta = .41) between the SSI (our measure of objective stress) and the PSI. Remember that the SSI is based on a set of macro-level statistics for states, whereas the PSI is based on individual survey responses for the same states. This is a solid finding considering that the data are from quite distinct sources and that the survey data are subject to small sample variability. (Although 6,002 is large for a national survey, the sample size for some states is small, thereby potentially contributing to measurement error.) Moreover, Landou (1988) reports that in the few studies that have investigated the connection between objective and subjective stress, relationships have been weak.

TABLE 5-3.   REGRESSION OF SUICIDE RATE ON SIX INDEPENDENT VARIABLES, 1982–1983

Independent Variable	b	beta	se(b)	t
State Stress Index	.09	.58	.02	3.9**
Perceived Stress Index	−.05	−.11	.06	−0.9
Thought about Suicide	.26	.27	.12	2.1*
% Poor	.05	.19	.05	0.3
% Metro	−.01	−.08	.03	−0.6
% African-American	−.19	−.53	.05	−3.3**

Note: *p < .05, **p < .01 (one-tailed tests). Labels used by the State and Regional Indicators Archive for the independent variables are given in the note to table 5-2.

The finding of a significant link between the SSI and the PSI is important for a number of reasons. Prior to this finding, we could only infer a relationship between the rate of stressful events in a state and the subjective experience of stress. Events within the SSI are known to be stressful based on research with individuals, and the SSI is consistently correlated with the rates of maladaptive behaviors. The findings shown in table 5–2 help to establish a cognitive link between the concentration of stressor events within social systems (the SSI) and the behavioral outcome of suicide. This finding supports the construct validity of the principal independent variable of the study, the SSI. It appears that populations living in states with a high concentration of stressful events (high SSI scores) do appear to experience their environment as stressful.

Perceived Stress and Suicidal Thoughts

The path from Perceived Stress to Suicidal Thoughts in figure 5–1 also shows that populations that subjectively experience greater stress show significantly higher levels of suicide ideation (beta = .28). This relationship is not as strong as the association between the SSI and perceived stress. Although both of these indicators are derived from the same set of data, there are reasons why a weaker relationship might be anticipated, such as the extremely skewed measure of suicidal thoughts. The more important reason, however, is because, on theoretical grounds, there is a more direct connection between stressful events and feeling stressed than there is between feeling stressed and thinking about suicide.

Suicidal Ideation and Suicide

The right side of figure 5–1 shows that the level of suicidal ideation in a state population is significantly linked to the total suicide rate for the state. The beta

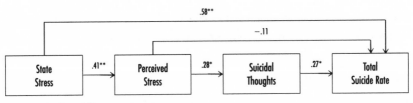

Note: *p ≤ .05, **p ≤ 1.01.

Figure 5-1.   Path Analysis of Suicide Rate

of .27 is remarkable in view of the fact that the proportion of a population who thinks about suicide is much larger than the proportion who actually commits suicide; there is a potential error in measuring suicidal thoughts; and this coefficient is net of the effect of five other variables.

As a number of researchers have shown, the potential responses to stress are legion. Suicidal behavior is only one. Responses may take extremely violent and outwardly directed aggressive forms, as we shall see in later chapters. Or, as we saw earlier, they may take other self-destructive forms such as fatal accidents, alcoholism, and tobacco abuse. Other responses to stress have been shown to include deaths from ulcers, asthmatic attacks, or other psychogenic illnesses.

The various outcomes of the stress process may be based on the tendency of individuals to respond to stress in different ways. In addition, as we suggested in chapter 1, different cultures and subcultures may channel the response to stressful conditions and events in particular directions through the socialization process and through strong normative controls over behavior.

An example of the role of culture is found in a study of alcohol abuse and violence reported in chapter 7. Those findings show that norms regarding the legitimacy of violence and norms surrounding drinking help to explain state-to-state differences in violent drinking in response to stress. Thus, the cultural context in which the stress is played out is important in predicting what outlet individuals may take.

Perceived Stress and Suicide

The path analysis shows only a small tendency (beta = .11) for populations who report subjectively experiencing stress to respond to that stress with higher levels of suicidal thoughts and more actual suicides. This may be because considering suicide and going through with suicide are only two highly extreme forms of coping with the feelings of being under stress. Again, there are many other less lethal responses to perceptions of stress. The outcomes of subjective stress would depend on the entire arsenal of coping styles permitted or encouraged within a culture, that is, normatively directed forms of responses.

Stressful Events and Suicide

The direct path of .58 between the SSI and total suicide rate is much stronger than the indirect path through Perceived Stress and Suicidal Thoughts. This might be explained by a number of factors. One possibility, of course, is that the relationship may be stronger in reality than in this analysis because of the crude measurement of the cognitive variables. There could also be some other more relevant indirect paths involving other micro-processes not measured here intervening between objective stress and suicide.[1]

CONCLUSIONS

We found a continuous albeit modest path from the objective social stress experienced by a population through the perception of that stress and suicidal thoughts, leading eventually to suicide rates. At the same time, there is still a strong direct path between our objective social stress measure, the SSI, and suicide that is not explained by the more cognitive intervening variables. In the broad sense Durkheim may be correct that the suicide *rate,* as a characteristic of a social system, may be better explained by factors external to individuals—that is, by other social-level processes than by psychological constructs. These other factors could include the sociocultural climate of states that may make it more or less likely that objective and subjective stress will eventuate in a higher suicide rate. Such sociocultural variables include the social-control and social-integration factors discussed by Durkheim, such as religious climate, the openness or closeness of communities, and the stability of the relational systems.

1. It would, for example, be useful to include attempted suicide as a path between stress and suicide. Although information on suicide attempts was available in the survey data, the incidence was too small for dependable state-by-state estimates. Similarly, depression has been linked in individual-level research to both stressful events (Paykel, Prusoff, and Myers 1975; Warheit 1979) and suicide (Arieti 1959). Consequently, we originally included an additional variable in the path analysis, a four-item depression inventory derived from the same set of survey data. In the path between self-perceived stress and suicidal thoughts, however, depression created a confusing pattern. It correlated positively with both our objective and subjective measures of stress, as expected, but negatively with suicidal thoughts and the rate of suicide, contrary to expectations. We plan to examine the measure of depressive symptomatology further as part of an effort to determine what is responsible for this pattern. We mention it here in case researchers with experience in this area should wish to share their knowledge with us.

CHAPTER 6

Gender Differences in the Links between
Stress, Suicide, and Homicide

In this chapter we continue to examine the nature of the connection between the stress of society and rates of violent activities, with particular attention to gender differences.

PHYSIOLOGICAL AND COGNITIVE MODELS

Most research on the effects of stress, especially in the area of illness, relies on either a direct physiological model or a cognitive model of stress. In the direct physiological model, accumulating stressors are seen as operating directly on the physical organism (including neurophysiological processes), but at a preconscious level; sometimes these stressors result in pathological processes (Selye 1980, Holmes and Rahe 1967). In the cognitive or psychological model, various cognitive or psychological appraisal processes such as threats to identity (Burke 1991), interrupted expectations, psychological discomfort, and anxiety are seen as mediating the effects of stress on various outcomes (Lazarus 1966). Research in this tradition has tended to focus on the relation of these cognitive variables, especially self-perceived threat, to various outcomes; whereas research in the direct-physiological-model tradition examines primarily correlations between objective stressors and various purported outcomes of stress. Seldom are both the objective stressors and the subjective perceptions of that stress included within the same design, as they are in this study, so that their separate and joint effects can be determined.

GENDER DIFFERENCES

The primary purpose of this chapter is to examine the question of whether women and men resident in the same communities are sensitive to the same or different environmental stressors. Do the same social stressors bother men and women similarly? Are there different cognitive factors that mediate stress for men and women? Are there classes of stressors to which men appear more sensitive or vulnerable than women, and vice versa?

Studies of gender differences in response to stress have sometimes yielded surprising findings. Not only do women and men frequently play different roles, but even when they play the same role such as parent, worker, or neighbor, they may experience those roles quite differently (Barnet, Beiner, and Baruch 1987; Umberson, Wortman, and Kessler 1992; Simon 1991). For example, the meaning of being an adult child of an elderly parent could be far different for women than for men because of differing expectations that both they and others have for themselves in that situation. Aneshensel and Pearlin (1987, p. 76) argue that such "structured differences have their origins not in the psyches of individual women and men . . . but in the sex stratification of the social system." They go on to suggest that it is important to understand not only how social roles determine the exposure to stress but also how stressors occur at the junctures of multiple roles. The role of wife and mother is more likely to be time-consuming and expansive and more disruptive of other social roles than the role of husband and father. There is therefore a greater potential for inter-role conflict with work roles.

In our previous research we found that the relationship between stress and a number of maladaptive behaviors were stronger for women than for men (Linsky and Straus 1986). This includes a stronger link to motor vehicle accidents, total accidents, suicide, heavy smoking, heavy drinking, and deaths from asthmatic attacks and peptic ulcers. Thus, women appear to be at greater risk from the effects of social stressors than men for these disorders.

One explanation for a possibly closer association of maladaptive behavior and disease with stress in women lies in the nature of some of the stressful events included in the ssi. Several events in the index relate closely to women's family and reproductive roles (infant deaths, fetal deaths, abortions, and illegitimate births). Other events such as divorce, recent migration, and new housing could also have a greater impact on women than on men. Divorce tends to impose greater economic hardship on women; residential moves are frequently made because of husbands' changing jobs; and wives may bear the brunt of adjustment to the new community. Even economic and job-related stressors such as work stoppages and unemployment, which appear to affect men more than women owing to traditional centrality of labor market roles for men, may be extremely stressful for women because of the strains these stressors place on entire families and because of women's special responsibility for the well-being of the family.

We are not suggesting that the stronger relationship between stress and disorders is simply a measurement artifact resulting from the particular set of stressful events in the SSI. The items that make up the SSI were chosen partly because of the convenience of the available data. But more important, they were chosen because of their inclusion in previous stressful life-event scales and because, in our view, such events as the death of an infant, moving to a different community, divorce, and job loss represent some of the most stressful experiences in American life. The fact that women appear more vulnerable than men to the effects of this group of stressors may be a function of women's particular position within the structure of American society.

In this chapter, we examine the way men and women respond differentially to stress; do men or women have a higher proclivity for either internal or external aggression? Specifically, we extend the analysis from the last chapter by performing a path analysis linking objective stress (as measured by the SSI) with gender-specific indexes of perceived stress and to gender-specific rates of homicide and suicide. Additionally, we use victim-offender relationships (family, acquaintance, stranger) for gender-specific homicide offense rates. In this way, we can identify whether men and women respond differentially with aggression toward selves or toward others as the result of stress. Also, when the aggression is directed outward, we are able to assess who is most vulnerable to that aggression. For example, are men more likely to be violent to those close to them or to strangers? Who are the most likely targets of aggression by women?

METHODS

This section describes key variables and also gives the rank order of states on each theoretically relevant variable. Because these data are not available in published sources, the tables enable readers to gather information on important social indicators and also make the data available for use in other studies.

Familial, Economic, and Community Sources of Stress

The analysis up to this point employed the entire fifteen-item State Stress Index rather than the subgroups of economic, familial, or community events. We did this for two reasons. First, it is more consistent with Holmes and Rahe's (1967) theory that stress arises from the cumulation of stressful events from diverse

TABLE 6-1. STATE STRESS AND PERCEIVED STRESS, BY GENDER

| | | | Perceived Stress | | | |
| | State Stress Index | | Females | | Males | |
Rank	State	EVNTINDX	State	VB63YP2F	State	VB63YP2M
1	NEV	100	ND	30.0	NH	20.0
2	GA	85	WVA	29.0	VT	20.0
3	ALAS	83	ALA	27.4	NEV	17.6
4	ALA	82	UTAH	26.5	ALAS	14.3
5	ARIZ	75	KY	26.5	MONT	12.5
6	MISS	73	RI	25.0	MASS	11.4
7	TENN	73	MISS	23.6	OHIO	10.8
8	WASH	72	VA	23.5	ARK	10.4
9	CAL	70	NY	23.3	INDI	9.1
10	SC	70	KANS	23.3	MO	9.0
11	COLO	69	ARIZ	23.2	UTAH	8.8
12	MICH	69	OREG	22.4	KY	8.8
13	OREG	65	IDA	22.2	MICH	8.7
14	FLA	60	COLO	22.0	CAL	8.7
15	VA	58	LA	21.7	NM	8.6
16	ILL	56	ARK	21.5	OREG	8.4
17	LA	56	WYO	21.4	NJ	8.4
18	INDI	54	NJ	21.3	OKLA	8.3
19	OKLA	54	INDI	20.9	NC	7.9
20	TEX	54	SC	20.5	LA	7.8
21	HAWA	53	SD	20.0	FLA	7.2
22	NM	52	TENN	19.8	WVA	7.0
23	KY	51	MD	19.7	MD	6.8
24	NC	51	MO	19.6	KANS	6.8
25	OHIO	51	OKLA	19.3	ALA	6.8
26	WVA	51	ILL	18.8	WASH	6.7
27	IDA	50	OHIO	18.7	NY	6.6
28	NY	50	PA	18.7	PA	6.5
29	DEL	49	CA	18.6	ARIZ	6.3
30	PA	49	GA	18.2	DC	6.3
31	MO	48	NEV	17.6	TEX	6.1
32	MD	45	WASH	17.1	GA	6.1
33	RI	40	TEX	17.1	IOWA	5.9
34	UTAH	40	NEBR	16.7	NEBR	5.9
35	VT	39	MINN	16.5	TENN	5.7
36	ME	38	NC	16.4	IDA	5.6
37	NJ	38	DC	15.6	CONN	5.5
38	KANS	35	FLA	15.2	MISS	5.5
39	MINN	32	WIS	15.0	ILL	5.2
40	ARK	31	ALAS	14.3	MINN	4.9
41	MASS	31	MICH	14.1	WIS	4.6
42	NH	31	NH	13.3	DEL	4.3
43	CONN	30	MONT	12.5	SC	4.2
44	MONT	29	MASS	12.4	COLO	4.1
45	WYO	29	ME	12.0	ME	4.0
46	ND	24	CONN	11.8	VA	3.4
47	WIS	23	NM	11.4	ND	0.0
48	NEBR	15	VT	10.0	RI	0.0
49	IOWA	10	HAWA	10.0	WYO	0.0
50	SD	10	IOWA	8.9	SD	0.0
51	DC		DEL	8.7	HAWA	0.0

sources that overwhelm the capacity of individuals to adjust. The content of stressor events is seen as less important than their cumulative impact.

Our findings are consistent with that assumption. We found that the cumulative SSI correlated more highly on average, and more consistently, with various maladaptive outcomes than either single items or the separate economic, familial, or community subindexes (Linsky and Straus 1986).

The second reason we used the total index is economy. As this chapter illustrates, it would greatly complicate and possibly clutter the book to substitute three separate component indexes (or possibly fifteen separate items) in each of the chapters as compared to the single SSI, without a clear gain in our view.

Because the focus here is on gender differences, however, it seemed important to separate the index into its components. First, as we discussed above, women and men often occupy different roles in the familial and economic spheres. And even when they do occupy the same roles, they may experience them roles differently. Thus, the analysis of gender differences in the stress process would seem to benefit from the separation of these areas of potential stress. Table A–7 shows the states in rank order of their scores on the three component stress indexes. Table 6–1 shows the rank order of the states on perceived stress by gender, and also for comparison, the rank order of the states on the State Stress Index.

Homicide Data

Williams and Flewelling (1988, p. 421) criticize the use of total homicide rates in comparative studies of homicide. They suggest that some of the inconsistent findings in such research is attributable to the "failure to disaggregate the overall homicide rate into more refined and conceptually meaningful categories of homicide." For example, most previous homicide research used either the published FBI data on homicides or the homicide death rates from *Vital Statistics of the United States*. Consequently, they have used homicide *victimization* rates, despite the fact that the primary issue has usually been theories that explain homicide *offenses*. In this research we use data that has heretofore not been available on homicide rates for men and women—the Comparative Homicide File, or CHF. These data allow a much more precise analysis of the relationship of social stress to homicide.

The CHF is based on the Supplemental Homicide Report made up of data files obtained from the Federal Bureau of Investigation for the years 1976–1984; this report contains records on over 157,000 homicides. Williams and Flewelling (1987) converted this data to rates for each of the fifty states.

TABLE 6-2.   RELATIONSHIP-SPECIFIC HOMICIDE RATE FOR MALE OFFENDERS, PER 100K

Homicides Committed by Males

Rank	Family		Acquaintance		Stranger	
	State	R8F106	State	R8F107	State	R8F108
1	DC	8.85	DC	21.11	DC	24.42
2	TEX	5.02	TEX	13.53	NY	7.71
3	NEV	4.55	GA	12.99	LA	7.67
4	MISS	4.49	FLA	11.95	NEV	6.77
5	LA	4.46	ALAS	11.78	TEX	5.51
6	SC	4.40	MISS	11.33	FLA	5.41
7	GA	4.31	NEV	11.31	CAL	4.84
8	ALA	4.21	LA	11.06	ILL	4.03
9	ALAS	4.18	NM	10.49	ARIZ	3.52
10	OKLA	4.06	CAL	10.23	NM	3.37
11	NM	4.04	ALA	10.14	OHIO	2.97
12	FLA	3.99	SC	9.40	MD	2.91
13	KY	3.89	MD	9.15	MO	2.83
14	NC	3.56	MICH	8.74	SC	2.80
15	TENN	3.43	NC	8.72	ALAS	2.76
16	CAL	3.17	TENN	8.60	TENN	2.72
17	ARIZ	3.14	MO	8.37	MISS	2.66
18	MO	3.01	ILL	8.10	MICH	2.51
19	NY	2.90	KY	7.98	OKLA	2.48
20	ARK	2.82	OKLA	7.91	GA	2.46
21	MICH	2.74	NY	7.40	COLO	2.39
22	VA	2.64	ARK	7.29	INDI	2.35
23	DEL	2.55	VA	7.27	VA	2.13
24	WVA	2.45	ARIZ	7.09	WYO	2.09
25	MD	2.36	COLO	5.64	HAWA	1.96
26	KANS	2.33	NJ	5.55	NJ	1.94
27	INDI	2.29	INDI	5.15	ALA	1.86
28	ILL	2.27	DEL	4.93	PA	1.84
29	WYO	2.22	OHIO	4.86	NC	1.80
30	COLO	2.09	WVA	4.74	KY	1.64
31	PA	1.98	PA	4.72	KANS	1.61
32	HAWA	1.94	CONN	4.61	WASH	1.46
33	OHIO	1.93	WYO	4.39	OREG	1.44
34	NJ	1.91	KANS	4.27	CONN	1.41
35	UTAH	1.82	WASH	4.01	MASS	1.39
36	WASH	1.64	HAWA	3.91	MONT	1.33
37	MONT	1.62	OREG	3.62	RI	1.07
38	OREG	1.45	RI	3.48	UTAH	1.06
39	RI	1.37	MASS	3.36	DEL	1.03
40	NH	1.19	IDA	3.28	NEBR	.99
41	CONN	1.18	NEBR	2.59	ARK	.96
42	ME	1.16	UTAH	2.55	WVA	.85
43	MASS	1.14	VT	2.49	WIS	.75
44	WIS	1.13	WIS	2.37	VT	.62
45	NEBR	.98	MONT	2.26	MINN	.56
46	IDA	.88	ME	2.03	NH	.50
47	IOWA	.84	SD	1.82	IDA	.46
48	ND	.64	NH	1.81	IOWA	.44
49	SD	.59	IOWA	1.78	ME	.43
50	MINN	.55	MINN	1.75	SD	.43
51	VT	.32	ND	.67	ND	.30

In contrast to the homicide rates published by the FBI, which are confined to the overall incidence of homicide, or the rates published by the National Center for Health Statistics, which are confined to homicide mortality, the Comparative Homicide File specifies homicide rates by situations, and most relevant to the current chapter, by the relationship of victims and offenders. These detailed rates allow us to examine the more specific mechanisms that link such broad explanatory variables as social stress to homicide. Tables 6–2 and 6–3 display those detailed homicide rates.

Suicide

The gender-specific suicide rates used as the dependent variables were computed from the number of suicides in each state for the years 1982 and 1983 as given in the *Vital Statistics of the United States* (National Office of Vital Statistics 1985). We used the mean rate per 100,000 population for these two years because the one-year rates for small states are unreliable. Table 6–4 displays these gender-specific rates of suicide.

Statistical Analysis

The main analysis for the study takes the form of separate path analyses for each gender. Each analysis tests a model, starting with objective stress in a state (SSI), leading to the subjective experience of that stress by the state's population, which leads in turn to rates of homicide and suicide. Examination of the diagrams (figures 6–1 to 6–3) do not show paths for any of the control variables, because that would make already complicated diagrams almost unreadable. Readers should keep in mind, however, that all the coefficients were estimated with controls for urbanizaton, the percentage of African-Americans in the state population, and poverty.

Table 6–5 presents a zero-order correlation matrix for all of the stress measures employed in this chapter, including the SSI, the three subindexes of economic, family, and community stressors, and perceived stress for females and males. The SSI is not significantly correlated with any of the three subindexes, nor with male and female perceived stress separately. Moreover, the three subindexes are not significant. There is a modest but significant correlation between economic stressors and female perceived stress (.39) and a significant negative association between economic stressors and male perceived stress (−.38). This paradoxical finding is explored further later in this chapter in the discussion of the path analysis.

TABLE 6-3. RELATIONSHIP-SPECIFIC HOMICIDE RATE FOR FEMALE OFFENDERS, PER 100K

	Homicides Committed by Females						
	Family			Acquaintance		Stranger	
Rank	State	R8F109	State	R8F110		State	R8F111
1	TEX	2.66	DC	5.76		DC	1.70
2	ALA	2.57	MISS	2.13		LA	.54
3	LA	2.53	NEV	2.00		TEX	.25
4	MISS	2.49	GA	1.84		ALAS	.22
5	GA	2.33	TEX	1.65		NM	.20
6	ALAS	1.92	FLA	1.53		FLA	.19
7	SC	1.89	ALA	1.41		MICH	.18
8	FLA	1.79	NC	1.40		MISS	.17
9	ARK	1.65	ARK	1.39		NY	.13
10	OKLA	1.62	LA	1.37		CAL	.12
11	MO	1.44	SC	1.32		ARIZ	.12
12	TENN	1.41	TENN	1.26		SC	.12
13	NEV	1.40	MICH	1.20		OHIO	.11
14	MICH	1.38	VA	1.11		ARK	.10
15	NC	1.37	CAL	1.04		INDI	.09
16	WYO	1.36	OKLA	.92		OKLA	.09
17	KY	1.23	INDI	.88		GA	.09
18	COLO	1.12	NY	.88		ILL	.08
19	ILL	1.08	ILL	.85		ALA	.08
20	CAL	1.07	OHIO	.84		WVA	.08
21	DC	1.06	MD	.83		PA	.07
22	VA	1.05	DEL	.82		MD	.07
23	OHIO	.95	MO	.81		WIS	.07
24	NY	.93	KY	.76		NJ	.07
25	ARIZ	.93	VT	.71		NC	.07
26	INDI	.89	ARIZ	.64		NEBR	.06
27	NM	.85	PA	.61		KANS	.06
28	MONT	.82	WVA	.60		WASH	.06
29	MD	.78	KANS	.58		MO	.06
30	KANS	.76	COLO	.55		HAWA	.05
31	IDA	.74	NJ	.54		COLO	.04
32	WVA	.70	NM	.54		MINN	.04
33	PA	.69	OREG	.53		VA	.04
34	CONN	.55	WASH	.51		OREG	.03
35	RI	.54	CONN	.47		UTAH	.03
36	DEL	.51	NEBR	.35		TENN	.02
37	NJ	.51	WIS	.33		MASS	.02
38	WASH	.50	MASS	.29		KY	.02
39	HAWA	.49	IDA	.28		NEV	0.0
40	NH	.49	IOWA	.26		DEL	0.0
41	OREG	.36	ALAS	.23		VT	0.0
42	UTAH	.35	UTAH	.22		CONN	0.0
43	MINN	.32	RI	.17		IDA	0.0
44	VT	.30	NH	.15		IOWA	0.0
45	NEBR	.29	HAWA	.15		RI	0.0
46	ND	.28	MINN	.14		NH	0.0
47	MASS	.26	ND	.12		ND	0.0
48	ME	.25	WYO	.10		WYO	0.0
49	WIS	.24	SD	.07		SD	0.0
50	IOWA	.21	MONT	.07		MONT	0.0
51	SD	0.0	ME	.07		ME	0.0

TABLE 6-4. GENDER-SPECIFIC SUICIDE RATES

	Suicide per 100 K			
	Male		Female	
Rank	State	SD8283MR	State	SD8283FR
1	NEV	44.07	NEV	13.66
2	WYO	33.88	FLA	8.94
3	NM	32.08	ARIZ	8.88
4	COLO	29.46	WYO	8.30
5	ARIZ	28.55	CAL	8.12
6	MONT	28.14	NM	8.02
7	FLA	27.81	COLO	7.83
8	VT	27.50	WASH	6.71
9	IDA	25.36	OKLA	6.62
10	OREG	24.29	OREG	6.51
11	UTAH	23.46	LA	6.49
12	CAL	23.29	DEL	6.34
13	OKLA	23.23	VA	6.23
14	SD	22.31	TEX	6.20
15	ALAS	22.30	IDA	6.03
16	WASH	22.15	ME	5.96
17	ME	21.78	NC	5.83
18	KY	21.77	GA	5.81
19	VA	21.77	MO	5.78
20	TEX	21.34	TENN	5.64
21	WVA	21.00	MONT	5.58
22	LA	20.91	OHIO	5.53
23	NC	20.81	SC	5.49
24	TENN	20.75	KY	5.48
25	WIS	20.73	KANS	5.43
26	MO	20.50	MICH	5.28
27	ARK	20.46	RI	5.14
28	GA	20.20	WIS	5.08
29	NH	20.07	INDI	5.06
30	KANS	19.10	PA	5.03
31	ND	19.03	UTAH	5.02
32	MICH	18.62	MINN	4.84
33	DC	18.45	MD	4.69
34	INDI	18.31	DC	4.67
35	IOWA	18.29	ALA	4.57
36	PA	18.20	ILL	4.52
37	ALA	17.85	MISS	4.29
38	MINN	17.84	ARK	4.27
39	DEL	17.78	NH	4.24
40	OHIO	17.74	WVA	4.18
41	MD	17.67	NEBR	4.17
42	RI	17.29	HAWA	4.15
43	SC	17.23	ALAS	3.97
44	NEBR	15.93	IOWA	3.91
45	HAWA	15.36	MASS	3.88
46	MASS	15.31	SD	3.86
47	ILL	15.30	VT	3.81
48	MISS	14.99	NJ	3.71
49	CONN	13.12	CONN	3.42
50	NY	12.55	NY	3.21
51	NJ	12.14	ND	2.31

TABLE 6-5.   CORRELATION OF STRESS INDICATORS FOR FIFTY STATES

Stress Measure	1	2	3	4	5	6
1. State Stress Index						
2. Economic Stressors	−.26					
3. Family Stressors	−.19	.08				
4. Community Stressors	.24	−.23	−.01			
5. Stress as Perceived by Females	.18	.39*	−.11	−.29		
6. Stress as Perceived by Males	.19	−.38*	.24	.12	−.28	

Note: *p < .01, **p < .001 (one-tailed significance).

GENDER DIFFERENCES IN THE RELATION BETWEEN OBJECTIVE AND SUBJECTIVE STRESS

In chapter 5, we reported that the perception of stress by a state's population correlates significantly with objective stress as measured by the SSI. In this chapter we examine this relationship for men and women separately. In figure 6–1, the two paths from Stressful Events (far left) to Perceived Stress (center) show that perceived stress is significantly linked to stressful events for men (.38) but not for women (.10).

STRESS AND HOMICIDE

Because family has been the traditional domain of women and because almost all homicides by women occur within the family, we assumed that the link between stress and homicide within families would be accounted for mostly by women. That assumption was incorrect, however. The path of .37 (at the top of figure 6–1) and the path of .41 (fourth down) indicate that the relationship between stressful events and family homicide is practically the same for both men and women.

Turning to the indirect paths, that is, those from Perceived Stress (at the center) to the homicide rates (at the right), it can be seen that none of these paths are statistically significant for women, but two of the three are significant for men. Thus, figure 6–1 suggests that perceived stress is a mediating variable in the link between stressful events and homicide only for men. Perceived stress experienced by men adds a small increment of explained variance to the male homicide rate. It also adds a bit of confusion, because it is linked significantly with homicides of strangers as well as homicides of acquaintances and is not significantly related to family homicides. In sum, the hypothesis that the effect of stressful life events is mediated by subjectively experienced stress was only

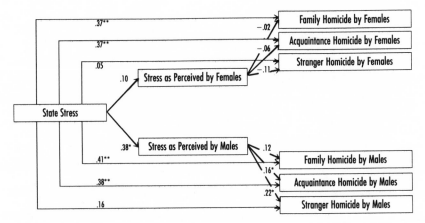

Note: *p ≤ .05, **p ≤ .01.

Figure 6-1.   Path Analysis of Family, Acquaintance, and Stranger Homicides Using Overall Stress Index

weakly and inconsistently supported. Instead, the results replicate previous findings in chapter 5 of a direct link between objective stress and violence and show
that these effects apply to both men and women. That is, stressful life events
explain a significant part of the state-to-state variance in homicides of family
members and acquaintances by men and women. However, stress is not significantly related to homicides of *strangers* by either men or women. Thus, it appears
that objective stress at the state level is associated with an increased rate of lethal
violence between intimates and acquaintances for both men and women but
not between strangers. The role of subjective or perceived stress in the stress-
homicide process is inconsistent, however.

Source of Stress and Type of Homicide

When the fifteen-item State Stress Index was partitioned into three separate
subindexes or areas of stress (economic, family, and community), we found that
the three subindexes are only somewhat correlated with each other (see table 6–
5). Consistent with those low correlations, figure 6–2 shows substantial differences in how the subindexes relate to homicide.

Economic stressors (section A of figure 6–2) are significantly related to
homicides of strangers, but not to other homicides. This finding, which applies
to both men and women, makes a certain degree of sense. Homicides of strangers
are more likely to occur in economically motivated crimes such as robbery and
burglary. Homicides of family members and acquaintances are less likely to be
directly motivated by economic concerns.

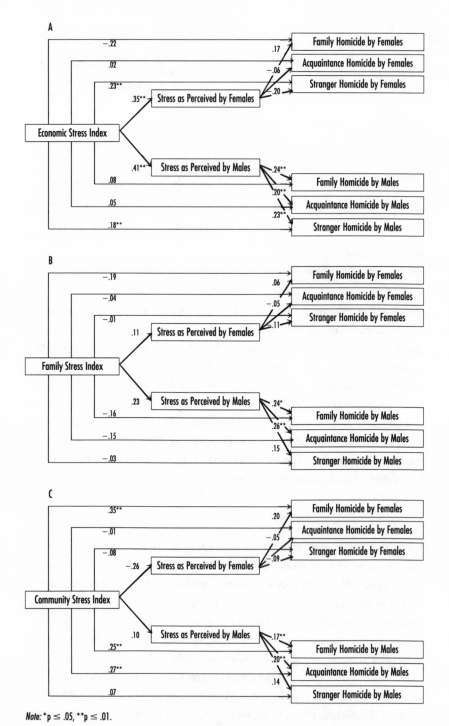

A

Economic Stress Index

path	value
→ Family Homicide by Females	−.22
→ Acquaintance Homicide by Females	.02
→ Stranger Homicide by Females	.23**
→ Stress as Perceived by Females	.35**
→ Stress as Perceived by Males	.41**
→ Family Homicide by Males	.08
→ Acquaintance Homicide by Males	.05
→ Stranger Homicide by Males	.18**

Stress as Perceived by Females → Family Homicide by Females .17
Stress as Perceived by Females → Acquaintance Homicide by Females −.06
Stress as Perceived by Females → Stranger Homicide by Females .20

Stress as Perceived by Males → Family Homicide by Males .24**
Stress as Perceived by Males → Acquaintance Homicide by Males .20**
Stress as Perceived by Males → Stranger Homicide by Males .23**

B

Family Stress Index

−.19
−.04
−.01
.11
.23
−.16
−.15
−.03

Stress as Perceived by Females → .06, −.05, .11
Stress as Perceived by Males → .24*, .26**, .15

C

Community Stress Index

.35**
−.01
−.08
−.26
.10
.25**
.27**
.07

Stress as Perceived by Females → .20, −.05, −.09
Stress as Perceived by Males → .17**, .20**, .14

Note: *p ≤ .05, **p ≤ .01.

Figure 6-2.   Path Analysis of Family, Acquaintance, and Stranger Homicides Using Subindexes of Stress

Family stressors (section B), on the other hand, show no direct path to any of the types of homicide, including family homicide, for either men or women. Community stressors (section C) are linked directly to *family* homicides for both men and women. Community stressors are also significantly related to *acquaintance* homicides for men.

Indirect Paths

The indirect effects of stress on homicide are shown by the paths from the center of figure 6–2 to the right side. These paths follow a similar pattern for each of the three separate subindexes, as was previously established in figure 6–1 for the overall State Stress Index.

Although objective stress is related to the homicidal behavior of both men and women about equally, it occurs in a somewhat different fashion. For men, seven out of the nine paths in figure 6–2 from perceived stress to homicide are statistically significant; whereas for women, none of these nine paths are significant. From this, one can conclude that the relationship between stress and homicide is partly mediated by subjective or perceived stress, but not so with women. Thus, external social stressors either act directly on women without mediation of perceptions, propelling them in the direction of lethal violence, or operate through other cognitive or social processes not examined in this study.

STRESS AND SUICIDE

So far in this chapter we have examined gender difference in regard to the process leading from stress to lethal violence directed against others. We now turn to the other end of the spectrum of aggression—gender differences in the stress processes leading to the most extreme form of violence directed toward self, suicide.

The results of the path analyses of the effects of a stressful social environment on suicide rates are given in figure 6–3. Section A of figure 6–3 uses the overall SSI as the measure of objective stress and shows highly significant direct paths between the State Stress Index and suicide for both men (.61) and women (.53). However, almost nothing is added by the indirect paths through subjective stress for either men or women. Thus, stress does not appear to have an impact on suicide rates through conscious cognitive processes, that is, through awareness and concerns about these stressors and their impact. Rather the findings are more consistent with a model that supposes that stress affects outcomes such as

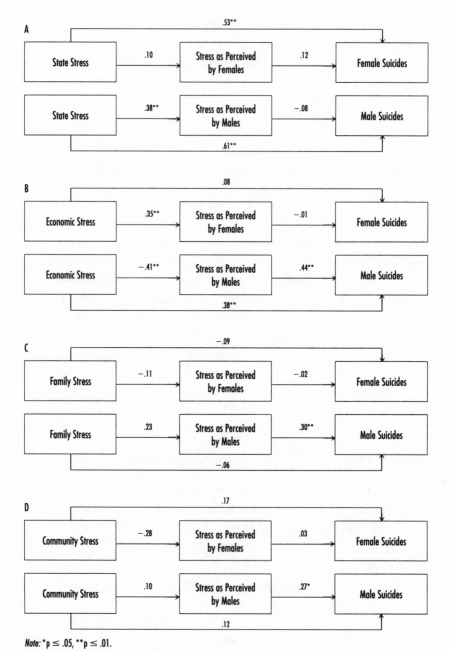

A

State Stress — .10 → Stress as Perceived by Females — .12 → Female Suicides
.53** (top path from State Stress to Female Suicides)

State Stress — .38** → Stress as Perceived by Males — −.08 → Male Suicides
.61** (bottom path from State Stress to Male Suicides)

B

Economic Stress — .35** → Stress as Perceived by Females — −.01 → Female Suicides
.08 (top path from Economic Stress to Female Suicides)

Economic Stress — −.41** → Stress as Perceived by Males — .44** → Male Suicides
.38** (bottom path from Economic Stress to Male Suicides)

C

Family Stress — −.11 → Stress as Perceived by Females — −.02 → Female Suicides
−.09 (top path from Family Stress to Female Suicides)

Family Stress — .23 → Stress as Perceived by Males — .30** → Male Suicides
−.06 (bottom path from Family Stress to Male Suicides)

D

Community Stress — −.28 → Stress as Perceived by Females — .03 → Female Suicides
.17 (top path from Community Stress to Female Suicides)

Community Stress — .10 → Stress as Perceived by Males — .27* → Male Suicides
.12 (bottom path from Community Stress to Male Suicides)

Note: *p ≤ .05, **p ≤ .01.

Figure 6-3.   Path Analysis of Male and Female Suicides

homicide and suicide by direct preconscious processes or perhaps some other intervening group- or individual-level process not considered here.

Sections B, C, and D of figure 6–3 provide the results of partitioning the State Stress Index into economic, family, and community stressors. Only one of the six direct paths indicates a significant relationship to suicide (economic stress for men, .38), and even that is considerably weaker than the corresponding path using the overall SSI.

As for indirect paths, none of those in sections B, C, and D are significant for women. For men, however, all three of the paths from perceived stress to suicide are significant, and there is a significant indirect path from economic stressors to perceived stress and suicide. Thus, as in the case of the link between stressful events and homicide, there is a tendency for the link between stressful events and suicide to be mediated by subjectively experienced stress, but only for men.

DISCUSSION

In this chapter we have examined the impact of both subjective and objective stress on suicide and homicide rates for men and women. First, we tested the hypothesis that the relationship between stress and these two types of violence is mediated by subjectively perceived stress. We found support for this hypothesis only for men: the more stressful events that occur in a state, the greater the percentage of male residents who perceive themselves to be stressed. It should be reiterated, however, that this may be an artifact of our measure of subjective stress. Future research should investigate these issues as they differentially relate to men and women.

We also found that the relationship between stressful events and homicide is stronger for homicides involving family members or acquaintances than for homicides of strangers. There could be several reasons for this. Perhaps family members become "targets of convenience" for aggressive behavior because of their proximity and accessibility. Or perhaps violent passions in response to stress are more easily ignited within the context of relationships that are already infused with the intensity and intimacy of the family (see Straus and Hotaling 1980 and chapter 8 for a more detailed discussion). Either way, the family appears to act as a collection point for stressors emanating in the wider society. This view is contrary to the model of the family as a safe haven that moderates or buffers its members against the exigencies of the wider world, at least as far as homicide is concerned.

We had a special interest in how gender might affect the response to different subgroups of stressful events such as those indicating an unstable economic environment (rates of business failures, new unemployment claims, striking workers, bankruptcies, and mortgage foreclosures) and those emanating from an unstable family environment (rates of divorce, abortion, illegitimate births, infant deaths, and fetal deaths). The findings proved paradoxical. Family stress was not found to be significantly related to women's perceived stress, nor was the economic stress index positively related to men's. Women's perceived stress was, however, significantly related to the economic stress at the state level. What is further perplexing is that although men in states with a high level of economic stressors do not perceive themselves to be under more stress than men in other states (or at least do not articulate this attitude), there is a strong relationship between the economic-stressor index and suicides by men. Perhaps men tend to respond to stressful economic environments by denying that they feel under stress or that they have trouble coping. In fact, the greater the objective economic stress, the less likely men are to admit that they feel stress or that they experience special difficulty in coping ($-.41^{**}$). This reaction occurs despite the fact that men are presumed to have their egos heavily invested in the economic area (Linsky 1968). Regardless of the views they vocalized, however, the suicide rate among men rose in direct relationship to the objective economic stressors in their environments.

Women responded differently. They admitted to feelings of being under stress in direct proportion to the level of economic stress within their states. In high-stress states, they felt more stressed but, interestingly, were not propelled toward suicide as men were by those economically based stressors. At least two interpretations are possible here. One is that women's ability to recognize and admit that they are under stress, that is, to express emotional concerns in the face of environmental conditions outside of their power to control, serves ultimately as a protector against the most extreme consequence of that stress—suicide. They may be better able to cope with stress through better emotional management, the first step of which is to comprehend vulnerability clearly and, in doing so, to head off its ultimate devastation. Perhaps the perception of being under stress acts as an early warning system for women and enables them to better mobilize their psychic energies in combating the most self-destructive aspects of their stress (Lazarus 1981). This appears to parallel the frequently observed phenomenon in mental health epidemiology, that women score more poorly than men on most mental health scales, perhaps because women are able to admit more freely to emotional troubles than are men. But it is men who outnumber women in admission to mental hospitals (Cleary 1987). However, the explanation offered above, based on more adaptive cognitive processes in women, and a purportedly mediational effect of perception of stress, does not appear to be supported by our data. Overall, men do not appear less willing or less able to acknowledge the external stressors in their environments. They "correctly" perceive the objectively stressful conditions as measured by total State Stress Index; their "blind spot" appears limited to the subindex of economic stressors. Except for this one area, men overall appear more realistic in their assessment of objective stressful conditions than do women, but that realistic assessment does not appear to protect them from the risk of suicide.

An alternative explanation that does seem to fit better with our data is that men may suffer greater loss of self-esteem from the consequences of economic stress than do women but do not perceive it (or if they do perceive it, they do not articulate it). Women, on the other hand, are clearly stressed by economically unstable environments both directly, because of job loss engendered by their participation as actors in the economic sphere, and indirectly, because of the responsibility they feel to maintain family functioning despite the loss of economic support. We suspect that in spite of these severe stressors, women do not believe that these external conditions are their fault, nor are others likely to fault them. Consequently they may suffer less ego damage and diminished self-esteem. We suspect that a greater number of men take such externally generated changes personally and suffer intolerable loss of self-esteem in the process, ending in suicide for some. Thus, economic events may have different meaning for men and for women.

Other explanations are possible. Because women and men still differentially participate in the economic and family spheres in our society, their differing involvement may ultimately affect the perceived stress they experience. Specifically, many women are less involved in the economic sphere than are their husbands. This lower level of participation may produce feelings of helplessness and lack of control over objective economic stressors. This might explain the stronger relationship between economic stress and perceived stress for women than for men.

The same type of process may explain the unexpected finding that men experience family stressors more subjectively than do women. If women, on average, are more involved in family roles, the other side of the coin is that men are less involved. Lack of involvement may mean less control, and lack of ability to do anything about untoward events is extremely stressful.

These elaborate interpretations derived from somewhat skeletal facts are of course highly speculative. Neither the aggregated official statistics nor the national sample survey is ideally suited to pursue questions of the personal meanings of events in the lives of actors. Thus the issue remains a question for future resolution, one that offers intriguing possibilities concerning the relationship of investment in roles, objective and perceived stressors, and resulting vulnerability to suicide. Nevertheless, our findings suggest that populations are at greatest risk from stressful events that have an impact on their most invested roles. On a cognitive level they may respond to such events by refusing to acknowledge them as sources of stress. Regardless of the response, however, individuals may not easily avoid the potentially destructive impact.

PART 3 *Assault, Rape, and Homicide*

CHAPTER 7

Culture, Stress, and the Drinking-Violence Connection

In this chapter, we examine the cultural contexts conducive to aggression toward others. The primary question investigated here is why heavy drinking is sometimes linked to violent behavior and sometimes not. Our approach to both questions is to examine, within different cultural contexts, the correlation between social stress on the one hand and various combinations of heavy drinking and alcohol abuse on the other.

The major hypothesis discussed briefly in chapter 1 is that what people do when under stress is scripted or channeled by culture into particular directions. In this chapter, we look at subcultural differences within the United States in norms favorable to drinking and norms supportive of violence. More specifically, we test the hypothesis that stress is especially likely to eventuate in violence-prone drinking within areas where the cultural norms favor drinking and also support violence.

Two multi-indicator indexes of normative contexts make this type of study possible: a Legitimate Violence Index (Baron and Straus 1987) and a Restrictive Norm Index (Linsky, Colby, and Straus 1986a). The analysis employs a combination of macro-level data on states for drinking norms and violent subcultures and individual survey data on self-perceived stress, violence, and drinking.

As we noted earlier, very little research on stress has explicitly included culture as a variable. Part of the reason is that a great deal of the early research in this area was done by psychologists and psychiatrists, who, quite naturally and appropriately, tended to focus on the psychological and physiological characteristics of individuals. Cultures and social structures, however, affect stress in several important ways.

- Events that place people under stress are for the most part the result of the organization of a given society, and the risk of encountering stressful events varies with one's location within the social structure.
- Cultural norms to a large extent define what will be considered stressful.
- How people deal with stress is determined as much by social rules and social organization as by the personality of the person experiencing a stressful event. In some societies, people learn to deal with stress by withdrawal and passivity; in others, they tend to respond to stress by aggression (Berkowitz 1993; MacAndrew and Edgerton 1969).

It follows from the last of these propositions that within any society, different subgroups tend to respond to stress in different ways. Thus, how a person deals with or reacts to stress is, to a considerable extent, a function of the society or of the part of society in which a person is located.

Observations of the association of heavy drinking and violent behavior are commonplace, but that link is not universal, and explanations for the link are far from settled. Perhaps the most common explanation is the "disinhibition" theory. Essentially this theory argues that alcohol, by virtue of its toxic assault upon the higher brain centers, causes the drinker to lose control and do things he or she would not otherwise do. Examples of such behavior include sexual permissiveness and acting out of character. Especially relevant to the present subject, such disinhibition is believed to increase hostility and aggressiveness. However widely that view is held, there is no consistent evidence for it, and it remains only one of several possible explanations (MacAndrew and Edgerton 1969; Collins 1981, Coleman and Straus 1983).

MacAndrew and Edgerton describe many societies where consumption of alcohol and even drunkenness do not have a disinhibiting effect. If the disinhibition theory is true, neurochemical effects should be relatively constant. Instead, the effects of alcohol appear to vary widely from individual to individual and society to society.

A research review by Blum (1981) suggests that the alcohol-violence relationship is much too complex to be explained through neurochemical processes alone. He cites the importance of social settings and cues present in those settings, group structure, whether drinking norms are integrated with other norms, the meaning of alcohol, beliefs and expectations about the loss of control when drinking, and whether persons are held accountable for their misbehavior while intoxicated. Laboratory experiments (Lang et al. 1975) on the effects of alcohol on aggression find that research subjects' beliefs about whether there was gin in their fruit juice was a more important factor in determining their aggressiveness than whether the alcohol was in the drink or not.

The evidence appears to better fit at least two alternative theories for the alcohol-violence connection. "Learned-behavior" theory suggests that violent behavior by those who drink is learned like other culturally prescribed behavior. "Deviance disavowal" theory suggests that it is because drinkers are not viewed as responsible for their deviant behavior that they are able to engage in reprehensible behavior while preserving a favorable self-image and their social standing.

Although the present research is not aimed at directly untangling these alternative explanations, the point that we take from the studies and reviews cited is the potentially strong molding impact of cultural conditions on the linking of alcohol with violence. (See Coleman and Straus [1983] and Kantor and Straus [1987] for a more complete description of these theories.) There are, of course, interesting exceptions to the general inattentiveness of the research community to the influence of cultural forces in stress outcomes. Robert Bales's classical theory of comparative alcoholism rates (1946) posits that is the combination of stressful conditions built into the structure of a society *plus* a normative system that supports the use of alcohol to deal with stress and tensions of the society that leads to high rates of alcoholism within populations. As we saw in chapter 4, the correlation of social stress and alcoholism problems reached its highest point within states that were normatively permissive to drinking, thus supporting Bales's theory.

INDIVIDUAL-LEVEL DATA

The approach used in this chapter is "contextual analysis," which requires data on differences in social context as well as data on the behavior of individuals within those contexts. The social-context data refer to differences in cultural norms concerning drinking and violence and are described in the next section. The data on the behavior of individuals were obtained from the National Family Violence Survey and were described in greater detail in chapter 5.

Measurement of Heavy Drinking

Heavy drinking was measured in two ways in this study: by assessing frequency of drunkenness and by using a drinking index, which is sensitive to heavy chronic drinking that may not imply as much loss of control as drunkenness. In this exploratory analysis we felt it was preferable to use multi-indicators of the dependent variable, because differences between indicators might provide a basis for further theoretical development.

The Drinking Index, developed by Kantor and Straus (1987), combines data from survey questions on the frequency of drinking and the quantity of alcohol drunk:

1) In general, how often do you consume alcoholic beverages—that is, beer, wine or liquor? Never, less than 1 day a month, 1–3 days a month, 1–2 days a week, 5–6 days a week, daily? (The median frequency of drinking was 1–3 times a month.)
2) On a day when you drink alcoholic beverages, on average, how many drinks do you have? By a "drink" we mean a drink with a shot of ½ ounces of hard liquor, 12 ounces of beer, or 5 ounces of wine. (The median number of drinks per day was two.)

These questions were used to develop six categories of drinking:

  0 = Abstinent: Never drinks (30.6%).
  1 = Low: Drinks on infrequent occasions, ranging from less than once a month up to 1–2 times a week; never more than 1 drink at a time. Drinks less than once a month and no more than 2 drinks at a time (26.8%).
  2 = Low Moderate: Drinks from 1 to 3 times a month up to daily; never more than 2 drinks (22.1%).
  3 = High Moderate: Drinks less than once a month up to 1 to 2 times a week; 3–4 drinks a day (10.5%).
  4 = High: Drinks 3–4 times a week up to daily; 3 or more drinks a day (4.9%).
  5 = Binge: Drinks on infrequent occasions—once a month up to 1 to 2 times a week; 5 or more drinks a day (4.65%).

The distribution of the Drinking Index reveals that over half the sample were abstinent or low drinkers, and for the individuals who did drink, moderate patterns predominated. Significant gender differences in drinking patterns were also present. Two-thirds of women were abstinent or infrequent drinkers, and less than 5% of women were high or binge drinkers. Kantor and Straus (1987) report that these findings are comparable to previous national surveys that investigate drinking patterns (Cahalan 1970; Gallup 1978).

The second measure of alcohol use and misuse is how many times individuals reported being drunk during the previous year. Among husbands, 68.3% reported that they had never been drunk during that time; the comparable figure for wives was 80.4%. The percentage of husbands who were drunk two or more times in the previous year was 23.0% as compared to 11.6% for wives.

The Perceived Stress Index was created from three questions in the National Family Violence Survey (Straus and Gelles 1990). Respondents were asked to indicate how often in the preceding twelve months each of the following occurred: 1) Felt nervous or stressed; 2) Felt difficulties were too great; 3) Could not cope. The response categories were: Never = 0; Almost Never = 1; Sometimes = 2; Fairly often = 3; Very often = 4. The index is the sum of the response scores.

Three control variables were employed in the partial correlations. Socioeconomic status was a factor score obtained from a principal-components analysis using respondent's education, occupation, and total family income. One factor was extracted, with no matrix score falling below .70. We controlled for race using a dichotomous variable indicating whether respondent was African-American or white and for residential population by using a variable that indicated the size of the community or city in which the respondent lived.

MEASUREMENT OF STATE CONTEXT

One problem in evaluating the impact of norms on behavior at the macro-level is that some research fails to measure separately the normative conditions and the behavior in question. When that shortcoming occurs, it reduces the issue of the consequences of culture to circular reasoning. In the current study, we employ two measures of normative conditions at the macro-level: an Index of Restrictive Alcohol Norms and a Legitimate Violence Index, each of which is measured independently of the behavior it is intended to explain.

Restrictive Norm Index

This index (described more fully in chap. 4) combines the following four indicators of restrictive sentiment toward the use of alcohol:

- The percentage of fundamentalist or Mormon church members in a state population.
- The percentage of a state's population residing in legally dry areas.
- The number of on-premise liquor outlets per 1 million population.
- Restricted drinking hours for on-premise liquor outlets.

Table 1 in chapter 4 arrayed the states in rank order according to this index and also briefly discussed which states and regions are high and low in norms that restrict drinking.

Cultural Norms Governing Violence

The level of violent crime in a society is influenced not only by the level of stressful events but also by preexisting response patterns built into the culture and thus into the response repertory of individuals through socialization. In some societies, a larger portion of people may learn to deal with stress through withdrawal and passivity rather than through aggression, whereas in other societies the response pattern may be the reverse. This idea is consistent with those put forth by Wolfgang and Ferracuti (1967), Gastil (1971), Glaser (1971), and Hackney (1969), all of whom report regional differences in several types of deviance. For example, although the rate of property crime is low in the South, the rate of violent crime is high. They attribute these differences to a regional pattern of culture that implicitly legitimizes a violent response to personal affronts.

The theory that cultural norms can legitimize violence and therefore lead to a high level of actual violence need not be restricted to criminal acts such as punching someone who is insulting. An equally or more powerful process is what Baron and Straus (1989) call cultural-spillover theory, which holds that the more a society uses violence for socially legitimate purposes such as physical punishment of children or capital punishment of serious offenders, the greater the probability that some members of the society will use violence for their illegitimate criminal purposes.

If violence is defined as an act intended to cause physical pain or injury to another person, a great many types of violence are socially legitimate in the sense that they are permitted or required by cultural norms. The severity of such normatively permitted or required violence can be minimal, as in physical punishment of a child, or lethal, as in capital punishment of murderers.

Archer and Gartner (1984), Baron and Straus (1989), and Bowers (1984; brutalization theory) have tested different aspects of this theory and shown that the higher the level of culturally legitimate violence, the greater the level of criminal violence. They argue that this is because of a spillover of the legitimacy of using violence for socially approved ends to its use for ends that the society defines as criminal.

Legitimate Violence Index

We measured cultural support of violence in using Baron and Straus's (1989) Legitimate Violence Index (LVX), a multi-indicator measure based on the assumption that if there are group differences in values concerning violence, they should be observable in many different activities such as education, recreation, and law enforcement. Consequently, indicators were selected that might reflect an underlying belief in the efficacy and desirability of physical force. However, to avoid the circularity of inferring a subculture of violence from high rates of violent crime, Baron and Straus restricted such indicators to violent activities that are noncriminal and socially approved. The twelve indicators included in the LVX can be grouped in the following categories:

Governmental Use of Violence. The 5 variables in this category include laws permitting corporal punishment by school teachers in 1979, executions per 100 homicide arrests for the years 1940–1959, executions per 100 homicide arrests for the years 1960–1978, African-Americans sentenced to death per 100 African-Americans arrested for homicide in 1980, and whites sentenced to death per 100 whites arrested for homicide in 1980.

Mass-Media Preferences. The two variables included in this group are the 1979 circulation rates per 100,000 population of 5 magazines depicting violence, and an index of the most violent television programs in the fall of 1980.

Participation in Socially Approved Violent Activities. The 5 variables making up this category are hunting licenses sold per 1,000 population in 1980, the state of origin of college football players per capita in 1972, National Guard enrollment per 100,000 population in 1976, National Guard expenditures per capita in 1976, and lynchings per 1 million population during the years 1882–1927.

Prior to computing the LVX, the 12 indicators were Z-scored. The indicators were then summed and the composite index was standardized through a procedure called ZP-scoring. Through the ZP-scaling method, index scores acquire the characteristics of both Z-scores and percentages. Thus a change of 1 ZP score point can be interpreted as a change of 1% of the 0 to 100 scoring range, whereas a change of 20 ZP score points can be viewed as a change of one standard deviation (mean = 50). The internal-consistency reliability of the LVX was tested with the SPSS reliability program. Cronbach's standardized alpha for the 12 composite indicators is .71.[1]

1. There are many questions that can be raised about this index, some of which have been discussed in Baron and Straus (1989). For example, at first glance it might seem inappropriate to use lynching as one indicator of legitimate violence. However, Brown's (1979) analysis of vigilante violence suggests that, although illegal, lynching in post-Reconstruction America had cultural support among dominant groups in society. Moreover, because lynching is a historical indicator, it provides

CULTURAL EFFECTS

The main hypothesis, it will be recalled, deals with the impact of the cultural *context* on behavior under stress. First, however, we thought it useful to examine the impact of the cultural milieu of states, that is, the effect of alcohol and violence norms separate from the effects of stress. In other words, we shall first examine the impact of culture as a direct effect rather than as a contextual variable for understanding the consequences of stress. The following analysis investigates whether differences among states in restrictive alcohol norms and cultural legitimation of violence are related to the rate of alcohol abuse and familial and nonfamilial violence, and whether these two normative dimensions are related to the combination of drinking with violent behavior.

Figure 7–1 describes the four possible normative contexts by using the drinking-norms index to classify each state as permissive or restrictive and using the LVX to classify each state as low or high. The next step was to group the respondents in the National Family Violence Survey (as described in chap. 5) into the four cells, depending on the state in which they lived. Of the original sample of 6,002 cases, 5,159 were available for this particular analysis.

Contextual Analysis of Violence in Conjunction with Drinking

The data on drinking and violence in the survey permitted us to create eight variables to measure behavior involving both drinking and violence, as shown in table 7–1. Included are violence by husbands against wives, wives against husbands, and violence outside the home combined with either the frequency of drunkenness or heavy drinking.

The issue addressed here is whether cultural or subcultural factors alone—in this case, restrictive or permissive drinking norms and a high level of culturally legitimate violence—are associated with a tendency to combine alcohol and violence. Cultural-norms theory predicts that the highest scores should occur in cell A, which includes the states where permissive drinking norms coincide with

---

a measure of the historical legacy of violence in states. It might also seem inappropriate to include items reflecting state statutes permitting use of violence, such as capital punishment and corporal punishment in schools, because the existence of a statute does not indicate how frequently, if at all, it is invoked. However, the Legitimate Violence Index is intended as a cultural or normative indicator rather than as a behavioral indicator. Such statutes per se are important as a symbolic indicator of community values (Gusfield 1963) whether they are actually invoked or not and are therefore appropriate for an index designed to measure cultural norms. See Straus (1985) or Baron and Straus (1989) for further conceptual and methodological issues in construction of the Legitimate Violence Index, sources for all indicators, and state-by-state listings of each indicator.

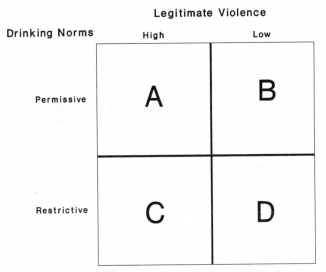

Figure 7-1.   Four Normative Contexts Based on Restrictiveness toward Alcohol and Legitimate Violence (State-Level Indicators)

the approval of legitimate violence. This would indicate that those living in a permissive environment in terms of both drinking and violence are engaging in both behaviors.

Table 7–1 provides somewhat mixed support for the hypothesis. The cell order is in the predicted direction for four of the eight indicators of combined alcohol and violence (DV1, DV5, DV4, and DV8). Two of the means were significant by Duncan's Multiple Range Test at the .05 level: the combination of husband's drinking index and husband-to-wife violence, DV1; and the combination of wife's drunkenness and wife's violence outside the home, DV4. In the latter case, although differences are significant, the mean scores are extremely small because of the relatively low frequency of women's drunkenness and women's physical aggression outside the home.

At the other end of the cultural spectrum, among families living in states with a low level of culturally legitimate violence and restrictive drinking norms (cell D), the findings are more consistent. Column 4 of table 7–1 shows that, in seven of eight tests the behavior that combines alcohol abuse with violence is lowest in cell D, as expected.

The average scores for culturally mixed environments (cells B and C), that is, states that were high on only one of the two cultural dimensions, for the most part fall in between the scores for cells A and D, as expected by the theory. Thus normative conditions alone do appear to have at least some

TABLE 7-1. MEAN SCORE ON EIGHT MEASURES OF ALCOHOL-VIOLENCE MIX, BY CULTURAL CONTEXT

		Cultural Context				
		A	B	C	D	
		Permissive Drinking— Violent	Permissive Drinking— Nonviolent	Restrictive Drinking— Violent	Restrictive Drinking— Nonviolent	
Behavioral Configuration		Subcultures	Subcultures	Subcultures	Subcultures	
DV1	Husband's Drunkenness and Husband-to-Wife Physical Aggression	12.22	10.78	7.24	6.00	NS
DV3	Wife's Drunkenness and Wife-to-Husband Physical Aggression	2.32	5.05	5.61	1.81	NS
DV5	Husband's Heavy Drinking and Husband-to-Wife Physical Aggression	4.54	2.04	1.43	.39	.05
DV6	Wife's Heavy Drinking and Wife-to-Husband Physical Aggression	3.57	3.98	2.34	1.28	NS
DV2	Husband's Drunkenness and Nonfamily Physical Aggression	.44	1.37	1.17	1.79	NS
DV4	Wife's Drunkenness and Nonfamily Physical Aggression	.13	.02	.06	.01	.05
DV7	Husband's Heavy Drinking and Nonfamily Physical Aggression	.11	.11	.13	.08	NS
DV8	Wife's Heavy Drinking and Nonfamily Physical Aggression	.04	.03	.04	.02	NS

Note: Significance tests are Duncan's Multiple Range Test in which Cell A (Permissive Drinking—Violent Subculture) is significantly different from one or more of the means listed above.

direct impact on the tendency to combine alcohol abuse with violent behavior, regardless of stress.

Contextual Analysis of Drinking and Violence as Separate Dimensions

We also examined separately the impact of normative systems on the level of alcohol abuse and violent behavior. Here the prediction from the cultural-determination theory is somewhat different from the previous model. In this case, the theory leads to the hypothesis that alcohol abuse considered on its own is highest among populations resident in areas with permissive drinking norms (cells A and B), as compared with residents of restrictive states (cells C and D).

Table 7–2 lists the drinking and the violence scores for each of the four social contexts. The data partly support the cultural-determinism hypothesis.

If we look first at drinking behavior, cell B (pro-alcohol norms and non-violent subculture) has the highest scores for two of these tests (Husband Drunk and Drinking Index) and the second highest for the remaining index (Wife

TABLE 7-2. MEAN SCORES FOR DRINKING PATTERNS AND PHYSICAL AGGRESSION, BY CULTURAL CONTEXT

Dependent Variable	Cultural Context				
	A Permissive Drinking— Violent Subcultures	B Permissive Drinking— Nonviolent Subcultures	C Restrictive Drinking— Violent Subcultures	D Restrictive Drinking— Nonviolent Subcultures	
	Drinking				
Husband Drunk	2.40	3.95	2.60	2.57	*
Wife Drunk	.56	1.30	1.37	1.13	NS
Drinking Index Respondent	1.43	1.54	1.27	1.27	*
	Physical Aggression				
Husband to Wife	2.84	1.32	.91	.56	*
Wife to Husband	2.68	1.52	1.38	.80	*
Nonfamily Aggression: Husband	.06	.05	.05	.06	NS
Nonfamily Aggression: Wife	.03	.01	.02	.02	NS

*Significant at .05 by Duncan's Multiple Range Test.

Drunk). However, cell A, which is also characterized by pro–alcohol norms (but linked with violent subculture) does not rank highly in average levels of drinking.

When we examine the theory that legitimate violence is related to personal violence by the respondents, an interesting pattern emerges. The hypothesis derived from this theory is that the highest levels of personal violence should be in cells A and C (a high level of culturally legitimate violence). In four tests of the hypothesis, however, cell A alone (pro–alcohol norms and high index of legitimate violence) is always highest, even though we would have expected cell C (high index of legitimate violence linked with restrictive alcohol norms) to be equally high.

The hypotheses of disinhibition and deviance disavowal discussed earlier may help to explain this pattern. Only in one of the two cells with high legitimate violence (A, where norms of high legitimate violence are combined with pro-alcohol norms) is legitimate violence linked with spousal violence. Why would proviolence norms not be sufficient on their own to provoke the highest levels of personal violence? Perhaps it is because the LVX measures norms of *legitimate* violence. Thus, violence against a wife, a husband, or others within a person's private sphere would not qualify as "legitimate violence" in the eyes of the subjects. Perhaps this is where alcohol has its impact. Other studies have found pro–alcohol norms to be linked to heavy drinking behavior (Linsky, Colby, and Straus 1987). The consumption of alcohol may somehow facilitate the violence being directed at illegitimate targets.

The purported disinhibition effects of alcohol were discussed earlier as a possible explanation for violence under the influence of alcohol. There is some doubt, however, over whether the direct chemical impact of alcohol is sufficient to explain such complex changes in human behavior as the dropping of previous moral restraints on deviant behavior. It was also suggested that the drinkers' expectations concerning the effects of alcohol may be more important than the alcohol itself in determining whether alcohol is linked to aggressive behavior. In addition, alcohol and certain settings together may promote the expression of aggression (Blum 1981). There is also the presence of a strong cultural belief in the United States, as in several other societies, that one is not fully responsible for antisocial behavior exhibited while one is under the influence of alcohol. Thus, both the expectation on the part of the drinkers that they are likely to become violent under the influence, coupled with the belief that they are not morally culpable for their actions when in such a state, may combine to produce a higher level of physical abuse while they are drinking. Communities where the consumption of alcohol has a high level of approval and where violence is modeled according to socially legitimate purposes may be particularly fertile ground for the expression of violence toward illegitimate targets. Thus violence may be redirected from legitimate to illegitimate targets by the successful neutralization via alcohol of that important moral distinction.

STRESS, VIOLENCE, AND ALCOHOL ABUSE: A CONTEXTUAL ANALYSIS OF FOUR CULTURAL CONFIGURATIONS

We now move on to the more complex and central issue of how normative contexts shape and script the behavioral response to stress. The central hypothesis is that the combination of alcohol abuse and physical violence is more likely to occur when stress is experienced within certain subcultural configurations, that is, within states where cultural norms support both drinking and at least some forms of violence. Conversely, stress is less likely to trigger such a compound reaction within other cultural configurations, such as within states that are high on only one of the two normative dimensions. The alcohol-violence response should be especially low among those living in areas characterized by nonviolent subcultures and restrictive alcohol norms. The following data are most relevant to our central hypothesis. We examine, for husband and wife separately, the relationship of drunkenness or heavy drinking, combined with two types of physical aggression to perceived stress: aggression against the spouse and nonfamily physical aggression (see table 7–4). The analysis contains

TABLE 7-3. PARTIAL CORRELATIONS BETWEEN PERCEIVED STRESS AND COMBINATIONS OF ALCOHOL USE AND INTERSPOUSAL VIOLENCE WITHIN CULTURAL CONTEXTS

		Cultural Context			
		A Permissive Drinking— Violent Subcultures	B Permissive Drinking— Nonviolent Subcultures	C Restrictive Drinking— Violent Subcultures	D Restrictive Drinking— Nonviolent Subcultures
Dependent Variable					
DV1	Husband's Drunkenness and Husband-to-Wife Physical Aggression	.178 <.001	.158 <.001	.079 <.001	.052 NS
DV3	Wife's Drunkenness and Wife-to-Husband Physical Aggression	.214 <.001	.079 <.001	.017 <.001	−.077 NS
DV5	Husband's Heavy Drinking and Husband-to-Wife Physical Aggression	.157 <.01	.167 <.001	.144 <.001	.023 NS
DV6	Wife's Heavy Drinking and Wife-to-Husband Physical Aggression	.129 <.010	.106 <.001	.060 <.010	.008 NS
N		299	2,585	1,464	453

a total of eight tests of the main hypothesis concerning cultural context and correlations of the relationship between stress and the combination of violence with alcohol abuse.

PHYSICAL AGGRESSION WITHIN THE FAMILY

Three of the four tests in table 7–3 support the central hypothesis that outcomes of stress are shaped by the cultural context within which the stress is experienced. In DV1, DV3, DV6, the rank order of the magnitudes of the partial correlation coefficients is exactly as predicted, with the highest correlations occurring in cell A, the lowest in cell D, and intermediate correlations in cells B and C. The sixteen partial-correlation coefficients are small, with all but one in the predicted direction. Additionally, they are almost all statistically significant, owing perhaps to large sample size. The important point here, however, is not the magnitude per se but the relative size of the correlations between different cultural contexts. Thus, when we are describing husband-to-wife violence, the hypothesis about stress outcome is supported.

A different picture emerges when we shift the focus to violence directed outside the family. Table 7–4 presents data on nonfamily physical aggression. Our central hypothesis is supported in only one of the four tests. Thus, subcultural context is a poor predictor of the outcome of stress involving violence outside the family but does predict the outcome of stress within the family.

The contrast in outcome is consistent with what we observed in the last

TABLE 7-4. PARTIAL CORRELATIONS BETWEEN PERCEIVED STRESS AND COMBINATIONS OF ALCOHOL USE AND PHYSICAL AGGRESSION OUTSIDE THE HOME WITHIN CULTURAL CONTEXTS

| | | Cultural Context | | | |
		A Permissive Drinking– Violent Subcultures	B Permissive Drinking– Nonviolent Subcultures	C Restrictive Drinking– Violent Subcultures	D Restrictive Drinking– Nonviolent Subcultures
DV2	Husband's Drunkenness and Nonfamily	.057	.085	.046	.040
	Physical Aggression	<.060	<.026	<.020	<.034
DV4	Wife's Drunkenness and Nonfamily	.060	.026	−.020	.034
	Physical Aggression	NS	NS	NS	NS
DV7	Husband's Heavy Drinking and Nonfamily	.021	.063	.014	.036
	Physical Aggression	NS	NS	NS	NS
DV8	Wife's Heavy Drinking and Nonfamily	.040	.001	.023	.063
	Physical Aggression	NS	NS	NS	NS

chapter and what we shall observe in chapter 8. Objective stress, it appears, is consistently linked with homicide of family and acquaintances but not with homicide of strangers.

CONCLUSIONS

The findings reported in this chapter generally support the theory that the link between alcohol abuse and violence is not a neurochemical given but is governed by the cultural context within which the behavior occurs. Specifically, heavy drinking and physical aggression are most likely to occur together in a society with a cultural configuration that supports or tolerates both types of behavior. This pattern was demonstrated with regard to the effects of these two cultural dimensions alone, as well as with regard to their joint effects on the link between stress and violence. Thus, this research suggests that the experience of stress is at least partially scripted by the particular cultural context within which it occurs. Although this analysis focused on one context specifically—a high level of legitimate violence in combination with permissive drinking norms—future research might profitably test hypotheses about the effects of other cultural contexts on the way people behave under stress.

CHAPTER 8

Stress and Homicide of Family Members,
Acquaintances, and Strangers

We now examine the relationship between stress and one of the most violent forms of outward aggression—criminal homicide. As a legal category, criminal homicide is the killing of one human being by another without legal justification or excuse. This act is generally considered first-degree murder when one person causes the death of another with premeditation and intent and second-degree murder when death occurs with malice and intent but without premeditation. Nonnegligent manslaughter usually involves intent to inflict bodily injury but without deliberate intent to kill, whereas involuntary manslaughter is reckless or negligent killing without intent to harm. The category of noncriminal homicides includes excusable killings, usually in self-defense, or justifiable homicide, for example, the killing of an individual by a police officer in the line of duty (U.S. Department of Justice 1985a).

This chapter uses data on the incidence of murder and nonnegligent manslaughter. Even within these limited categories, there are a great variety of situations and motives behind aggregate rates of homicide. The situations range from brutal killing in the course of a trivial quarrel or crime of passion to the premeditated and skillfully planned homicide. Moreover, there are important differences in the relationship between victim and perpetrator. One of our purposes in this chapter is to examine if the effect of stress depends on whether victim and perpetrator are strangers, acquaintances, or members of the same family.

ANALYSIS ON THE INDIVIDUAL VERSUS SOCIAL-SYSTEM LEVEL

Almost all of the existing research on stress and homicide is at the individual level of analysis (e.g., Humphrey and Palmer 1986; Petrick and Hart 1980). They relate stressful events within the biographies of individuals (or families) to criminal or violent acts by those same persons. There are, however, a few studies of the effects of stressful events in social systems on rates of violence (Steinberg, Catalano, and Dooley 1981; Brenner 1976 and 1980). (For a description of these studies and a discussion of how these ecological correlations of stressor events and rates of violence could arise, see chapter 1.)

COMPETING THEORIES OF HOMICIDE AND THEIR MEASUREMENT

Stress Theory

Linsky and Straus (1986) found that the the State Stress Index of 1976 was strongly related to the state homicide rate ($r = .69$, $p < .001$) for the same year. That relationship was confirmed by a multiple regression analysis with ten other variables controlled. This finding was replicated using the 1982 version of the ssi and average homicide rates for the period of 1980–1984. The correlation for this period was .75 ($p < .001$).

The findings mentioned above are so remarkably strong and stable that they beg closer scrutiny and interpretation. This chapter provides that examination in two ways. First, we specify the model more adequately by including indicators of three major alternative theories that purport to explain differences in homicide rates: control theory, culture-of-violence theory, and economic-deprivation theory. We also included two control variables: urbanization and the percentage of African-Americans in the population of each state. This design makes it possible to examine the relation of stress to homicide in the context of the more widely investigated explanations of homicide.

Second, we examine the relationship of social stress to specific types of homicide by disaggregating the overall homicide rate into three categories, based on the relationship between offender and victim: homicides of strangers, acquaintances, and family members. Recent studies (Smith and Parker 1980; Straus 1988; Williams and Flewelling 1988) suggest that use of such specific homicide rates, rather than the total rate, is likely to yield increased understanding. Moreover, Williams and Flewelling (1988, p. 421) suggest that some of the inconsistent findings in homicide research may be attributable to the "failure to disaggregate the overall homicide rate into more refined and conceptually meaningful categories of homicide." Our use of more refined rates can help clarify the nature of the link between social stress and homicide. For example, does the relationship apply to all types of homicide, or is it found only or mainly for certain types, such as intrafamily homicides or stranger homicides?

On the one hand, there are plausible grounds for expecting that stress would be most highly related to intrafamily homicide. Mounting stress levels in communities may have an impact on intimate relationships, thereby increasing the homicide rate mainly among family and friends. Persons in such relationships could become targets of opportunity for displaced aggression resulting from socially generated stressors. Stress may well trigger lethal aggression within the intimate and dependent relationships of the family, because such relationships are already charged with high levels of affect.

On the other hand, a recent analysis of family versus nonfamily homicides by Straus (1988) throws some doubt on that reasoning. Straus found that rates of intrafamily homicide are relatively stable over time and from state to state. Most state-to-state variation in homicide is explained by the rate of nonfamily homicide. The latter finding seems to suggest that stranger homicides may account for our previously reported correlations (Linsky and Straus 1986). This and other related issues should be illuminated by using the relationship–specific rates of homicide.

Cultural and Economic Theories

Some investigators have posited cultural theories to explain homicide differentials (Gastil 1971; Hackney 1969; Huff-Corzine, Corzine, and Moore 1986; Messner 1983; Wolfgang and Ferracuti 1967). The argument is that murder occurs more often among certain groups because they endorse or at least tolerate the use of physical force in settling quarrels. Gastil (1971) attempted to test the theory of regional cultures of violence by employing a Southernness Index based on the percentage of the population who had migrated to the state from the South as the independent variable. He found that the higher the score on this index, the higher the homicide rate.

Loftin and Hill (1974) criticized this study because the Southernness Index is a measure of region, not a measure of culture per se. In addition, they believe that Gastil incorrectly specified the relationship between homicide rates and socioeconomic status by assuming that the relationships are linear when they are not. After replicating the analysis with the inclusion of a Structure of Poverty Index, Loftin and Hill found that both the dummy variable for the Confederate South and Gastil's Southernness Index are reduced to nonsignificance. They cautiously state, however, that "a more definitive assessment of the role of cultural and situational variables on interpersonal violence will require specifying a theoretical model which would allow for a full range of cultural and situational variables" (Loftin and Hill 1974, p. 724).

The study by Loftin and Hill motivated research by others attempting to measure more accurately the independent contributions of poverty and sub-cultural orientations on homicide rates (Smith and Parker 1980; Blau and Blau 1982; Blau and Golden 1986; DeFronzo 1983; Williams 1984; Williams and Flewelling 1988; Huff-Corzine, Corzine, and Moore 1986; Dixon and Lizotte 1987) with results remaining equivocal, in part because none of these studies employed a measure of cultural orientation concerning violence. Although some investigators have measured cultural support for violence at the individual level (Dixon and Lizotte 1987; Ball-Rokeach 1973), aggregate-level indicators have usually been regional-location measures or demographic proxies. The research reported in this chapter attempts to overcome that limitation by using the Legitimate Violence Index.

Control Theory

The importance of social control, or the hold that societies or groups are able to exert over their members, has been a persistent theme in sociological explana-tions of deviance since Durkheim's classical study of suicide (Durkheim [1897] 1951). What is known as control theory (Hirschi 1969) focuses on the strength of the bond between the individual and society as the central explanatory variable in deviant behavior. Some investigators have employed measures such as divorce, mobility, and urbanization as indicators of commitment to the group and its norms to explain differences between social units in homicide (Blau and Blau 1982; Crutchfield, Geerken, and Gove 1982; Wilkinson 1984; Williams and Flewelling 1988). Contemporary control theories of crime and deviance may be conceptually similar to social-disorganization theories, because the degree to which behavior is effectively regulated by group norms is also one of the major emphases within the social-disorganization approach to deviance. In social-disorganization theory, the concern is with the processes by which a deterioration of social control leads to norm violations. As is true of social-disorganization theory, control theory focuses our attention on the circumstances that weaken primary group controls and, consequently, reduce constraints against nonconfor-mity (Hirschi 1969; Reckless 1973). Although both control theory and social-disorganization theory contain certain unique elements (for example, they make different assumptions concerning deviant motivation and the nature of the soci-ety) they share a concern with the individual's bonds to society and the conditions under which social regulation is effective in implementing conformity to norms.

It is also important to clarify the difference between stress theory and control theory. Control theory asserts that crime is more likely to occur when the ability of a society to prevent crimes is reduced because individuals are not involved in stable relationships that can regulate their behavior. Social-stress theory asserts that the accumulation of stressor events creates extreme demands for adjustment within the community and within its members that sometimes exceed their capacity to cope. The resulting psychological or physical strain may then manifest itself through violent responses on the part of some members of the community.

MEASURES

Testing these three theories of the social origins of homicide required development of new empirical measures, each of which is described below. In addition, we used newly developed rates of homicide that enabled us to investigate whether the effect of social stress on homicide differs for murders of strangers, acquaintances, and family members.

Homicide

The homicide rates for each state are from the Comparative Homicide File (CHF). The CHF is based on the "Supplemental Homicide Report" from the Federal Bureau of Investigation for 1976–1984. The procedures for computing the CHF rates for each state are given in Williams and Flewelling (1988).

Table 8–1 arrays the states in rank order according to the overall homicide rate and according to the rate of homicide between family members, between acquaintances, and between strangers.

In addition to the revised State Stress Index (see chapter 2 for detailed description), the following variables were used.

Legitimate Violence Index

An adequate test of the culture-of-violence theory requires direct evidence on cultural norms supporting violence, and such a measure has not been available. Straus therefore created the Legitimate Violence Index (LVX) for each of the fifty states. The twelve indicators in the LVX reflect socially acceptable preferences for noncriminal violence in three broad areas: mass media having high violence content, such as the Nielson rating for the six most violent prime-time television programs; governmental use of violence, such as laws authorizing corporal pun-

TABLE 8-1.   RANKING OF STATES ON HOMICIDE RATES, 1980–1984

Rank	Total		Family		Acquaintance		Stranger	
1	DC	29.75	DC	4.12	DC	11.75	DC	13.88
2	TEX	14.15	TEX	3.80	TEX	7.48	NY	4.73
3	LA	13.53	MISS	3.41	GA	6.93	LA	4.34
4	NEV	13.13	LA	3.34	NEV	6.58	NEV	3.71
5	FLA	12.07	ALA	3.33	MISS	6.52	CAL	3.58
6	GA	11.75	GA	3.18	FLA	6.41	FLA	2.93
7	MISS	11.38	ALAS	3.15	ALAS	6.33	TEX	2.87
8	ALAS	11.03	SC	3.09	LA	5.86	MO	2.11
9	CAL	10.12	NEV	2.83	NM	5.69	ILL	2.10
10	ALA	9.90	OKLA	2.80	ALA	5.57	ARIZ	2.07
11	SC	9.79	FLA	2.73	SC	5.23	INDI	1.71
12	NM	9.63	KY	2.54	NC	4.96	NM	1.69
13	NY	9.57	NC	2.42	CAL	4.79	MD	1.67
14	TENN	8.52	TENN	2.36	TENN	4.75	GA	1.65
15	OKLA	8.41	NM	2.25	MICH	4.74	OHIO	1.61
16	NC	8.30	ARK	2.18	MD	4.68	MICH	1.61
17	MICH	8.24	ARIZ	1.93	OKLA	4.34	ALAS	1.56
18	MO	8.03	MICH	1.89	ILL	4.29	SC	1.46
19	ILL	8.01	MO	1.88	KY	4.26	MISS	1.45
20	MD	7.85	VA	1.80	ARK	4.20	TENN	1.41
21	KY	7.63	CAL	1.75	VA	4.06	OKLA	1.27
22	ARIZ	7.62	WYO	1.72	MO	4.04	COLO	1.23
23	VA	7.02	ILL	1.62	ARIZ	3.62	VA	1.16
24	ARK	6.97	COLO	1.59	NY	3.30	WYO	1.07
25	COLO	5.89	NY	1.55	COLO	3.06	NJ	1.07
26	INDI	5.71	WVA	1.54	NJ	2.89	HAWA	1.03
27	OHIO	5.70	MD	1.50	DEL	2.79	KANS	1.02
28	WYO	5.17	DEL	1.48	OHIO	2.71	ALA	1.00
29	NJ	5.09	KANS	1.43	INDI	2.69	PA	.98
30	PA	4.81	OHIO	1.37	WVA	2.59	NC	.92
31	DEL	4.80	INDI	1.31	PA	2.55	MASS	.85
32	KANS	4.73	PA	1.27	CONN	2.42	KY	.83
33	WVA	4.61	HAWA	1.22	WYO	2.38	WASH	.82
34	HAWA	4.34	MONT	1.22	KANS	2.29	OREG	.77
35	WASH	4.07	NJ	1.13	WASH	2.21	CONN	.76
36	CONN	4.00	WASH	1.04	HAWA	2.09	UTAH	.73
37	OREG	3.68	UTAH	.99	OREG	2.02	MONT	.66
38	RI	3.19	OREG	.89	RI	1.84	ARK	.59
39	MASS	3.10	RI	.84	IDA	1.78	NEBR	.54
40	MONT	3.05	CONN	.83	MASS	1.65	DEL	.53
41	UTAH	2.99	IDA	.81	VT	1.60	RI	.51
42	IDA	2.81	NH	.80	NEBR	1.43	WVA	.47
43	NEBR	2.59	ME	.69	WIS	1.32	WIS	.43
44	WIS	2.41	WIS	.66	UTAH	1.27	MINN	.33
45	VT	2.19	NEBR	.62	MONT	1.17	NH	.29
46	NH	2.03	MASS	.61	ME	1.02	SD	.28
47	ME	1.93	IOWA	.50	IOWA	.97	VT	.27
48	IOWA	1.73	ND	.46	NH	.94	IOWA	.26
49	MINN	1.65	MINN	.42	MINN	.90	IDA	.23
50	SD	1.44	VT	.31	SD	.89	ME	.21
51	ND	1.01	SD	.27	ND	.40	ND	.15

ishment in the schools; and participation in legal or socially approved violent activities, such as enrollment per 100,000 population in the National Guard. Unlike the Southernness Index or the Structure of Poverty Index used in previous research, the LVX has the advantages of being measured independently of region.[1] The second column of table 8–2 arrays the states in rank order on the Legitimate Violence Index.

Baron and Straus (1989) investigated the concurrent validity of the LVX and found a correlation of .40 with a Violence Approval Index based on attitudes toward violence measured by the General Social Survey. They concluded that a correlation of .40 can be taken as evidence of concurrent validity, because despite the vast difference in the types of data used for the two measures, it is somewhat higher that the average of published validity coefficients. The construct validity of the LVX is indicated by Baron and Straus's finding that it is a significant predictor of both rape and homicide rates after controlling for many other variables. We decided to use the Legitimate Violence Index rather than the Violence Approval Index because the latter is available for only forty states and because of sampling and other problems with the measure described in Baron and Straus (1989, pp. 167–168).

Measure of Economic Deprivation

The percentage of families below the poverty line established by the Bureau of the Census (1986) was used as the indicator of resource deprivation and poverty, as shown in the fourth column of table 8–2. The choice of this indicator was guided by previous research that found that the absolute level of poverty is an appropriate measure of economic deprivation when explaining variations in homicide differentials (Williams 1984; Williams and Flewelling 1989).

Economic deprivation as measured by the percentage of those below the poverty level involves some common elements with stress theory. Both involve difficult circumstances or hardships to which residents must adjust. Economic deprivation, however, differs in two important regards from the State Stress Index. The SSI includes a variety of family and community events in addition to several different economic events. More important, the SSI is based on the stressful life-events approach, which emphasizes new demands or changes in people's lives that require adaptation. The percentage of people living in poverty, on the other hand, involves ongoing or chronic strains in response to ongoing condi-

1. The theoretical rationale of the Legitimate Violence Index, and of each of the twelve indicators, is given in chapter 7.

TABLE 8-2. RANKING OF STATES ON INDICATORS OF FOUR THEORIES

Rank	Stress Index		Legit. Viol.		Weak Controls		Poverty	
1	NEV	100.00	WYO	98.00	NEV	3.00	MISS	18.70
2	GA	85.00	MONT	87.00	WYO	1.92	DC	15.10
3	ALAS	83.00	MISS	85.00	ALAS	1.64	LA	15.10
4	ALA	82.00	IDA	83.00	VT	1.55	ALA	14.80
5	ARIZ	75.00	UTAH	83.00	COLO	1.53	ARK	14.70
6	MISS	73.00	GA	78.00	HAWA	1.38	KY	14.60
7	TENN	73.00	NEV	77.00	WASH	1.36	NM	14.00
8	WASH	72.00	ARK	74.00	OREG	1.21	GA	13.20
9	SC	70.00	VT	71.00	FLA	1.18	SC	13.10
10	CAL	70.00	LA	66.00	CAL	1.11	SD	13.10
11	MICH	69.00	ALAS	64.00	MONT	1.07	TENN	13.10
12	COLO	69.00	FLA	63.00	ARIZ	.89	WVA	11.70
13	OREG	65.00	ALA	62.00	IDA	.60	NC	11.60
14	FLA	60.00	OKLA	62.00	DEL	.50	TEX	11.10
15	VA	58.00	TEX	61.00	NH	.49	NY	10.80
16	LA	56.00	ARIZ	60.00	ME	.39	OKLA	10.30
17	ILL	56.00	SC	60.00	NM	.23	FLA	9.90
18	TEX	54.00	SD	59.00	MICH	.13	ME	9.80
19	OKLA	54.00	ND	57.00	VA	.04	ND	9.80
20	INDI	54.00	OREG	56.00	MD	−.06	IDA	9.60
21	HAWA	53.00	COLO	54.00	TEX	−.17	ARIZ	9.50
22	NM	52.00	NM	54.00	KANS	−.18	MONT	9.20
23	KY	51.00	DEL	54.00	OKLA	−.22	VA	9.20
24	WVA	51.00	KANS	52.00	GA	−.25	MO	9.10
25	NC	51.00	VA	47.00	INDI	−.34	DEL	8.90
26	OHIO	51.00	NC	47.00	ARK	−.35	VT	8.90
27	NY	50.00	WASH	45.00	SD	−.36	CAL	8.70
28	IDA	50.00	HAWA	45.00	NY	−.36	ALAS	8.60
29	DEL	49.00	TENN	44.00	MO	−.40	ILL	8.40
30	PA	49.00	NEBR	42.00	ND	−.43	MICH	8.20
31	MO	48.00	OHIO	41.00	MINN	−.43	NEBR	8.00
32	MD	45.00	IOWA	41.00	SC	−.46	OHIO	8.00
33	RI	40.00	WVA	38.00	LA	−.54	HAWA	7.80
34	UTAH	40.00	KY	36.00	ILL	−.54	PA	7.80
35	VT	39.00	PA	35.00	NEBR	−.54	OREG	7.70
36	ME	38.00	ILL	34.00	OHIO	−.56	RI	7.70
37	NJ	38.00	ME	34.00	IOWA	−.57	UTAH	7.70
38	KANS	35.00	CAL	33.00	NC	−.61	MASS	7.60
39	MINN	32.00	MINN	32.00	WIS	−.72	NJ	7.60
40	ARK	31.00	INDI	31.00	WVA	−.74	IOWA	7.50
41	MASS	31.00	MO	30.00	TENN	−.78	MD	7.50
42	NH	31.00	NH	30.00	MISS	−.88	COLO	7.40
43	CONN	30.00	MICH	29.00	KY	−1.01	KANS	7.40
44	MONT	29.00	CONN	29.00	UTAH	−1.05	INDI	7.30
45	WYO	29.00	NY	27.00	ALA	−1.05	WASH	7.20
46	ND	24.00	WIS	27.00	NJ	−1.08	MINN	7.00
47	WIS	23.00	MD	26.00	MASS	−1.20	NEV	6.30
48	NEBR	15.00	NJ	22.00	CONN	−1.25	WIS	6.30
49	SD	10.00	MASS	19.00	PA	−1.42	CONN	6.20
50	IOWA	10.00	RI	18.00	RI	−1.69	NH	6.10
51	DC	—	DC	—	DC	—	WYO	5.80

tions within a population, a somewhat different conceptualization of stress (cf. Pearlin et al. 1981).

Social Control Index

As an indicator of weak social control, we employ a revised version of an index developed by Baron and Straus (1987, 1989) for use in their study of rape in the United States. The operationalization of control theory has, in the past, been methodologically limited to the individual level. This index permits investigation of the same phenomena at the macro-level. The theoretical rationale for the Social Control Index and a review of the literature is given in Baron and Straus (1989). The third column of table 8–2 ranks each state on the measure of weakness of social control.

The three indicators that were combined to create this version of the Social Control Index are:[2]

1) The percentage of respondents not affiliated with a religious organization. Durkheim ([1912] 1954) argued that religion promotes social cohesion through its divine legitimation of existing norms and values. Many studies have examined the effect of religiosity on such things as delinquency but the findings remain equivocal (Hirschi and Stark 1969; Rhodes and Reiss 1970; Albrecht et al. 1977). Stark and his colleagues (Stark, Doyle, and Kent 1980) more recently have used a measure of church membership in an analysis of crime rates of the Metropolitan Statistical Areas (MSA) and found that it is inversely related to every major property and violent crime. The percentage not affiliated with a religious organization could be interpreted as both weakening the commitment to conventional beliefs about how one should act, and also as weakening attachment of individuals to the collectivity thus releasing them to engage in crime.

2) The percentage of nonfamilied male-only householders and the percentage of single-parent female households with children under 18. These two categories were included in the index because they contradict the idealized social norms that expect all adult men and women to marry and live with a spouse. In addition, because of fewer opportunities for stable adult associations and residential instability, men who live alone are likely to have weak domestic attachments and be subject to low levels of informal social control. There are also

2. Two of the original six items in the Baron and Straus Social Disorganization Index, geographic mobility and divorce, were dropped because of overlap with items in the State Stress Index. Also, two of the other original indicators, households headed by a male with no female present and households headed by a female with no male present, were combined into one indicator to avoid having an index dominated by family-structure variables.

studies suggesting that solitary living poses a serious threat to the physical and mental well-being of single householders, especially men (Kobrin and Hendershot 1977). For these reasons, populations with higher proportions of males with no family or families headed by a single female may indicate a climate of social instability and less effective social control.

3) The ratio of tourists to residents. Faris (1955) characterizes the tourist as a "temporary migrant" and notes that "the folkways and mores of [the tourist's] home community lose some of their power to control him when he is away from home." Thus, the short-term release of tourists from the rules and regulations of their local communities may reduce restraints against nonconforming behavior. Tourism has also been shown to have adverse affects on the resident population of tourist centered communities. The nonconforming behavior of tourists with regard to clothing and entertainment may serve to weaken commitment to local norms. Nicholls (1976) reports that tourism fosters a number of illegal activities such as prostitution, fraud, and theft. After reviewing the literature, Pearce (1982) concluded that the residents of vacation areas sometimes come to resent tourists for violating local norms and may retaliate by assaults, swindling, or theft. Thus, to the extent that tourism undermines normative constraints, it represents an appropriate indicator of social control.

The Overlap among Independent Variables

Although the conceptual difference between stress theory, social-control theory and economic-deprivation theory is clear at the empirical level, there appears to be a possible overlap. For example, we employ infant deaths as one of fifteen indicators (stressor events) in the State Stress Index. Loftin, however, used the infant mortality rate as an indicator of poverty to explain homicide differentials (1974). Although infant mortality is higher in poorer populations, it is not confined to poor families and is stressful no matter what the social class of the family. Death of a close family member is adjudged to be one of the most stressful events conceivable (Holmes and Rahe 1967; Dohrenwend et al. 1978).

The rate of initial unemployment claims, another item in the SSI, also appears to overlap with our poverty measure (the percentage of families below the federally defined poverty level), because they both belong to the economic sphere. But new unemployment cases as well as several other economic events included in the SSI (for example, personal bankruptcies or business foreclosures) again relate to discrete events that demand major adjustments consistent with the life-events conceptualization of stress. On the other hand, low income relates to a more structural and ongoing aspect of poverty. Both may be stressful, but

TABLE 8-3. CORRELATION OF INDEPENDENT VARIABLES IN THE MODEL

Independent Variable	1	2	3	4	5	6
1. Stress						
2. Control	.35*					
3. Legit. Viol.	.22	.43**				
4. % African-American	.49**	−.32	−.18			
5. % Poor	.26	−.29	.31	.34*		
6. % Metro	.24	.06	−.27	.32*	−.40*	

Note: *p < .01, **p < .001 (one-tailed significance).

only the newly unemployed face demands for adjustments in the face of what is experienced as a traumatic event for most persons.

The conceptual distinctiveness of the ssi and our measure of economic deprivation is also revealed empirically. Table 8–3 shows that the correlation of the ssi with the percentage of families below the poverty line is only .26. Although this level indicates that the two are associated, the low correlation suggests that they are not measuring the same phenomenon. Further, in the multivariate analysis, all reported relationships between stress and homicide are net of other relationships, including economic deprivation.

There are parallels also with certain items from the ssi and items from the Social Control Index. The rate of divorce is included within the State Stress Index because the rupturing of such central relationships normally requires major personal adjustments. For example, within weighted individual life-events scales such as that of Holmes and Rahe (1967), divorce is considered one of the most stressful life events possible, ranking only behind death of a spouse or a close family member in severity of stress.

On the other hand, the proportion of individuals living in normatively incomplete households, one of the items from our Social Control Index, refers to an ongoing condition of a social structure (that is, a reduced density of stable adult relationships, a condition that is presumed to lessen effective social control).

Previous research by Linsky and Straus (1986) using an earlier version of the State Stress Index lends additional empirical support for maintaining the inclusion of the specific items within the ssi. They performed a factor analysis that resulted in three factors: two were related to family, and one to economic problems. They then computed factor-weighted indexes for each of the three; these indexes were not as highly or as consistently correlated with the dependent variables as the overall State Stress Index. This is consistent with the life-events theory, which suggests the critical factor is not so much the content of the

stressor events but the sheer number of events that characterize the social climate of a state.

An additional reason to include the specific items discussed within the ssi is
for continuity with extensive previous research that relates the ssi for 1976 and
1982 to many other types of crime, illness, and maladaptive behavior (Linsky and
Straus 1986; Linsky, Colby, and Straus 1987; Linsky, Straus, and Colby 1985).

Control Variables

Homicide has been found repeatedly to be related to urbanization and minority
status (Curtis 1974; Plass and Straus 1987; Williams 1984). Because these two
variables also may be related to our measures of stress, social control, and legitimate violence, the percentage of individuals living in a census-defined MSA and
the percentage of nonwhites are included in the regression analysis.

CORRELATIONS

Table 8–4 presents the bivariate correlations between the homicide variables and
each of the exogenous variables. Of the explanatory variables, only social stress is
consistently significantly related to all four homicide categories. Correlations
range from a high of .75 for total homicide to a low of .63 for stranger homicides,
and all are significant at the .001 level. The percentage of those who are poor is
correlated significantly with three of the homicide variables, total, family, and
acquaintance, but the correlations are in the more moderate range of .41 to .46.
The correlation of poverty with stranger homicide is not significant. Neither the
Legitimate Violence Index nor the Weak Social Control Index, the other two
explanatory variables, are significantly correlated with any of the homicide variables, although all correlations are in the expected direction. Of the two control
variables, the percentage of African-Americans is significantly correlated with all
four types of homicide, whereas the percentage of urbanization retains significance with stranger homicides only.

The bivariate analyses just presented strongly support the stress theory of
homicide and also the economic-deprivation or poverty explanations. In addition, the percentage who are African-American is also shown to be strongly
related to all four homicide measures. On the other hand, the cultural-norms
theory and social-control theory are not supported at the bivariate level. However, neither the support for the stress and economic-deprivation theories nor
the lack of support for the cultural-norm and social-control theories are reliant.
Stress and poverty, for example, might be confounded with urbanization, and

TABLE 8-4. CORRELATION MATRIX OF HOMICIDE VARIABLES AND SIX INDEPENDENT VARIABLES FOR FIFTY STATES, 1980–1984

Homicide Variables	Independent Variables					
	STRESS	LEGVIO	PCTPOOR	CONTROL	PCTBLCK	PCTURB
TOTAL	.749**	.172	.408*	.109	.781**	.343
FAMILY	.723**	.284	.462**	.081	.717**	.221
ACQUAINT	.745**	.159	.429*	.092	.787**	.278
STRANGER	.634**	.027	.162	.148	.686**	.588**

Note: *p < .01, **p < .001 (two-tailed significance). STRESS = Stress Index; LEGVIO = Legitimate Violence Index; PCTPOOR = % Poor; CONTROL = Social Control Index; PCTBLCK = % African-American; PCTURB = % Metro; TOTAL = Total Homicide Rate; FAMILY = Total Family Homicide Rate; ACQUAINT = Total Acquaintance Homicide Rate; STRANGER = Total Stranger Homicide Rate.

the relationship of stress and the percentage of African-Americans to homicide might be explained because of poverty. Further, the lack of relationship to social control and cultural norms may be masked by failing to specify the other variables. Consequently, a multivariate analysis is needed to examine the effect of stress and the effect of the percentage of African-Americans after controlling for other variables such as poverty.

MULTIVARIATE ANALYSIS

Four regression analyses, one for each of the four homicide rates, are presented in table 8–5.[3] The first panel gives the results of regressing the total homicide rate on the exogenous variables and shows an adjusted R-squared of .849 (p < .0001). Three of the four major explanatory variables were found to be statistically significant: the State Stress Index, the Weak Social Control Index, and the poverty measure. Both control variables, the percentage of African-Americans and the percentage of persons living in metropolitan areas, are significantly related to total homicide with the percentage of African-Americans showing the strongest effects.

Family Homicide

The second analysis in table 8–5 uses family homicides as the dependent variables. Here 76% of the variance is explained with all of the independent variables together. With regard to family homicide, both the ssi and Legitimate Violence Index show significant relationships. However, neither the social control nor the

3. The homicide rates and the percentages of African-Americans, poor, and urban have all been transformed to log 10.

TABLE 8-5. REGRESSION ANALYSES OF HOMICIDE RATES ON SIX INDEPENDENT VARIABLES FOR FIFTY STATES, 1980–1984

Homicide Variables	Independent Variables					
	STRESS	LEGVIO	PCTPOOR	CONTROL	PCTBLCK	PCTURB
TOTAL						
b	.0070	.2807	.6377	.1720	.0034	.5925
beta	.2102	.1018	.2663	.2588	.6211	.2070
se(b)	.0029	.0025	.2089	.0595	.0394	.2119
t	2.412*	1.372	3.051**	2.891**	7.127**	2.796**
FAMILY						
b	.0093	.0083	.4558	.0677	.2501	.3134
beta	.2799	.2522	.1917	.1026	.5572	.1103
se(b)	.0036	.0030	.2589	.0737	.0488	.2625
t	2.575**	2.727**	1.761	0.919	5.125**	1.194
ACQUAINT						
b	.0076	.0025	.5893	.1751	.3018	.3134
beta	.2255	.0726	.2414	.2585	.6551	.1091
se(b)	.0031	.0026	.2248	.0640	.0424	.2279
t	2.453**	0.928	2.622**	2.736**	7.124**	1.396
STRANGER						
b	.0036	.0009	.7335	.2585	.2829	1.731
beta	.0881	.0221	.2466	.4870	.5037	.4870
se(b)	.0047	.0040	.3394	.0966	.0639	.3442
t	0.773	0.228	2.161*	2.674**	4.421**	5.029**

Note: *p < .05, **p < .01 (two-tailed significance). STRESS = Stress Index; LEGVIO = Legitimate Violence Index; PCTPOOR = % Poor; CONTROL = Social Control Index; PCTBLCK = % African-American; PCTURB = % Metro; TOTAL = Total Homicide Rate; FAMILY = Total Family Homicide Rate; ACQUAINT = Total Acquaintance Homicide Rate; STRANGER = Total Stranger Homicide Rate.

poverty measures were significantly related to family homicide. Of the two variables included for statistical control, the percentage of African-Americans is significant but the percentage metropolitan is not.

Acquaintance homicide is significantly related to both the ssi and the Weak Social Control Index. In this case the Legitimate Violence Index drops out. The percentages of African-Americans and poverty remain highly significant but the percentage metropolitan is not significantly related to acquaintance homicide.

The last analysis in table 8–5 focuses on stranger homicide. This category appears to be at the opposite end of the continuum in terms of the intensity and intimacy of the offender-victim relationship (Straus 1988). To the extent that this is the case, there is little reason to believe that stranger homicide would be associated with the same pattern of explanatory variables. For example, more than half of stranger homicides occur during commission of another crime such as robbery (Straus and Williams 1988), an activity that is more instrumental than expressive. Accordingly, we would not expect the type of visceral response often associated with high stress to be linked to homicides associated with instrumental crimes. Yet this in fact proves to be the case. Stranger homicide is the only type of homicide with which the State Stress Index is *not* significantly correlated once other exogenous variables are controlled.

The strongest of the explanatory variables in the case of stranger homicide is the Weak Social Control Index, which is significant at the .01 level. The percentage of poor and both of the control variables (the percentage of African-Americans and percentage metropolitan) are significantly related to stranger homicide. Recall that the percentage metropolitan was not significantly correlated with either family or acquaintance homicide.

The above pattern of relationships makes a certain degree of sense in terms of a plausible connection with stranger homicides. For example, one would be more likely to encounter strangers in urban settings than in rural or small-town locations. Consequently, strangers would be more likely to be targets of opportunity. Similarly, the presence of weak social ties in a community, as indicated by the Social Control Index, would increase the likelihood of contacts with strangers and indicate a weakened community capacity to prevent homicidal events from occurring.

One reason for the significant relationship of poverty to stranger homicide may be that economic deprivation motivates economically oriented crimes. As noted above, stranger homicides frequently occur during the commission of crimes such as robbery. This contrasts with family homicides where the lethal violence is usually unrelated to commission of other crimes and is not associated with poverty when other factors are controlled in the regression analysis.

SUMMARY AND CONCLUSIONS

This chapter tested four theories that might account for the large differences between states in the incidence of homicide. These theories hold that homicide is a function of social stress, of cultural norms that support violence, of economic deprivation, and of a weak system of social control. The regression analysis also included controls for urbanization and racial composition of the states. The regressions were replicated for the overall homicide rate and for homicides of family members, acquaintances, and strangers.

These analyses confirmed our previous finding of a strong relationship between the State Stress Index and total homicide rate based on data for 1976. They also extend the earlier study with the finding that the stress-homicide relationship primarily reflects a relationship between stress and primary-group homicides, that is, murders of family members and acquaintances. Moreover, we found that the stress-homicide relationship holds even when the model includes some of the other major variables that have been used to explain homicide, such as cultural support for violence, weak social control, economic deprivation, urbanization, and a large minority population. This finding suggests that the stress theory is not simply a restatement of some of the better established theories of homicide reported, since stress has a significant relationship to homicide net of variables representing these other theories.

Distinctive Effects of Stress

There appears to be strong demarcation between the independent variables in terms of their relationship to homicide. Social stress is significantly related to both family and acquaintance homicides, but not to stranger homicides. This contrasts sharply with the relationship of poverty and weak social control to homicide. The latter are significantly related only with stranger and acquaintance homicides but are not significantly related to homicide of family members and thus have their major impact on the less intimate end of the relationship continuum. Thus, what appeared previously to be competing theories of comparative homicide rates may each be valid within their separate domains. The findings further support the value of disaggregating rates for comparative study of homicide (Williams and Flewelling 1988).

Links between Stress and Intrafamily Homicide

In some ways it seems surprising that the State Stress Index is most strongly related to homicide within the family, and we shall therefore suggest two theoretical models of possible mediating processes.

Differential Impact of Stress on Family Relationships. The first model holds that the effect of stress on interpersonal relationships is greater for family relationships than for nonfamily relationships. Indeed, families may be stress-collection points not only for stressful events created inside the family but also for stresses originating outside of the family, such as community disasters, business failures, or work stoppages. This view of families as a channel through which stress becomes translated into lethal violence contrasts with, but is not necessarily inconsistent with, the view of families as mediators or safe havens from the stressors of the outside world. The haven view of the family is partly based on the idea that people can "be themselves" in the bosom of the family. They can express their anger and frustration in ways that would be unacceptable outside the family (Gottman 1979; Raush et al. 1974). However, a possibly negative side effect of the permission to ventilate frustrations within the family may be that a certain proportion of the ventilated verbal aggression becomes physical aggression (Straus 1974a) and that a certain proportion of those situations in turn become lethal.

Differential Impact of Stress on Women. The second theoretical model that might explain the greater link of stress with family homicide starts with the proposition that stressful life events have a greater impact on women than men. This proposition is consistent with our earlier research on the links between stress and mortality from various causes (Linsky and Straus 1986). We found stronger relationships for women than for men for all accidental deaths, motor-vehicle deaths, suicide, heavy smoking (respiratory cancer), and alcohol abuse (cirrhosis). Ironically the death rate for most of the above disorders is substantially higher among males than among females, but the link with stress is higher among females. For deaths due to asthma and peptic ulcers, the relationship with stress was significant only for females. Thus, social stressors seem to put women at greater risk of death from a number of disorders than men. (The concluding chapter discusses explanations for the closer association of stress and disorder for women.)

The second proposition in the gender-difference model is based on the finding that homicides committed by women, although less frequent than those committed by men, are primarily directed toward members of their family (Browne and Williams 1989). Homicide of strangers, on the other hand, is an almost exclusively male pattern.

Finally, if women are indeed more affected than men by the stressful events included in the ssi, and if women are most likely to direct their lethal aggression within the family and to rarely engage in assaults on strangers, an increasing level of stress would have a greater impact on the intrafamily homicide rate than on the stranger homicide rate.

Whatever the intervening process, there is a marked contrast between the strong relationship of the ssi and homicide of acquaintances and family members and the absence of a relationship between the State Stress Index and homicide of strangers. Socially generated stress seems to have its major impact on homicide by propelling established and sometimes intimate interactions in the direction of lethal violence.

CHAPTER 9

Legitimate Violence, Gun Availability, and Methods of Homicide

In the previous chapter we examined the link between stress and relationship-specific homicide. This chapter continues the examination of the stress-homicide process by looking more closely at weapon-specific forms of homicide. Specifically, we examine the relationship that stress and violent cultures have to homicides committed with handguns, shoulder guns, and sharp or blunt instruments. In addition, we look at the role that weapon availability plays in stress, culture, and lethal violence.

STRESS AND THE RELATIONSHIP OF VICTIM TO OFFENDER

In the last chapter we determined that social stress is significantly related to total homicide rates net of all other control variables. The controls included a subculture of violence, social control, economic deprivation, the percentage of African-Americans, and the percentage metropolitan. This overall relationship was replicated for family and acquaintance homicide separately but not for stranger homicide. Thus, socially generated stress appears to have its major impact on homicide by propelling established, and sometimes intimate, interactions in the direction of lethal violence.

In the present chapter we examine additional issues in the stress-homicide relationship. Namely, we focus on the question, Does the strong overall relationship between the SSI and homicide apply to all methods of killing, or is it limited to only some? The answer will reveal important clues regarding the dynamics of the stress-homicide relationship.

The variety of weapons used in homicide may imply various motivational processes intervening between stressors and homicidal response. In the literature on stress, the "fight or flight" concept is prominent (Selye 1980). As we discussed in the first chapter, survival mechanisms that prepare the organism for flight or fight are activated when organisms are faced with external threats (Cannon 1963). There is an emergency discharge of adrenalin, a quickening of the pulse, an increase in blood pressure, stimulation of the central nervous system, temporary suspension of digestion, a quickening of blood clotting, and a rise in the blood sugar. Hence, the organism is prepared by these physiological responses to engage in physically demanding or violent activity, which may result in homicidal behavior involving any of a number of weapons.

Advocates of gun control, for example, argue that the ready availability of handguns results in some homicides that would not occur otherwise, because handguns require only a sudden and momentary arousal to precipitate a lethal response (Wright, Rossi, and Daley 1983). Put another way, some unwanted or unforeseen homicides may occur under conditions of stress as a function of the "heat of the moment" coupled with the availability of suitable weapons. Thus, according to this reasoning, if guns were not available and a more time-consuming method requiring sustained effort was employed, the heat of the moment might elapse prior to completion of the fatal act.

At the same time, one can argue an almost opposite case that would support a stronger link between stress and slower means of homicide, such as attacks with knives or blunt instruments. For example, such homicides may be linked to the powerful emotional states triggered by stress, because they may require a stronger and more sustained motivation and physical exertion to complete the lethal act. Following this line of reasoning, we should expect the strongest link of stress and homicide to be with knives and blunt instruments. This issue will be investigated with a nondirectional hypothesis, in that the case can be argued plausibly in both directions. Tables 9–1a and 9–1b array the states in rank order on the weapons-specific homicide rates used for this analysis.

In addition to social stress, a measure of the subculture of violence was also included as an explanatory variable in relation to weapon-specific homicide. The concept of the subculture of violence and its measurement through the Legitimate Violence Index (LVX) were discussed extensively in the previous chapter, which also gives a table arraying the states in rank order on the LVX. Several demographic variables are also included for control purposes because of their well-established relationship to homicide: the percentage of African-Americans, percentage of urbanization, and percentage of poor (those families with an income below the poverty line established by the U.S. Social Security Administration; Bureau of the Census 1987).

TABLE 9-1A.   RANK ORDER OF STATES ON WEAPON-SPECIFIC HOMICIDE RATES, PER 100*K* POPULATION, 1980–1984

Rank	Handguns State	R8V13	Shoulder Guns State	R8V14	Sharp Instruments State	R8V15
1	DC	16.46	ALAS	2.81	DC	7.57
2	LA	6.85	LA	2.76	TEX	2.87
3	TEX	6.59	TEX	2.75	NY	2.54
4	NEV	6.06	MO	2.65	LA	2.47
5	MISS	5.83	GA	2.54	CAL	2.46
6	FLA	5.55	MISS	2.24	NEV	2.26
7	GA	5.26	NC	2.22	FLA	2.10
8	ALA	4.76	SC	2.11	GA	2.00
9	NY	4.71	ALA	2.07	ILL	1.94
10	SC	4.44	FLA	1.98	MISS	1.94
11	ALAS	4.31	TENN	1.93	MD	1.92
12	ILL	4.08	ARK	1.74	ALA	1.89
13	CAL	4.07	OKL	1.58	SC	1.81
14	TENN	4.06	KY	1.58	NM	1.67
15	KY	3.99	MICH	1.57	MICH	1.65
16	OKL	3.75	CAL	1.56	ALAS	1.58
17	MD	3.74	VA	1.33	NJ	1.57
18	NM	3.70	NM	1.33	NC	1.52
19	MICH	3.48	NEV	1.26	ARI	1.47
20	NC	3.42	WV	1.24	TENN	1.47
21	ARK	3.37	ARI	1.01	COL	1.45
22	VA	3.22	WYO	.99	VA	1.34
23	ARI	3.15	IND	.97	DEL	1.34
24	IND	2.96	DEL	.93	OKL	1.31
25	OHIO	2.90	MD	.83	MO	1.29
26	MO	2.38	KAN	.75	PA	1.22
27	COL	2.32	ORG	.68	HAWA	1.15
28	PA	2.12	DC	.64	OHIO	1.05
29	KAN	2.05	COL	.64	MASS	.98
30	WYO	1.97	ILL	.63	ARK	.96
31	WV	1.95	MONT	.63	KY	.92
32	NJ	1.86	OHIO	.63	RI	.91
33	CONN	1.62	ME	.60	WASH	.90
34	MONT	1.45	WASH	.60	CONN	.89
35	WASH	1.31	VT	.55	IND	.88
36	DEL	1.30	CONN	.52	KAN	.79
37	HAWA	1.17	PA	.49	OREG	.77
38	ORG	1.12	RI	.49	NEB	.66
39	IDA	1.08	IDA	.48	WYO	.66
40	MASS	1.04	NY	.45	UTAH	.61
41	UTAH	1.02	HAWA	.44	WV	.56
42	NEB	.92	NH	.44	WIS	.55
43	WIS	.90	WIS	.38	MONT	.52
44	RI	.70	UTAH	.37	MINN	.47
45	VT	.63	NEB	.35	IOWA	.45
46	IOWA	.60	SD	.34	IDA	.40
47	SD	.53	IOWA	.33	VT	.39
48	NH	.49	NJ	.32	NH	.35
49	ME	.47	MINN	.31	ND	.28
50	MINN	.45	ND	.31	ME	.27
51	ND	.15	MASS	.24	SD	.23

TABLE 9-1B. RANK ORDER OF STATES ON WEAPON-SPECIFIC HOMICIDE RATES, PER 100K POPULATION, 1980–1984

Rank	Blunt Instruments State	R8V18	Total Gun Rate State	TOTGUNRT
1	DC	3.66	DC	17.10
2	NEV	1.75	LA	9.61
3	NY	1.41	TEX	9.34
4	CAL	1.36	MISS	8.07
5	FLA	1.30	GA	7.81
6	ARI	1.20	FLA	7.53
7	OKL	1.19	NEV	7.32
8	HAW	1.13	ALAS	7.12
9	TEX	1.11	ALA	6.83
10	GA	.98	SC	6.55
11	MICH	.97	TENN	5.99
12	NM	.96	NC	5.64
13	SC	.95	CAL	5.63
14	ALAS	.92	KY	5.57
15	LA	.91	OKL	5.34
16	MISS	.91	NY	5.16
17	MD	.90	ARK	5.11
18	WYO	.89	MICH	5.05
19	COL	.87	MO	5.03
20	MO	.86	NM	5.03
21	ILL	.86	ILL	4.72
22	NJ	.85	MD	4.57
23	DEL	.82	VA	4.55
24	ALA	.82	ARI	4.16
25	KAN	.79	IND	3.93
26	KY	.77	OHIO	3.53
27	UTAH	.74	WV	3.20
28	RI	.74	WYO	2.96
29	OHIO	.74	COL	2.96
30	TENN	.70	KAN	2.80
31	WASH	.69	PA	2.61
32	NC	.66	DEL	2.23
33	PA	.65	NJ	2.18
34	ARK	.62	CONN	2.14
35	CONN	.61	MONT	2.08
36	IDA	.59	WASH	1.90
37	VA	.56	OREG	1.80
38	OREG	.52	HAWA	1.61
39	NH	.51	IDA	1.56
40	WV	.50	UTAH	1.39
41	MASS	.49	WIS	1.28
42	IND	.48	MASS	1.28
43	VT	.47	NEB	1.27
44	NEB	.43	RI	1.18
45	WIS	.35	VT	1.17
46	MONT	.33	ME	1.07
47	ME	.31	NH	.92
48	MINN	.28	IOWA	.92
49	SD	.26	SD	.87
50	IOWA	.23	MINN	.77
51	ND	.09	ND	.46

TABLE 9-2.   CORRELATION MATRIX OF INDEPENDENT AND CONTROL VARIABLES AGAINST WEAPON-SPECIFIC HOMICIDE RATES, 1980–1984

Homicide Variables	Independent Variables					
	EVNTINDX	ZLEGVIO	ZGUNMAG	PBPPOOR	PCTBLCK	PCTURB
Handguns	.69**	.30	−.01	.41*	.77**	.29
Shoulder Guns	.65**	.44**	.12	.58**	.59**	−.08
Total Guns	.71**	.35*	.02	.48**	.76**	.20
Sharp Inst.	.69**	.14	−.18	.26	.83**	.56**
Blunt Inst.	.67**	.26	.01	.11	.57**	.53**

Note: $^*p < .01$, $^{**}p < .001$ (2-tailed significance). EVNTINDX = State Stress Index; ZLEGVIO = Modified Legitimate Violence Index; ZGUNMAG = Gun Magazine Subscriptions per 100 K; PBPPOOR = % Poor; PCTBLCK = % African-American; PCTURB = % Metro.

HOMICIDE DATA

We again use the same new source of data on homicide we did in chapter eight, the Comparative Homicide File (CHF). As we mentioned there, the CHF specifies homicide by situation, by the relationship of victim and offender, and, most relevant to the current chapter, by the specific weapons involved.

CORRELATION OF STRESS, LEGITIMATE VIOLENCE, AND WEAPON-SPECIFIC HOMICIDE

Table 9–2 presents the bivariate correlations between the homicide variables and each of the independent variables. Of the two explanatory variables, social stress is the most consistently correlated to all of the homicide categories. Correlations range from a high of .71 for total gun homicides to a low of .65 for homicides by shoulder gun. All homicide variables are significant beyond the .001 level.

Legitimate violence, on the other hand, is significantly correlated with shoulder guns (.44), but the correlations with handguns, and blunt or sharp instruments, though in the right direction, are smaller and not significant.

Three control variables are included in the matrix. The percentage of African-Americans is strongly and significantly correlated with all homicide variables. The percentage below the poverty line, on the other hand, is significantly correlated only with gun homicides, whereas the percentage metropolitan, in contrast, is significantly correlated only with homicides by sharp or blunt instruments.

The bivariate relationships just presented suggest that the social stress–homicide relationship operates strongly across all weapons categories, whereas the subculture of violence correlates mainly with homicides using firearms.

TABLE 9-3. REGRESSION ANALYSES OF WEAPON-SPECIFIC HOMICIDE RATES AGAINST FIVE INDEPENDENT VARIABLES FOR FIFTY STATES, 1980–1984

Homicide Variables	Independent Variables				
	EVNTINDX	ZLEGVIO	PBPPOOR	PCTBLCK	PCTURB
Handguns					
b	.004	.10	.20	.15	.22
beta	.21	.26	.15	.59	.13
se(b)	.002	.03	.12	.02	.14
t	2.41*	3.37**	1.65	6.24**	1.55
Shoulder Guns					
b	.004	.09	.19	.10	.13
beta	.29	.30	.17	.49	−.21
se(b)	.002	.02	.11	.02	.13
t	2.97**	3.40**	1.66	4.58**	−2.17*
Total Guns					
b	.004	.09	.21	.13	.06
beta	.250	.27	.17	.59	.04
se(b)	.001	.02	.10	.02	.12
t	3.07**	3.68**	2.03*	6.60**	.567
Sharp Inst.					
b	.003	.03	.15	.10	.48
beta	.230	.12	.15	.54	.40
se(b)	.008	.01	.06	.01	.07
t	3.87**	2.32*	2.47**	8.47**	6.68**
Blunt Inst.					
b	.004	.04	.040	.04	.40
beta	.350	.19	.040	.26	.40
se(b)	.001	.02	.100	.01	.11
t	3.02**	1.86	.417	2.12*	3.48**

Note: $^*p < .05$, $^{**}p < .01$ (two-tailed significance). EVNTINDX = State Stress Index; ZLEGVIO = Modified Legitimate Violence Index; PBPPOOR = % Poor; PCTBLCK = % African-American; PCTURB = % Metro.

Before definitive statements can be made, however, multivariate analysis must first be performed.

REGRESSION ANALYSIS

Four regression analyses were computed, one for each of the four homicide rates; that is, each of the weapon-specific types of homicide was regressed on the State Stress Index, the Index of Legitimate Violence, and the three control variables.

Handguns and Shoulder Guns

The top panel of table 9–3 reveals that both the State Stress Index and the Legitimate Violence Index are significantly related to homicide rates by handgun. One of the three control variables, the percentage of African-Americans, is

also related significantly to handgun slayings, while the relationship of urbanization and poverty with handgun homicide fails to reach significance. All of the
exogenous variables together result in an adjusted R-squared of .78.

With regard to homicide by shoulder guns, the ssi and the lvx continue to
be related significantly to deaths from shoulder guns, as shown in table 9–3.
Again, only one of the three control variables, the percentage of African-Americans, is significantly related. Urbanization is related negatively to shoulder-gun
deaths. This finding is consistent with the fact that long guns are more likely to
be available in rural areas (Wright, Rossi, and Daley 1983; Dixon and Lizotte
1987). Here 71% of the variance is explained with all of the independent variables together.

Sharp Instruments

The ssi continues to retain high significance with homicides by knives and sharp
instruments (p < .001) net of all other variables. Legitimate violence is also
related significantly to knife deaths, but the relationship is not as strong as in the
case of guns. All three control variables, the percentage of African-Americans,
metropolitan, and poor, are significantly related to deaths by stabbing. Together
the two explanatory and three control variables account for 90% of the variance
in sharp-instrument homicides.

Blunt Instruments

The relationship of the ssi and the homicide rate for blunt objects is highly
significant again. The relationship of the lvx to blunt-object homicides, however, fails to attain significance. Of the control variables, the percentages of
African-Americans and of urbanization are significantly correlated with deaths
by blunt objects, while the relationship with poverty rate is insignificant. The
adjusted R-squared of the five exogenous variables on blunt-instrument homicides is 62%.

Overall Patterns

From our analysis, it appears that stressful life events, as measured by the ssi, are
strongly related to homicide deaths for all four types of weapons. Stress, therefore, appears to be implicated in homicides, regardless of the type of weapon.
This pattern includes homicides that require only momentary arousal or small
physical efforts, such as those committed with guns, as well as those homicides

that may require sustained arousal or greater physical effort. Both types appear to be increased by high levels of social stress. Thus, the opposing arguments advanced earlier in this chapter for the connection of stress with each type of homicide may both be right. That is, the motivations toward lethal violence engendered by stress are not dependent upon a particular type of weapon.

The stress-homicide relationship appears particularly robust, because it is consistently correlated with all four weapon-specific homicide rates and is also independent of the other important variables that are related to state variations in homicide.

In contrast, approval of violence (as represented by the LVX) is associated specifically with deaths from handguns, long guns and, to a somewhat lesser degree, sharp instruments. It is not, however, related to deaths by blunt instrument. This finding is anomalous because homicides involving blunt instruments appear to be at least as violent as gun deaths, if not more so. The lack of association between the LVX and homicides involving blunt instruments prompted us to reconsider the connection between approval of legitimate violence and homicide.

LEGITIMATE VIOLENCE, GUNS, AND HOMICIDE: A PATH ANALYSIS

Reconsideration of the links between approval of legitimate violence and homicidal violence suggested the possibility that the relationship of the LVX to gun-related homicides may be indirect. Specifically, a violent subculture may increase the likelihood of gun ownership, and it is this availability of guns that increases the rate of gun homicides. In contrast to guns, blunt instruments are ubiquitous and are probably available regardless of the cultural context. Hence, availability of this type of weapon could not serve as the intervening variable between the cultural approval of violence and homicide. Put another way, one cannot explain a variable such as weapon-specific homicide by a constant such as blunt-instrument availability.

The theory that acceptance of legitimate violence and gun-connected homicides were linked by the intervening variable of gun availability can be tested by path analysis, provided there is a state-by-state indicator of gun ownership. Although a census of privately owned guns would be the ideal, no such statistic exists for the entire set of states.[1] Instead we used the circulation rate of two gun

1. Wright, Rossi and Daly's extensive review of research on the relationship of weapons, crime, and violence concludes that at present "we do not know the total number of privately owned firearms in the United States except to the nearest few ten millions" (1983, p. 5). Alternatively, information

TABLE 9-4. RANK ORDER OF STATES ON INDEPENDENT VARIABLES

Rank	State Stress Index		Mod. Legitimate Violence Index		Gun Magazine Subscrip. per 100K	
	State	EVNTINDX	State	ZPLEGVIO	State	GUNMAG
1	NEV	100.00	ALAS	100.00	ALAS	1,842.33
2	GA	85.00	WYO	95.00	WYO	1,680.00
3	ALAS	83.00	NEV	80.00	NEV	1,028.47
4	ALA	82.00	GA	78.00	MONT	1,022.97
5	ARIZ	75.00	MONT	75.00	IDA	1,011.72
6	MISS	73.00	MISS	73.00	KANS	778.90
7	TENN	73.00	IDA	73.00	OKLA	761.23
8	WASH	72.00	UTAH	71.00	SD	730.48
9	CAL	70.00	OKLA	68.00	ND	719.42
10	SC	70.00	ARIZ	65.00	OREG	719.24
11	COLO	69.00	LA	65.00	ARIZ	716.44
12	MICH	69.00	FLA	64.00	TEX	659.85
13	OREG	65.00	TEX	64.00	VT	642.81
14	FLA	60.00	ARK	64.00	WASH	635.13
15	VA	58.00	COLO	62.00	UTAH	628.50
16	ILL	56.00	SC	60.00	COLO	615.51
17	LA	56.00	HAWA	58.00	ARK	588.38
18	INDI	54.00	VT	58.00	IOWA	571.56
19	OKLA	54.00	OREG	56.00	NM	571.43
20	TEX	54.00	VA	56.00	INDI	536.81
21	HAWA	53.00	NM	56.00	LA	525.14
22	NM	52.00	ALA	55.00	PA	523.55
23	KY	51.00	KANS	55.00	WV	509.36
24	NC	51.00	ND	53.00	NEB	502.39
25	OHIO	51.00	WASH	50.00	NH	483.42
26	WV	51.00	NC	50.00	OHIO	478.15
27	IDA	50.00	DEL	50.00	MO	471.33
28	NY	50.00	SD	50.00	KY	468.08
29	DEL	49.00	CAL	43.00	MINN	462.65
30	PA	49.00	TENN	40.00	ME	458.26
31	MO	48.00	OHIO	40.00	CAL	456.19
32	MD	45.00	NEB	40.00	DEL	445.29
33	RI	40.00	IOWA	36.00	MICH	441.60
34	UTAH	40.00	ILL	35.00	GA	435.34
35	VT	39.00	KY	35.00	HAWA	419.29
36	ME	38.00	ME	34.00	ILL	415.66
37	NJ	38.00	WV	33.00	WIS	407.70
38	KANS	35.00	MD	33.00	VA	405.75
39	MINN	32.00	NH	33.00	ALA	393.86
40	ARK	31.00	PA	32.00	TENN	378.40
41	MASS	31.00	MICH	31.00	DC	375.00
42	NH	31.00	CONN	30.00	MISS	355.60
43	CONN	30.00	INDI	29.00	FLA	353.75
44	MONT	29.00	NY	29.00	NC	337.76
45	WYO	29.00	MO	28.00	CONN	303.56
46	ND	24.00	MINN	27.00	SC	291.82
47	WIS	23.00	WIS	27.00	MD	284.40
48	NEBR	15.00	NJ	22.00	NY	272.67
49	IOWA	10.00	MASS	19.00	NJ	257.52
50	SD	10.00	RI	13.00	MASS	239.22
51	DC	—	DC	—	RI	217.24

magazines (*Guns and Ammo* and *Shooting Times*) as a proxy for gun ownership, because it seems reasonable to presume that gun owners would be the primary subscribers to such magazines. Table 9–4 arrays the states in rank order on gun-magazine subscriptions per 100,000 population.

The top half of figure 9–1 presents the results of the path analysis computed to test the hypothesis that the relationship between legitimate violence and the rate of homicide occurs because a high level of legitimate violence is associated with a high rate of gun ownership as measured by the circulation rate of gun magazines. For this test, we combined homicides by handguns and shoulder guns for a total rate of gun homicide.

The path analysis strongly supports the hypothesized model. The direct path from the LVX to gun homicides is only .03 and is not statistically significant. However, there are highly significant paths from the LVX to Gun Magazines (.82) and from Gun Magazines to Gun Homicides (.31). Thus, the indirect path is .25 [(.82) (.31)], which accounts for most of the .28 total effect (.25 + .03) of Legitimate Violence and Gun Magazines on gun-related homicides. Thus, this data supports the view that subcultures of legitimate violence are related to higher gun-homicide rates because there are more guns available among such populations and the availability of these guns in turn is linked to higher homicide rates.

These findings were internally replicated by a separate path analysis for homicides by handgun and shoulder gun (not shown here). In each case the patterns were almost identical with total gun homicides, although the effects were slightly stronger with the total gun homicides.

Test of an Alternative Model: Stress and Gun Ownership

The possibility still exists that the strong association of social stress and gun homicides may also reflect the intervening variable of available guns. For example, a high level of stressful events in a community could weaken relational systems and create an atmosphere of generalized anxiety and fear, which in turn could lead some citizens to buy guns for defensive purposes. This scenario, however, seems less likely, because stress is strongly associated with homicides from all the weapons examined, whether guns are involved or not.

---

on interview data was available to our study from a national sample of adults that included questions on ownership of weapons. However, when the total sample was aggregated to the state level, it was deemed too unreliable because the sample was too small in less populous states and because of a possible unwillingness of respondents to admit ownership of guns (Newton and Zimring 1969). The data on magazine circulation have the advantage of reflecting complete rather than sampled data and are not subject to the same types of social desirability that surveys on guns involve.

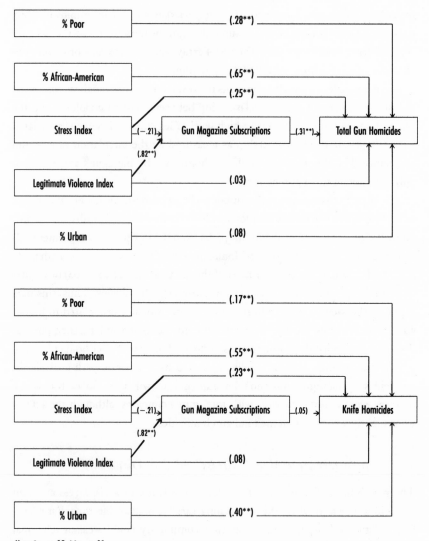

Note: *p ≤ .05, **p ≤ .01.

Figure 9-1.   Path Analysis of Gun Homicides and Knife Homicides

The path analysis presented in the upper half of figure 9–1 indicates that the effect of the SSI on gun homicides is a direct one, however, and is not linked through the intervening variable of gun ownership. This finding was also replicated separately for both handguns and shoulder guns (not shown here).

Because our indicator of gun availability is an indirect one (subscriptions to gun magazine), we are left with the possibility that we may be measuring something other than gun availability. To validate our findings, we tested a model that was identical to the previous model except for the substitution of knife homicides for gun homicides as the dependent variable in the path analysis. If the path analysis works with knife homicides as it did with gun homicides, then it would cast considerable doubt on the validity of gun magazine subscriptions as an indicator of gun ownership or availability. The path analysis in the lower half of figure 9–1, however, indicates almost no linkage (.05) between gun magazines and knife homicides. Thus, construct validity of gun magazines as an indicator of gun ownership is suggested, and we can rule out the possibility that the relationship between gun magazines and gun homicides in the first path analysis is spurious.

LEGITIMATE VIOLENCE, GUN OWNERSHIP, AND HOMICIDAL VIOLENCE

The association of the LVX with gun ownership at first glance appears contradictory to some recent individual-level research on gun ownership. Dixon and Lizotte (1987), analyzing patterns of gun ownership among individuals, conclude that gun ownership is unrelated to the violent values indicative of subcultures of violence. Their measure of violent attitudes was based on attitudinal items of a respondent's general approval of physical aggression in various situations. However, Dixon and Lizotte exclude from their indicators of violent attitudes items that reflect what they refer to as "defensive attitudes" (items reflecting approval of violence in self-protection or in protecting other innocent persons) as well as the reasonable use of violence by police in carrying out their duties. The excluded items appear not at all inconsistent in content with our macro-measure of legitimate violence. Dixon and Lizotte did in fact find a direct effect of defensiveness on gun ownership (p. 400).

In another related study, Wright, Rossi, and Daly (1983) reviewed survey-data research on gun ownership and concluded that there is little support for the explanation of gun ownership based on a subculture of violence. Citing the research by O'Connor and Lizotte (1978, p. 112) and others, they report that early socialization into what might be termed "gun culture," which glorifies not violence but rural values and activities and specifically the sporting use of guns, is the primary reason people own guns. However, Wright, Rossi, and Daly also acknowledge evidence from other studies indicating that two-thirds to three-fourths of gun owners report that they own them in part for self-defense, that is, for a normative and legitimate use. Therefore, the evidence from both of these reviews is not inconsistent with our own findings that legitimate violence is

associated with gun ownership, which in turn is associated with homicidal violence. These findings suggest that institutionalization of violence at the collec-
tive level for socially legitimate purposes provides a model that encourages
individuals to purchase guns for self-protection and that the presence of guns
increases the risk of fatal assaults.

DISCUSSION AND SUMMARY

In this chapter, two established theories of comparative homicide rates, social
stress, and subculture of violence were examined in terms of their ability to
explain weapon-specific types of homicide. Williams and Flewelling's (1987)
argument that many inconsistent findings in the comparative homicide literature
are attributable to treating homicide as if it were a single homogeneous category
was once again given credence here.

The relationship between social stress and homicide appears to be particularly robust, since stress is significantly related to homicide deaths from all
four types of weapons and is independent of four other variables commonly used
to explain homicide rates. Thus, social stress has an apparently broad impact on
lethal conduct, because it is linked with both the use of weapons that require
only a momentary state of arousal as well as those requiring more sustained,
strenuous action.

A subculture of violence, as represented here by the Legitimate Violence
Index, was associated significantly with homicide by handguns and shoulder
guns. To a lesser degree, it was associated with sharp instruments and was
unrelated to blunt instruments.

The finding that the Legitimate Violence Index was strongly associated
only with gun homicides suggested the possibility of an intervening variable
such as availability of guns in those states that have a subculture of violence. A
path analysis did in fact reveal a strong indirect path: the LVX was strongly linked
to the availability of guns, as indicated by gun-magazine subscribers, and availability of guns in turn was significantly linked to gun homicide. At the same
time, no direct path between the subculture of legitimate violence and gun
homicides was found. Thus, the impact of the two competing explanatory variables on homicide is quite distinct.

CHAPTER 10

Stress and Rape in the Context of American Society

Two important limitations in current research on social stress are addressed in this book. The first is the relative neglect of behavioral outcomes of stress. Variables such as rape and other forms of violent and criminal behaviors, for example, have been overlooked in favor of an almost exclusive concern with such consequences as mental and physical illness. The second is the nonspecificity in the prediction of stress outcomes. The perplexing problem of why stressful events lead to different patterns of outcomes within different populations deserves further attention. Although there are a few studies linking stress with such forms of violence as homicide (Humphrey and Palmer 1986; Bachman-Prehn et al., 1988; Linsky and Straus 1986; Landau and Raveh 1987) and assaults within families (Straus 1980b; Kantor and Straus 1987), there is to date almost no research linking stress with the propensity to commit rape.[1]

THEORETICAL GROUNDS FOR THE CONNECTION BETWEEN STRESS AND RAPE

Stress and Violent Crime

Researchers engaged in the comparative study of crime and violence have looked toward such broad cultural and structural conditions as economic deprivation, cultural support of violence, the efficacy of social control and, in the case of rape, the prevalence of pornography and gender inequality as explanations of that

1. For an important exception, see Mawson (1987).

behavior. Stress, however, has not been viewed as an important explanatory concept in this area.

The exclusion of social stress in comparative studies of rape may be due in part to the lack of broad-based objective measures of social stress in the past. Yet there are strong a priori grounds and some direct evidence for the assumption of a link between social stress and the rate of forcible rape. First, stress has been linked to both violent and nonviolent crime rates. Evidence suggests that a wide variety of criminal and delinquent acts can be precipitated by stressful life events (Mawson 1987; Linsky and Straus 1986; Schlesinger and Revitch 1980; Molof 1980). Further, rapists are often indistinguishable from the general population of felons (Bourque 1989) and frequently commit this crime during the commission of other crimes (Mawson 1987). On that ground alone, one would expect that stressful events or conditions that precipitate other forms of aggressive behavior and criminal activities would be linked to rape as well.

Irrational and preconscious motivations may be involved in the impact of stress on aggression, particularly violence (Brenner 1980). Mawson, drawing on psychophysiological formulations, argues that environmental stress may lead to arousal of the sympathetic nervous system, which in turn leads to stimulation-seeking behavior. Stimulation-seeking behavior includes both sex and aggression, which in turn are related to rape (Mawson 1987, p. 107). Mawson suggests that the decision to commit rape or some other crime depends partly on situational opportunities.

On a more sociological level, Wilkins (1980) explains how economic disruptions might lead to both criminal aggressions and self-directed aggressions. Economic disruptions among certain cultural groups may weaken community, neighborhood, and personal relationships in important ways; this weakening could, in turn, produce individual breakdowns that are manifested in sociopathic behavior (both passive and violent). We suggest that noneconomic stressors would also have these negative consequences, because they are also highly disruptive of personal relationships. Our research tests that proposition.

Cultural Norms and the Direction of Aggression

The central hypothesis of this chapter is that aggression arising out of stressful situations is channeled by cultural norms toward particular classes of victims. Ours is a complex model, but it is hardly a new theory. Several early studies summarized in Berkowitz (1962) demonstrated that year-to-year decreases in the price of cotton were associated with an increase in the number of African-Americans lynched in the South (Hovland and Sears 1940). Berkowitz suggests that the lynching of African-Americans posed a relatively low-risk outlet for whites who were frustrated by economic reversals because of the low power perceived among the target population.

The argument presented by Berkowitz is quite similar to the stress, culture, and aggression model we employ in our explanation of differences in the rate of rape. Our empirical data is based on use of the State Stress Index, which includes several indicators of economic disruptions, such as personal bankruptcies, plant closings, business failures, and new cases of unemployment. These are events that could pose economic threats similar to the severe economic reversals described in Berkowitz. The SSI, however, also includes a broad range of community and familial sources of stress. These economic and noneconomic stressors impose burdens and threats to the status and security of state residents that tend to be experienced as frustrating and stressful and thereby provide a context for stress-related rape. But other conditions included or implied in the Berkowitz model may also need to be present to explain the rate of rape, including a cultural tendency to express tension and frustration in the direction at violent aggression, an accessible and vulnerable class of victims, and finally, to explain this particular form of violence, a cultural disposition to sexually objectify the target population, that is, women.

Cultural Spillover

The cultural-spillover theory of violence (Baron and Straus 1987, 1989; Baron, Straus, and Jaffee 1988) suggests that high rates of rape may reflect an extrapolation or spillover from cultural spheres that permit or require violence. According to this theory, approval of violence for legitimate purposes (such as capital punishment of criminals, corporal punishment within schools, and other governmental use of violence) is part of a general cultural pattern that also tends to manifest itself in interpersonal violence. There is a spillover from legitimate violence to criminal violence, and vice versa. When criminal violence rates are high, the public tends to demand severe and often violent "crackdowns." Less obviously, when a society uses violence for legitimate purposes, it provides an example that spills over to private lives and results in a higher rate of violence in interpersonal disputes, criminal activities and, relevant to the present study, violence by men against women, such as rape. (See Baron and Straus [1987, 1989] for a more detailed description of this theory.)

Gender Inequality

The stress, culture, and aggression model can be illustrated by considering the effect of stress in states where the cultural definition and life circumstances of women accord them low power. There may be an implicit pattern of culturally directed aggression toward women, similar to the aggression directed against African-Americans because their low status makes them a vulnerable target.

The path of theoretical deduction is seldom without obstacles, however. In this case, women's status may act as a double-edged sword. A low status could create a vulnerability to criminal sexual aggression, because, as suggested above, such aggression is perceived as low risk. On the other hand, in states where the status of women is high, they may also be singled out as targets of aggression because of male resentment. Greater occupational and political equality may result in women being perceived by some males as threats to their own economic security and status, a condition that is again parallel to the way African-Americans were perceived and targeted in the South. Along this same line of reasoning, researchers suggest the changes in expectations and behaviors that occur as women move out of traditional roles increase their vulnerability to rape (Bourque 1989; Russell 1975). A number of recent studies have reported, for example, that more highly educated women (Russell 1984; Sorenson et al. 1987) were at greater risk of rape or sexual assault than the less highly educated, but results were by no means uniform.

Feminist perspectives on rape have been particularly salient for the past decade. Feminist theory as applied to rape is a theory of social control as well as of social conflict and stratification (Bourque 1989, pp. 14–15). Men deny women access to economic and social power structures and apply social, economic, and in some cases physical pressures to keep them in dependent roles. Rape and fear of rape, it is argued, is employed within patriarchal societies as a violent method of keeping women in their place (Russell 1975). Gender inequality would be positively linked to the incidence of rape based on this premise. Although it is not completely clear what impact the variable of gender inequality will have on the stress-rape relationship, we would expect, on balance, a low status for women to be linked to higher levels of rape.

Pornography

The theory that pornography causes rape is based on a number of interrelated assumptions that are discussed in detail in Baron and Straus (1989, chap. 5). First, it assumes that pornography depicts physical assaults against women and thereby serves as a behavioral model. Second, it assumes that male dominance pervades pornography. These images of women as objects of violent sexual and other exploitation tend to foster and legitimate rape. Even pornography that does not explicitly depict sexual violence portrays women as sexual objects. This sexual objectification, it is believed, dehumanizes and degrades women and therefore makes it psychologically easier for men to carry out sexual violence.

Although most earlier research on this subject failed to document any link between pornography and sexually violent behavior (Davis and Braucht 1973; Goldstein et al., 1974), contemporary research on this topic suggests that a relationship may exist (Donnerstein 1984; Baron and Straus 1989). Donnerstein's research has documented that sexually explicit materials with a distinctly aggressive content may cause males to develop hostile attitudes toward women and distorted beliefs about them. After reviewing his own and others' research, Donnerstein concludes that it is the aggression in films rather than the sexual explicitness that is linked to aggression and violence against women.

STATE-TO-STATE DIFFERENCES IN STRESS AND RAPE

In an earlier study we investigated the relationship between state-to-state differences in the stressfulness of life and crime (Linsky and Straus 1986). We found that the higher the score of a state on the State Stress Index, the higher the rate of each of the seven "index crimes" was in that state, as measured by the Uniform Crime Reports. Index crimes include both violent crimes and property crimes. Violent crimes were more highly correlated on average (.63) than were property crimes (.40). The correlation of the State Stress Index with rape (.73) was the highest of the seven correlations. Moreover, a multiple regression analysis that controlled for nine other variables that are plausibly related to both stress and crime found that the relationship between the ssi and rape remained highly significant. That striking finding was replicated using a new version of the ssi for the period 1980–1984. The correlation between the stressfulness of life and forcible rape rates for each state during this period was .71.

The strength and stability of the link between stress and rape strongly suggests the need for a closer examination of this relationship. In this chapter we provide that examination in two ways. First, we specify the stress–rape model more adequately by including along with our measure of social stress (the State Stress Index) indicators of four major alternative theories that purport to explain differences in rape rates: gender inequality, sex magazine readership, social disorganization, and cultural spillover from approved violence. We also include two control variables that have often been previously linked to the rate of rape, urbanization and poverty. This design makes it possible to examine the relation of stress to rape in the context of these more widely investigated explanations of this crime.

In chapter 1 we discussed in a general way how cultural factors encourage certain types of responses to stress while disallowing others. In this chapter we investigate specifically how the stress-rape relationship is influenced by culture. We suggest that the relationship between stress and rape will be maximized within populations in which the normative system is generally favorable to the expression of violence, where the status of women is especially low relative to men, and where woman are objectified as sexual objects.

METHODS

Rates of Rape

Rates for forcible rape for each state are based on statistics from the Uniform Crime Reports (UCR) on the number of rapes known to the police. The average number of rapes for the years 1980–1982 per 100,000 population is used as the dependent variable to avoid chance fluctuations for any given year. Data from the National Crime Survey indicates that only 47% of those who were raped in the six months prior to the survey reported their rape to the police (U.S. Department of Justice 1985a). Thus, underreporting is an important limitation of the UCR data. However, careful comparisons with the National Crime Survey statistics indicates that the UCR is reasonably accurate in terms of the relative ranking of states in the rate of rape (Hindelang 1974; Gove et al. 1985). The relative ranking of states is the present concern, because our purpose is to explain differences between states rather than to ascertain the absolute incidence of rape within each state. Table 10–1 gives the rank order of states based on the average rape rate.

Gender Equality Index

The empirical measure we used to assess the degree of equality between women and men, the Gender Equality Index (GEX), was developed by Yllo and Straus (1984) and later revised by Sugarman and Straus (1989). This index measures the extent to which women have parity with men in economic, political, and legal matters. It combines seven indicators of economic status (for example, the ratio

TABLE 10-1. STATES RANKED IN ORDER OF RAPE RATE AND INDICATORS OF FOUR THEORIES

	State	Rape Rate	State	Gender Equality	State	Sex Magazine Readership[a]	State	Legitimate Violence	State	Social Control
1	ALAS	83.3	OREG	93.31	NEV	97	WYO	98.0	NEV	3.00
2	NEV	64.5	HAWA	90.42	HAWA	94	MONT	87.0	WYO	1.92
3	FLA	55.5	ALAS	89.26	DC	90	MISS	85.0	ALAS	1.64
4	CAL	55.0	MD	75.44	OREG	84	IDA	83.0	VT	1.55
5	WASH	49.6	ARIZ	75.17	WYO	83	UTAH	83.0	COLO	1.53
6	COLO	47.5	CONN	71.66	ARIZ	79	GA	78.0	HAWA	1.38
7	MICH	46.9	ME	70.06	KANS	76	NEV	77.0	WASH	1.36
8	NM	46.3	CAL	69.15	NH	65	ARK	74.0	OREG	1.21
9	TEX	46.0	IDA	68.92	CAL	62	VT	71.0	FLA	1.18
10	GA	42.1	NH	68.25	GA	59	LA	66.0	CAL	1.11
11	LA	41.9	WASH	67.89	MD	56	ALAS	64.0	MONT	1.07
12	OREG	41.0	DEL	66.34	VT	55	FLA	63.0	ARIZ	.89
13	ARIZ	40.6	COLO	66.09	WASH	55	ALA	62.0	IDA	.60
14	MD	38.7	MINN	62.71	FLA	54	OKLA	62.0	DEL	.50
15	SC	37.5	MASS	62.06	IDA	54	TEX	61.0	NH	.49
16	TENN	36.8	KANS	60.86	ILL	54	ARIZ	60.0	ME	.39
17	OKLA	36.2	MONT	60.70	COLO	53	SC	60.0	NM	.23
18	HAWA	34.6	MICH	60.10	MICH	53	SD	59.0	MICH	.13
19	VT	32.3	FLA	56.99	TEX	53	ND	57.0	VA	.04
20	OHIO	31.7	KY	55.43	OKLA	53	OREG	56.0	MD	−.06
21	NJ	30.5	NEV	54.50	DEL	52	COLO	54.0	TEX	−.17
22	NY	30.4	IOWA	53.77	NM	52	NM	54.0	KANS	−.18
23	WYO	30.3	NY	52.13	VA	51	DEL	54.0	OKLA	−.22
24	INDI	30.1	WYO	51.66	OHIO	49	KANS	52.0	GA	−.25
25	MO	29.4	OHIO	49.75	NEBR	48	VA	47.0	INDI	−.34
26	KANS	29.0	WIS	48.93	NJ	48	NC	47.0	ARK	−.35
27	DEL	27.8	NEBR	48.51	MONT	47	WASH	45.0	SD	−.36
28	ALA	27.3	MO	48.25	ND	42	HAWA	45.0	NY	−.36
29	MASS	26.6	RI	45.51	MINN	42	TENN	44.0	MO	−.40
30	UTAH	26.6	NJ	43.32	INDI	41	NEBR	42.0	ND	−.43
31	VA	26.5	INDI	40.73	MASS	41	OHIO	41.0	MINN	−.43
32	ARK	26.3	WVA	40.55	SD	40	IOWA	41.0	SC	−.46
33	MISS	25.7	NC	39.91	NY	40	WVA	38.0	LA	−.54
34	ILL	24.0	SD	39.77	IOWA	39	KY	36.0	ILL	−.54
35	MINN	23.9	ILL	39.65	ME	38	PA	35.0	NEBR	−.54
36	NC	22.4	PA	39.48	LA	38	ILL	34.0	OHIO	−.56
37	PA	22.0	OKLA	38.16	WIS	37	ME	34.0	IOWA	−.57
38	CONN	21.8	VA	37.67	NC	36	CAL	33.0	NC	−.61
39	NEBR	21.4	VT	35.09	ALA	35	MINN	32.0	WIS	−.72
40	KY	20.0	ND	34.76	SC	34	INDI	31.0	WVA	−.74
41	IDA	19.8	NM	34.13	TENN	34	MO	30.0	TENN	−.78
42	MONT	19.3	GA	33.84	PA	34	NH	30.0	MISS	−.88
43	RI	18.1	UTAH	31.58	KY	33	MICH	29.0	KY	−1.01
44	NH	16.6	TEX	26.87	CONN	33	CONN	29.0	UTAH	−1.05
45	WVA	15.3	SC	26.80	WVA	29	NY	27.0	ALA	−1.05
46	WIS	14.9	TENN	23.65	RI	28	WIS	27.0	NJ	−1.08
47	IOWA	13.4	ARK	20.48	ARK	24	MD	26.0	MASS	−1.20
48	ME	13.0	LA	12.05	MO	20	NJ	22.0	CONN	−1.25
49	SD	11.8	ALA	11.33	MISS	19	MASS	19.0	PA	−1.42
50	ND	9.3	MISS	6.33	UTAH	19	RI	18.0	RI	−1.69

[a]Figures for sex magazine readership are expressed in ZP scores. See chap. 2, note 3.

of the median income of women to the median income of men), four indicators of political status (the percentage of women who are in the state legislature), and thirteen indicators of the legal status of women (laws that give married women the same property rights as married men). The alpha level of reliability of the Gender Equality Index is .60.

A perfect score on the GEX of 100 indicates full parity between men and women with respect to all the items making up the index. As table 10–1 shows, scores on the GEX range from a low of 6.3 in Mississippi to a high of 93.3 in Oregon. Even in Oregon, however, where women come closest to obtaining equality with men, women are still disadvantaged by 40%.

Index of Sex Magazine Readership

There is virtually no agreement on either the conceptual or operational definitions of *pornography* (Baron and Straus 1989). This situation leads some social scientists to follow the example of the Commission on Obscenity and Pornography (1970), which did not use the term pornography at all. Other authors substitute the term *erotica* for pornography. We think it is best to identify the measure we use as simply the Sex Magazine Readership Index (SMCX2).

The data for this measure are the number of copies of eight sexually explicit magazines (*Chic, Club, Gallery, Genesis, Hustler, Oui, Penthouse,* and *Playboy*). The data are for 1979 and include both subscriptions and sales of individual-copies. Baron and Straus (1987, 1989) obtained the data from the Audit Bureau of Circulation, which is an independent, nonprofit organization that audits and certifies magazine sales figures. These eight publications are by far the most widely read sexually oriented magazines in the United States. Several of them sell millions of copies every month. They reach a much wider audience than other sex literature and are therefore important for theoretical issues. Table 10–1 shows large differences between the states in the combined circulation rate of these magazines. (Figures for sex magazine readership in table 10–1 are in ZP scores; see note 2 in chap. 2.)

Legitimate Violence Index

The Legitimate Violence Index is again employed in this chapter. As discussed in chapter 7, Straus (1985) created this index for each of the fifty states. It has the advantage of measuring culturally legitimate aspects of violence rather than either such structural conditions as poverty (which might cause violence) or criminally violent behavior itself.

Social Control Index

As our indicator of social disorganization, we employ a revised version of an index developed by Baron and Straus (1987, 1989) for use in their study of rape in the United States. The Social Control Index is based on the presence or absence of religious affiliation; nonfamilied males; households headed by a single female; and the ratio of tourists to nontourists. Details and discussion of the measure are contained in chapter 8.

Control Variables

We included the percentage of the population living in metropolitan areas and the percentage of families with incomes below the poverty line in our analyses to control for possible confounding of these variables with the independent and dependent variables of theoretical interest.

FINDINGS

Bivariate Analysis

Table 10–2 presents the correlations between the exogenous variables with each other and with the incidence of rape. Column 1 shows that the State Stress Index is the most highly correlated with the incidence of rape of any of the explanatory variables (.71**). The variables of social disorganization and sex magazine readership are also correlated significantly with the incidence of rape, although not as strongly as in the case of the State Stress Index (.53** and .54**, respectively). The relationships of the Legitimate Violence Index and Gender Equality Index with rape, although in the predicted direction, are not significant.

The bivariate analyses just presented strongly support the stress theory of rape and also explanations based on pornography and social disorganization. On the other hand, neither legitimate violence nor gender equality, the other two explanatory theories, are supported at the bivariate level. However, the zero-order correlations in table 10–2 are not adequate tests of these theories. Both the presence and the absence of certain relationships might be due to the possible confounding among the variables. For example, the lack of relationship between rape and gender equality may be masked by failure to specify other variables related both to gender equality and to rape. Consequently, a multivariate analysis was undertaken to examine the net effect of stress and the other

**TABLE 10-2.   CORRELATION MATRIX OF THE RAPE RATE AND ALL
INDEPENDENT VARIABLES, FOR FIFTY STATES**

	1	2	3	4	5	6	7	8
1. Rape								
2. Stress Index	.71**							
3. Social Disorg.	.53**	.35*						
4. Legit. Violence	.16	.22	.43**					
5. Sex Magazines	.54**	.32*	.77**	.22				
6. Gender Equality	.20	−.02	.49**	−.26	.61**			
7. % Poor	.01	.25	−.29	.33*	.41*	−.65**		
8. % Urban	.24	−.41*	.08	−.29	.28	.30	−.41*	

Note: $*p < .01, **p < .001$ (one-tailed significance).

explanatory variables on the rate of rape after controlling for other variables
in the model.

The Cultural-Context Hypothesis

The multivariate analysis also permitted a more direct test of the theory that the
broad cultural context affects the relationship between stress and rape. We suggest that the relationship between stress and rape is maximized under the following cultural conditions:

1. The normative system is generally favorable to the expression of violence
    so that frustrations growing out of stressful conditions tend to be
    channeled into aggressive behavior.
2. The status of women is low, thus making women more-likely victims of
    that violence.
3. Sex magazine readership is high, which emphasizes women as sexual
    objects and thereby targets them for sexual aggression.

The statistical relationships implied above were tested by multiple regression analyses that included interaction terms to represent the relation between
stress and rape under the conditions of high and low values of each of the three
hypothesized contextual variables.

We did not include all the interaction terms in one regression equation,
because that would have meant a total of ten independent variables. Ten variables, together with the fact that each of the interaction term variables are highly
correlated with the variable measuring stress, posed a potential multicollinearity
problem. We minimized that problem by computing three regression analyses,
each of which included only one of the three interaction terms.

TABLE 10-3.   REGRESSION ANALYSIS OF RAPE ON STRESS, SOCIAL DISORGANIZATION, LEGITIMATE VIOLENCE, SEX MAGAZINE READERSHIP, AND CONTROL VARIABLES, FOR FIFTY STATES

Independent Variables	b	se	t	p <
State Stress Index				
When sex magazine readership is high	.31	.075	2.38	.021
When sex magazine readership is low	.17	*		
Legitimate Violence	−.08	.068	−1.26	.213
Social Disorganization	4.19	1.75	2.39	.021
% Poor	1.33	.547	2.43	.018
% Metro	.25	.092	2.75	.008

Note: *t = 2.48 (p < .01) for the significance of the difference between the stress-rape relationship when sex magazine readership is low (as given by the regression coefficient in the previous row) versus the stress-rape relationship when sex magazine readership is high (this row). The value for the high sex magazine readership row was obtained by computing a regression coefficient for the interaction of stress with sex magazine readership (b2 in the following equation):

$$Y = a + (b1)(x1) + (b2)(x2) + (b3)(x3) + (b4)(x4) + (b5)(x5) + (b6)(x6),$$

where x1 = State Stress Index, x2 = (x1)(d) and d = sex magazine readership converted to a dummy variable by coding states above the median as 1, and states below the median as 0, x3 = Legitimate Violence Index, x4 = Social Disorganization Index, x5 = % of families below the poverty line, x6 = % of the state population that is metropolitan. The value of b2 in this equation is .14. Thus, when sex magazine readership was high, the effect of stress on rape was increased by .14.

No significant interaction was found among stress, rape, and gender inequality. Thus, the stress–rape relationship was unaffected by the overall status of women. Similarly, there was not a significant interaction between stress and the LVX in regard to rape. Stress, it appears, is no more likely to result in rape in populations with a general acceptance of violence than in populations less accepting of violence. However, the regression analysis that tested for the interaction of stress and sex magazine readership was statistically significant and is shown in table 10–3. The regression model has an adjusted R-square of .74.

The coefficients in table 10–3 for the State Stress Index show that when sex magazine readership is high, there is a stronger relationship between stress and rape than when sex magazine readership is low. Specifically, when sex magazine readership is high, each increase of one point in the SSI is associated with an average increase of .31 rapes per 100,000 population, but in states where the sex-magazine readership index is low, the effect of stress on rape is only about half as great: each change of one point on the SSI is associated with an average increase of .14 rapes per 100,000 population.

In addition to the interaction of stress and sex magazine readership, four of the exogenous variables—stress, social disorganization, poverty, and urbanization—are also significantly related to the incidence of rape. Consistent with the zero-order correlations, neither gender equality nor legitimate violence was found to be significantly associated with the rate of rape.

SUMMARY AND CONCLUSIONS

This research tested the hypothesis that in the United States, the greater the number of stressor events that occur in a state, the higher the rate of rape; and that the relationship between stress and rape is greatest in states in which the status of women is low; violence is approved for socially legitimate purposes; a high level of social disorganization exists; and the readership of sexually explicit magazines is large.

The multiple regression analysis supported the hypothesis predicting a relationship between stress and rape. It also found that social disorganization, urbanization, poverty, and the interaction of stress and sex magazine readership are associated with rape. Of the three interaction-effect hypotheses tested, two were not supported: the hypothesized tendencies for rape to be most frequent when there is cultural support for the use of violence for socially approved ends and when the status of women is low.

We can only speculate as to why we did not find a significant interaction between stress and either cultural support for violence or gender equality. One possibility is that legitimate-violence norms may encourage many alternative forms of violent behavior besides forcible rape. Perhaps such general normative approval of violence is not culturally specific enough to direct aggressive behavior toward the sexual assault of women. That reasoning does not seem to apply, however, to the interaction of stress with gender inequality, which was also not statistically significant. Although gender equality is more specific than legitimate violence in identifying a class of victims as potential targets for violent aggression, it provides no direction as to the form that aggression might take. In addition, as mentioned in the introductory section, high or increasing status, as well as low status, may help create a special vulnerability for women, because they may be perceived by some men as a threat to their own status and their economic security. Because either high and low status may theoretically increase women's vulnerability to rape (for different reasons), the impact of these two variable effects may cancel each other out and accordingly blunt the interaction between stress and rape.

As for sex magazine readership, perhaps the significant main effect and interaction occur because sex magazines provide a specific context for sexual assault on women. Whatever the underlying process, a context of cultural beliefs reflected by sex magazine readership appears to channel the outcome of high levels of stressful events in the direction of sexual assault.

PART 4

Summary and Conclusions

CHAPTER 11

The Stress Process, Aggression, and Social Policy

It is surprising that the relationship between stress and aggression—the central concerns of this book—is neglected in the literature on those two subjects, especially when one considers the strong theoretical basis for assuming such a relationship. In chapter 1 we reviewed some of those theories, including physiological explanations, the frustration-aggression hypothesis, and Merton's theory of Anomie. All these theories are consistent with the stress-aggression theory. In response to outside threats, for example, physiological survival mechanisms may be mobilized to prepare the individual for flight or fight (Selye 1980) or, relevant to the current research, for aggressive action. The frustration-aggression hypothesis also suggests that when external events, particularly aversive events, block goal-related behavior, they lead to negative side effects, such as anger. This anger may in turn be directed toward others in the form of aggression (Berkowitz 1989, 1993).

SOCIAL STRESS AND AGGRESSION

The distinctive feature of the research in this book is that it focuses on the stressfulness of the social environment. In this sense, we follow in the tradition of Merton's theory of Anomie. Merton maintained that a major source of strain arises in American society because commonly held aspirations or goals, especially in the economic arena, cannot be realized for many owing to blocked opportunities. This blockage leads to predictable strains and frustrations, some of which eventuate in deviant behavior. Merton's theory placed the stress of blockage and frustration in a broader social context. The stressful life-events theory that guided this book also places the locus of stress in the social environment. The difference between our research and most research using the life-events approach is that we measured stress and other aspects of the stress process at the societal rather than the individual level.

Chapter 1 reviewed several empirical studies that linked the stressfulness of social environments with violence and aggression. Our own earlier research (Linsky and Straus 1986) on the fifty states found that the more stressful the social environment of a state, the higher the rate of several types of violent crime. This book extends and refines that macro-sociological approach in a number of ways.

Stressful Societies

The refinement and extension of research on the effects of a stressful social milieu were made possible by the development of techniques to measure *at the societal level* variables that are usually measured at the individual level. Foremost among these is the State Stress Index. The ssi measures differences in the rate at which stressful life events occur in the fifty states.

The ssi was calculated for our original study (Linsky and Straus 1986) and again five years later. (Straus, Linsky, and Bachman-Prehn 1988). After comparing the earlier and later versions of the index, we found considerable stability in the geographic patterning of social stress in the United States. States that were higher in stress originally continued to be high and vice versa. We also found that there was an average increase in the total ssi over this five-year period (around 17%). The increase was not completely surprising, because the second version of the ssi was calculated for 1982, which coincided with the peak year for a widespread economic recession in most states. Again, not surprisingly, the largest contribution to this increase came from the economic components of the index, such as workers who lost their jobs and the increasing number of business failures, personal bankruptcies, and mortgage foreclosures.

In addition to the State Stress Index, measures of several other societal level variables were developed for each of the states, including the level of subjectively experienced stress, cultural norms concerning drinking, cultural norms concerning violence, and the closeness of social control.

The Findings

The hypothesis that stress is linked to a wide range of aggression and violence was overwhelmingly supported. We included in the research a wide range of aggressive behavior and grouped each type of aggression according to whether it was directed against the self, in the form of suicide and abuse of alcohol and tobacco, or against others, in the form of homicide, violence when drunk, and rape. In all cases the analyses included controls for other important variables that have also been shown to be related to aggression, such as economic deprivation.

Smoking and Alcohol Abuse. In the analyses investigating the relationship between the State Stress Index and smoking and alcohol abuse, we controlled for between five and nine other variables. We also examined alternative measures of social stress (for example, measures of chronic stress) and different methods of controlling age, through both regression and age-standardization of mortality. In addition, we used alternative indicators of drinking and smoking based on different sources (taxes on alcohol and tobacco consumption, mortality rates from alcohol and smoking-related diseases and self-reports from national surveys). These alternative procedures provide a validity check on our original measures and increase the confidence we have in our findings. No matter how we measured social stress and substance abuse, and no matter which analytic measures we used, the results continued to support the stress-aggression hypothesis. The relationship between the stressfulness of a society and the two self-destructive types of behavior—smoking and alcohol abuse—must therefore be very robust and does not appear to be spurious.

Suicide. The stressfulness of the social environment was also found to be linked consistently to suicide, which is perhaps the ultimate form of inwardly directed aggression. As stress within certain social environments increased, so did rates of suicide for both men and women.

Homicide. Particular attention was paid to the link between social stress and homicide (chaps. 6, 8, and 9), because homicide, like suicide, represents one of the most extreme forms of aggression directed outward. The model we tested took into account three other leading comparative theories of homicide: economic deprivation, a subculture of violence, and control theory, as well as several other control variables. Stress and homicide were strongly and significantly linked, even after subtracting out the overlap of social stress with other variables that have been used to explain homicide rates.

When the analyses were replicated for specific types of homicide, they showed that stress was an explanatory factor principally for homicides in which offender and victim had a preexisting relationship (family and acquaintance homicide) but not for homicides among strangers. Economic deprivation and social control were both better able to explain stranger homicide. As pointed out in chapter 8, socially generated stress appears to have its major impact by propelling already established or intimate interactions in the direction of aggression and, in some cases, death.

We also attempted to answer the question of whether the strong overall relationship between stress and homicide applied to all methods of killing or only to some. We thought this information might reveal important clues regarding the dynamics of the stress process in relationship to homicide. Homicide by guns, for example, may require only momentary arousal to commit the homicidal act. Use of some other weapons such as blunt or sharp instruments may require a more sustained arousal to complete the homicide. We found that stress was significantly related to homicide regardless of the method used to kill the victim.

These findings are especially remarkable because of the consistency of the findings relative to the other explanatory theories we investigated: economic deprivation, a subculture of violence, and control theory. Social stress was the only theoretical indicator that was found to be significantly related to *all* methods of killing. Thus, similar to the relationship of stress to self-destructive behavior, the stress-homicide relationship is also particularly robust.

Rape. Rape was the final form of violent aggression directed toward others that we considered. Although most of the chapter on rape was concerned with how cultural and social structural factors encourage the channeling of aggression toward rape, the strongest relationship found was between social stress and the prevalence of rape. No other variable—neither an index of social disorganization, an index of legitimate violence, a pornography index, a broad measure of gender inequality, or a measure of economic deprivation and urbanness— showed nearly as strong a relationship with the rate of rape. The State Stress Index was significantly related to the rate of rape net of all the variables listed above.

Except for lethal violence directed toward strangers, then, the stressfulness of a given locale was significantly associated with every form of aggression we examined, namely, the abuse of alcohol and tobacco, suicide, the combination of alcohol with family violence, family and acquaintance homicide, and rape. Relationships tended to be strong and consistent, and they persisted with internal replications by gender. Moreover, the stress-aggression relationships remained, even when we statistically controlled for many other relevant variables, including indicators of alternative theories violence. Social stress explained state-to-state differences in homicide beyond what was explained by any other theory. This suggests that stress is not simply a restatement of other theories. Nor do we believe the results are simply an artifact of the way the variables are measured.

Many of the analyses employ multiple indicators of the dependent variables based on different data sources, including national survey data, state tax data, criminal-justice statistics, and vital statistics. Again, we obtained essentially parallel results. The conclusion that stress is implicated in aggressive behavior seems inescapable by this sheer preponderance of evidence.

THE STRESS PROCESS

Having established that the link between social stress and aggression is extremely strong, we next turned our attention to the processes that might account for that link. The question regarding the stress process primarily asks, How do stressor events or conditions combine with other variables to lead to stress outcomes? Sociologically oriented conceptualizations of this process have focused on the social supports and other social resources that potentially lessen the effects of stressors, whereas psychologically oriented conceptualizations tend to emphasize personality, cognitions, emotions, and coping skills as intervening variables between stressor events and outcomes (Ensel and Lin 1991).

Two of the most influential models of the stress process in the literature are the ones developed by Pearlin and his associates (Pearlin et al. 1981: Pearlin and Aneshensel 1986) and by Lazarus and his associates (Lazarus 1966; Lazarus and Folkman 1984). Pearlin et al. (1981) describe a process beginning with either stressful events or chronic life strains, such as role conflicts, that have an impact on self-concepts, including self-esteem and mastery. The effect of these variables on psychological depression is, in turn, mediated by coping skills and social resources.

Lazarus (1966, 1984) emphasizes a cognitive approach to the understanding of stress, whereby one's perception of a potentially stressful event, combined with knowledge of one's own coping resources, determines the amount of stress experienced. The main features of this model are two appraisal stages—one to appraise the potential threat associated with the event and a second to appraise coping strategies. Both of these factors intervene between the external event and the resulting stress reaction. Some elements of the stress process as modeled by Pearlin and Lazarus are included in our analysis, particularly aspects of coping and appraisal.

In our earlier research, we included as mediators between the ssi and outcome some macro-social equivalents of what coping and social support are to individuals. That is, we looked at institutional arrangements that supported adaptation to stressful conditions, including generosity of public assistance, average community educational levels, availability of psychologically trained counselors, and indicators of stable social relationships.

In this study, some models included an additional appraisal variable, a measure of perceived stress. This variable was derived by aggregating individual survey data from a national survey to the state level. Perceived stress was seen as intervening between the external environmental events and the eventual reaction to those events. Specifically, it was an indicator of the degree to which the external objective events that comprise the ssi are seen as harmful or threatening by residents at a conscious, cognitive level.

Culture and the Channeling of Aggression

Interestingly, no previous model of the stress process, including the Pearlin and Lazarus models, emphasizes the cultural context within which the stress operates. It is our view that cultural context is a central element in the process of channeling the effects of stress toward particular forms of aggression and violence. Some chapters therefore examined the relationship between the ssi and various stress outcomes within different cultural and subcultural settings. The context variables included state and regional differences in

- Cultural norms concerning drinking
- The use of violence for socially legitimate purposes
- The social and economic status of women
- Readership of pornography.

The hypothesis in each case was that the cultural or social context helps to determine or guide the expression of stress. In the case of alcohol, the cultural-context hypothesis was well supported (chap. 4). Although stress appeared to promote alcohol abuse everywhere, the link between stress and alcohol was especially significant within subgroups of states where the culture was the most favorable toward the use of alcohol.

We employed a measure called the Legitimate Violence Index (Baron and Straus 1989) to investigate the extent to which cultural approval of violence exacerbates the relation between social stress and violence. The LVX measures a state or region's acceptance of the use of violence, usually as a state-supported measure to achieve socially desirable goals. The index is based on indicators of such socially legitimate types of violence as capital punishment of criminals and corporal punishment of children in schools. We used the LVX in chapter 7, for example, to explore the supposition that a culture that tolerates the use of violence in some situations also increases the extent to which people become violent under the influence of alcohol. Specifically, we tested the hypothesis that stress is more likely to eventuate in violence-prone drinking if it occurs within cultural areas where normative systems that both favor drinking and support violence coincide. This hypothesis contrasts with a more medical interpretation of the relationship between alcohol and violence, namely, that alcohol serves as a disinhibitor, especially when consumed under stress (MacAndrew and Edgerton 1969). Under this theory, chemical assault on the higher brain centers causes drinkers to lose their internal controls and thereby increases the level of hostility and aggressiveness toward others, as well as other forms of deviant behavior normally kept under control.

One implication of the disinhibition theory is that because such chemical consequences are assumed to be constant, alcohol consumption should be linked to violence wherever it occurs, regardless of the normative context. On the other hand, according to the cultural-context theory, correlations should be highest where permissive alcohol norms coincide with violent subcultures, lowest where prescriptive norms correspond with nonviolent subcultures, and intermediate for states that are high on only one of the two cultural dimensions.

Our tests of the cultural-context theory of violent drinking produced mixed results. First, cultural context made little difference in the relationship between stress associated with drinking and nonfamily violence. Only one of the four tests supported the hypothesis. The relationships changed markedly, however, when the dependent variable changed to drinking accompanied by violence within the family. Within the cultural context of permissive drinking norms and approval of violence, perceived stress was significantly linked to violence-prone drinking for all four tests of the hypothesis using family violence as the outcome variable. Moreover, we computed the correlations between stress and the various combinations of drinking and violence in four cultural contexts (permissive alcohol norms and violent subcultures; permissive alcohol norms and nonviolent subcultures; prescriptive alcohol norms and violent subcultures; prescriptive alcohol norms and nonviolent subcultures) and found that the rank order of fifteen of the sixteen tests were in the predicted order of magnitude. That is, the correlations between social stress and violence were higher under cultural conditions favorable to violence.

The effect of the cultural context on the link between stress and the violence of a society was also examined using the prevalence of rape as the measure of violence. The contextual variables included the Legitimate Violence Index and a

Gender Equality Index to measure the status of women relative to men. The Gender Equality Index was included because the low status of women could affect the vulnerability that women have to victimization. A Sex Magazine Readership Index measuring the readership of pornography was also included as part of the cultural context when considering the relation of stress to rape. Pornography purportedly objectifies women as sexual objects and thereby may increase their vulnerability to sexual assaults (see the review of literature in Baron and Straus 1989).

The findings in our analyses of rape support the cultural-context hypothesis, but only in part. We tested the cultural-context theory by examining the interaction of each context variable with social stress. Neither the Legitimate Violence Index nor the Gender Equality Index significantly interacted with social stress to account for the relationship between stress and rape. However, one of the cultural context variables, the Sex Magazine Readership Index, did significantly interact with social stress. This interaction showed that the link between stressfulness within a population and rape is stronger with high levels pornography readership than with relatively low levels.

Summary of the Relationships among Stress, Culture, and Aggression

In general, some support was found for the cultural-context theory, but it was not consistent across the various measures of aggression by which the theory was tested. Cultural approval of drinking clearly played an important role in the case of alcohol consumption and abuse. The correlation of the State Stress Index with these items was highest within those states that most strongly encouraged or permitted residents to use alcohol.

Drinking accompanied by violence was most frequent, as predicted, in states with high scores on the Legitimate Violence Index and with permissive drinking norms, but only in the case of family violence. The hypothesis was not supported for violence occurring outside the family.

Using the prevalence of rape as the measure of societal violence, the link between social stress and rape was influenced by some cultural conditions but not others. The sexual objectification of women as indicated by sales of pornographic magazines significantly increased the likelihood that stress would eventuate in higher rates of rape. In this case, the cultural context does appear to influence the expression of stress. However, neither the variable of women's status nor that of subcultures of violence appeared to affect the link between social stress and rape. Evidence for the cultural-context hypothesis must, therefore, be considered mixed.

Subjective Mediation

On a subjective level, some individuals may not experience what are presumably traumatic events as stressful and therefore may not experience adverse effect. For instance, some may experience moving from one state to another as stressful, whereas others may see it as an escape from the stress of living in the place they left. Consequently, models of the stress processes typically include not only the occurrence of stressful events but also the subjective experience of being under stress. We therefore included in the research two measures of subjective stress: the score on an index that measures the perception of being under stress and the percentage of people in each state who had thought about suicide.

In addition to illuminating the stress process, these subjective measures provide a kind of construct-validity test of the SSI by allowing a comparison between the SSI (the measure of objective stressful events) and the subjective stress felt by residents of those states. It was encouraging that the SSI was significantly correlated with the subjective stress measures, especially since the two measures were based on completely different sources (official statistics for the SSI and aggregated survey findings for the Perceived Stress Index). The correlation, in fact, was as high as would be expected theoretically ($r = .41$), because stressful events and subjectively perceived stress represent different domains (Landau 1988). Stressful life events are indeed one cause of feeling under stress, but many other factors could potentially influence the degree to which a set of objective events are subjectively perceived or experienced as stressful.

With regard to suicide, it appears that stressful events within a social system (as measured by the SSI) are related to suicide rates indirectly through a path leading from objective stress to perceived stress to suicidal thoughts and finally to the act of suicide. However, the path from objective external stressors through these cognitive processes to suicide, although significant, was not as strong as the direct path between stressful events and the suicide rate. Thus, the cognitive path accounts for only part of the story. This pattern of findings suggests that Durkheim was perhaps correct in the broad sense that the suicide rate as a characteristic of a social system is best explained by other characteristics of a social system, that is, by characteristics that are external to individuals.

The Family

The family has special relevance for the stress process, because a high proportion of assaultive behavior takes place within the family (Gelles and Straus 1988; Straus and Gelles 1990). Two interesting findings emerged in this study related to the family. The central finding of chapter 8, which looked at stress and victim-specific homicide, is that the State Stress Index was significantly correlated only with those homicides in which the victim and perpetrator had some type of preexisting relationship, namely, with family and acquaintance homicide. In contrast, stranger homicide, although correlated with other independent variables often used to explain comparative homicide rates, was not significantly associated with stress.

Chapter 7 reported some interesting results that are consistent with those for lethal violence discussed above but are based on self-report survey data rather than on official crime rates. We used survey data for each state to obtain state-by-state rates for two types of assault: self-reported assaults inside the family by persons under the influence of alcohol; and assaults against nonfamily persons. These analyses found that although social stress is related to physical violence inside the family, it is a poor predictor of violence outside the family.

The implication of these combined findings is that stress has a major impact on family relationships. As we suggested in chapter 8, families may be stress-collection points not only for stressful events created within the family but also for stresses that clearly originate outside the family, such as economic disruptions in the community, natural and man-made disasters, and community instability.

The findings on alcohol-related violence using aggregated individual-level data on drinking and nonlethal assaults parallel the findings using official statistics on homicide. Thus, in the case of both the self-report survey of individuals and the study based on state-level crime statistics, it appears that social stress is associated with the rate of aggression by impelling already-intimate and affect-laden relationships in the direction of violence.

These findings on aggression within the family may at first seem to contrast sharply with the view of families as buffers or safe havens from the stressors of the outside world. The haven view of the family stems from the presumption that families are relatively tranquil compared to nonfamily groups and that family members are valued for themselves rather than for their performances of specific tasks. Thus, families are able to provide support, intimacy, emotional release, and esteem on a day-to-day basis. This view of the family is quite consistent with the "buffer theory" of social support in the social-stress literature. It has been observed in many studies that individuals who have strong social support are less likely to be affected by stress than more isolated individuals (Gore 1978, 1991; Lin et al. 1979; Turner 1981). Although serious questions have arisen over the causal priority between stressor events and support, support remains an important component of many studies of stress (Turner 1983;

Wheaton 1985; Aneshensel 1992). The protective function of the family has been a main assumption in sociology at least since Durkheim's classic study of suicide ([1897] 1951).

There has also been another stream of theory and research, however, about the nature of interpersonal relations within family. The family has been recognized by some psychologists as a potentially hostile and conflicted social unit, thereby making it a source of pathology, not tranquility (Day, Mishler, and Waxler 1965). The family has also been identified by some sociologists as one of the most conflict-prone, stressful, and violent institutions of our society (Collins and Coltrane 1991; Straus and Hotaling 1980; Gelles and Straus 1979).

These disparate views—of the family as haven and the family as hell—are not incompatible. Indeed, Straus and Hotaling (1980) and Gelles and Straus (1979) argue that the intimate primary-group nature of the family is part of the reason why there is so much conflict within families. For one thing, the primary-group nature of the family means that members are concerned with everything about other members, which creates limitless areas of potential conflict. As for its being a haven, members are able bring home their troubles and sometimes vent their anger on other members of the family in ways they would never do with individuals outside the family. Thus, the family serves as a stress-collection point for stressors emanating from the community. Evidence from the current study is consistent with the stress-enhancing and stress-collection aspects of the family.

Gender

Gender potentially affects almost every aspect of the stress process, including the relative risk of experiencing stressful events, cultural definitions of appropriate behavior, family involvement in stress, perceptions and reactions to stressful events, styles of coping with stress, and the types of behavior that result from experiencing an overload of stressful events (Barnett et al. 1987; Thoits 1991; Gore and Colten 1991; Conger et al. 1993; Avison and McAlpine 1992; Lennon and Rosenfield 1992). We took gender into account in most analyses by examining gender-specific rates of aggression. This section focuses directly on gender and stress by reviewing gender differences from this study and from our earlier research (Linsky and Straus 1986), which used several illnesses and maladaptive outcomes of stress not included in the current volume.

In five of the gender comparisons, stress was more strongly related to the outcome for women than for men (mortality from peptic ulcers, asthma attacks, all accidents, motor vehicle accidents, and the combined rate of mortality from alcoholism and alcoholic psychosis). On the other hand, the outcomes were approximately the same for both genders for mortality from cirrhosis of the liver and malignant neoplasms of the lungs and respiratory system (indicators of alcohol and tobacco abuse, respectively) and from both suicide and homicide. In only one case, that of alcohol-related violence, was the link with stress stronger for men than for women.

One possible explanation here is that many of the particular events selected for the SSI may relate more directly to women's roles in our society (for example, infant deaths, fetal deaths, abortions, and illegitimate births) than to men's. Others that may appear gender-neutral, such as moving to a new community and personal bankruptcy, may also be more stressful for women because of the strains these stressors place on entire families and because of women's special responsibility for the well-being of the family (Aneshensel, Pearlin, and Schuler 1993). This is sometimes referred to as the "cost of caring" (Kessler and Mac-Leod 1984).

Other explanations have been advanced as well. Markle and Troyer (1979), for example, attribute a slower decline in smoking for women than for men to the stress women experience in connection with the recent changes toward their fuller participation in the labor market. Presumably it is the strain of adopting a new role that creates high levels of stress. In the case of some women, add to this the special strains associated with managing job and home responsibilities (Barnett et al. 1987). It may be that such explanations could be applied to other stress outcomes as well, including those investigated in this book.

Another question arises here. Does stress only appear to have stronger negative consequences for women than for men because of the particular dependent variables we selected for the study? This does not seem to be the case, because the actual incidence of many of the stress-outcome variables, such as alcohol abuse, homicide, and suicide, is substantially higher among men. For example, there is a well-established fact that men commit suicide at a much higher rate than do women (Gerard 1993). Despite this difference in incidence, however, we found that social stress is as highly associated with suicide for women as it is for men.

These observations suggest another possible explanation, based on the normative structure surrounding male and female deviance. Because heavy drinking, violent drunkenness, or the extreme violence involved in suicide and homicide are more consistent with role expectations for males than for females, the circumstances during which men engage in these deviant acts may be less extraordinary than they would be for women. Women may engage in these non-normative forms of deviance less often and perhaps only under more desperate circumstances, such as being under extreme duress. This could account for the paradoxical contradiction between the higher incidence of such deviance for men, but the stronger link to stress for women. More research is clearly needed to clarify these issues.

CHRONIC STRESS

The State Stress Index employed in this study is based on the stressful life-events approach, which emphasizes the impact of an accumulation of important changes in people's lives, especially unwanted changes, that require major adjustments and adaptations. The SSI, however, is only one approach to social stress. A second emphasizes chronically stressful life conditions and situations (Pearlin et al. 1981). The emphasis here is on ongoing or chronic strains or conditions that exact a toll over time, not because of new adjustments required but because of the persistence of noxious or difficult factors in an individual's environment.

Sociological research in the chronic-stress tradition has focused on role strains of various kinds, including role conflicts, role overloads, and role underloads (Thoits 1983b). Role strains may be experienced as especially stressful, because a person's identity is so closely tied to the central roles that she or he plays, for example, gender roles, marital roles, worker roles, and so on (Burke 1991). Thus interruptions, or the threat of interruption, in such roles or the negative evaluation of role performances by oneself or others endangers the essential self. Other sources of chronic stress summarized in a recent review by Aneshensel (1992) include barriers to the achievement of life goals, inadequate rewards relative to investments, excessive or insufficient demands from the social environment, social and economic hardship, and inconsistencies between one's various roles.

The chronic-stress approach suggests that it is often the very chronicity of conditions that make them so stressful. For example, the informal role of care giver for frail or incompetent relatives may be more stressful primarily because of the continuing nature of the demand without prospects for relief.

A Chronic Stress Index

While the State Stress Index is based on the incidence of stressful events, it seems quite feasible to develop a similar societal-level index based on ongoing or chronic stressors. For instance, instead of using the rate of new unemployment cases (as used in the SSI), the average length of unemployment could be used.

Indicators of inadequate and overcrowded housing, as well as indicators of poverty, are available for geographic units, but other chronic stress indicators, such as homelessness, may pose a more daunting problem.

A high rate of crime may be both an effect of life in a high stress area (as shown in this book) and a source of chronic stress. We did not include crime as a stressor event in the State Stress Index, because the focus of this research was on testing the theory that social stress results in aggression, including criminal violence. Crime, however, acts as a stressor in the acute sense of someone's becoming a direct victim of crime and also in the more chronic form of fear of crime. From this perspective, crime rates would be an appropriate indicator to include in a chronic stress index at the societal level. Quality of life, for example, may be affected by crime in one's neighborhood, by the increased levels of fear and anxiety that result, or by forced changes in life-style (as when elderly persons no longer feel they can go out in their neighborhoods or parents no longer feel they can allow their children to play outside). Likewise, the fear of rape may restrict the range of activities that women are able to enjoy, and the combination of fear of rape and burdensome restrictions may be experienced as a chronic stress.

Status Integration

The level of chronic stress of geographic units in the United States has, in fact, been investigated using "status integration" as the indicator of chronic stress (Gibbs and Martin 1964; Dodge and Martin 1970). The Index of Status Integration is a complex measure of the degree of consistency between several statuses that individuals occupy at the same time (including such items as marriage, occupation, age–group, gender, and race). Rare combinations of the above, such as young widows or unemployed husbands (as compared to unemployed single men), are presumably stressful because individuals occupying such "poorly integrated" status combinations are impeded from forming stable relationships with others. This measure of stress has been found to be highly related to suicide, mental pathology, alcoholism, and death rates from a number of chronic diseases.

Relative Opportunity

Another macro-level measure of chronic stress is the Index of Relative Opportunities, or IRO (Linsky 1969). The IRO is based on the notion of status blockage or status frustration. Conceptually it is related to Parker and Kleiner's (1969) idea of "goal-striving stress" and Merton's (1957) concept of Anomie. Operationally, the IRO is based on the ratio of individuals in a community who have high aspirations and investment in achievement (as measured by educational level) to the opportunity for occupational attainment (based on the availability of high-status jobs in the community). Linsky (1969) used this index to investigate the mental health consequences of residence in communities in which the socially valued goal of upward mobility was threatened by the lack of an occupational-opportunity structure capable of sustaining such goals. He found that depressive mental disorders were one consequence of living in such a community. The Index of Status Integration and Index of Relative Opportunity are examples of measures of chronic stress that, like the SSI, can be calculated from census data or other data available to the public. We are currently using these indicators of chronic stress and additional indicators to explore the effects of living in a community characterized by a high level of chronic stress.

POLICY IMPLICATIONS

The research described in this book was not driven primarily by policy issues, yet several policy implications emerge. Most stress research, with a few notable exceptions discussed in chapter 1, focuses on stress and its consequences within the lives of individuals. Focus on the person as the unit of analysis tends to suggest intervention strategies (such as therapy and support services for individual victims of stress) and techniques of stress management that enable individuals to better cope with stress. Individually based policies might focus on promoting the acquisition of life skills to avoid stressful events and the teaching of better psychological and social coping skills to deal with stressful events.

Unfortunately, policies based on the individual leave intact the stressful conditions that lead to the problems in the first place and that will continue to create victims in the future. Individualizing stress processes and problems in this way may diminish the impetus for serious social change directed at removing the sources of the stress. In contrast, this research situates the problem clearly within the social and cultural structure of communities that produce stress and within the attitudes and values that serve to channel the outcome of stress in socially harmful ways. The findings in this volume therefore suggest a different strategy. We believe policy should be focused upstream—that is, by controlling some of the problems of stress closer to the source. For instance, policies could be directed at reducing such stressful events as work stoppages, mortgage fore-closures, and dropping out of school. In addition, reduction of infant mortality and stillbirths would be one realistic consequence of a universal prenatal-care program.

The State Stress Index also has practical applications. It could be used to measure the extent to which state policies directed at reducing the level of stressful events have actually attained that goal. Another use might be to help identify states or regions that may have the greatest need of support services for victims of stress. Such intervention, though undoubtedly expensive, may be cheap in comparison to the unchecked consequences of stress in the form of aggression and violence as described in the present research.

We have not suggested in this book that stress inevitably leads to aggression and violence. We have suggested that such outcomes of the stress process are most likely to occur when cultures direct those outcomes in particular directions. Accordingly, an additional strategy may be to implement programs designed to rechannel stress and tensions away from the most personally and socially harmful consequences described in this volume, including efforts to influence the cultural sphere, such as broad educational programs promoting nonviolent techniques to deal with public and private conflicts.

Our earlier book (Linsky and Straus 1986, pp. 58–62) investigated a number of buffering variables such as welfare-support levels, educational support, community integration, and availability of mental health services. We were primarily interested in the extent to which such buffering conditions would lessen the consequences of living in a high-stress state. We found that the adequacy of welfare support did soften the effects of stress on a number of outcomes, including accidental and motor-vehicle deaths, suicides, and deaths from asthma and respiratory disease. There was also, however, a somewhat ironic finding: the more stressful the social environment of a state, the less available the four buffer variables were to its residents. Thus, states whose populations were exposed to the most stress, which are the very populations most in need of supportive social arrangements and special resources for coping, were the states that were least likely to have such support. Rational public policy suggests reversing this pattern as a step toward diminishing the high levels of violence and aggression in the United States.

A further policy implication is suggested by contrasting the link between stress and aggression reported in this volume and the link between stress and illness that has been the focus of other research. Stress may be more socially tolerable as long as its effects are limited to such things as an individual illness. Stress then tends to be defined as a problem of unfortunate individuals, with no consideration of the cost to society of caring for those individuals. However, to the extent that stress is also perceived as linked to a higher level of crime and violence, it becomes increasingly difficult to ignore the social costs. When stress results in aggression, the number of victims is legion; it includes those who may be victims of self-directed acts of aggression and those who are the direct victims of this stress-induced aggression by others. Moreover, we must also include the large number of indirect victims whose quality of life is diminished because they live in high-crime communities. From this standpoint, it is hoped that stress may be seen more readily as not just an individual problem but a community problem as well, and therefore as a candidate for social policy.

APPENDIX A

State Rankings of Stress Indicators, Change in Stress Indicators, and Subindexes

TABLE A-1.   ECONOMIC STRESSORS, 1982

Rank	Business Failures per Million Pop.		Initial Unemployment Claims per 100 K Adults		Workers on Strike per 100 K Adults		Personal Bankruptcies per 100 K Pop.		Mortgage Foreclosures per 100 K Pop.	
	State	STR1R	State	STR2R	State	STR3R	State	STR4R	State	STR5R
1	OREG	440.03	NC	38.81	WVA	6.81	NEV	336.79	NEV	103.39
2	WASH	268.01	SC	38.56	MINN	2.43	TENN	318.78	MICH	76.73
3	COLO	212.70	MICH	27.30	PA	1.73	CAL	275.87	ARIZ	74.03
4	NEV	208.43	TENN	25.31	DC	1.65	ALA	275.19	IDA	71.57
5	TENN	174.72	RI	25.24	NH	1.63	GA	239.62	UTAH	59.31
6	ARIZ	174.68	ALAS	24.83	MONT	1.61	IDA	239.61	WASH	55.50
7	OKLA	173.01	PA	24.23	ILL	1.49	INDI	235.08	ALA	43.55
8	ALAS	159.91	OREG	24.01	KY	1.07	UTAH	232.78	INDI	42.39
9	NM	158.74	ALA	22.48	ND	0.96	OREG	222.23	COLO	38.12
10	KANS	150.39	WIS	22.16	RI	0.93	ILL	218.41	SC	31.05
11	CAL	148.72	IDA	22.05	WASH	0.89	OHIO	216.68	CAL	30.19
12	HAWA	146.44	OHIO	21.01	COLO	0.83	WASH	212.91	HAWA	30.01
13	MICH	133.41	ME	20.94	OHIO	0.77	MISS	203.23	GA	29.36
14	SD	123.92	GA	20.91	VA	0.75	COLO	198.08	OREG	28.73
15	WVA	122.90	ARK	20.33	VT	0.74	KY	184.73	OHIO	28.69
16	ND	114.58	MISS	20.01	UTAH	0.70	ARIZ	182.32	ILL	26.33
17	MO	111.49	INDI	19.72	TENN	0.67	KANS	178.56	FLA	24.74
18	OHIO	108.14	WASH	19.64	MASS	0.66	OKLA	177.10	DEL	23.25
19	MINN	104.07	CAL	19.61	NEBR	0.65	VA	167.72	TENN	22.61
20	VA	100.07	KY	19.18	ALA	0.64	LA	156.85	NJ	21.64
21	KY	99.35	MO	18.71	NJ	0.56	WIS	153.26	TEX	21.51
22	GA	97.33	NEV	18.52	NY	0.53	WYO	151.37	OKLA	21.22
23	ALA	95.64	VT	18.47	OREG	0.51	NEBR	144.12	DC	20.69
24	ILL	94.80	DEL	17.65	INDI	0.51	MO	141.95	NEBR	20.50
25	UTAH	93.57	ILL	16.71	IOWA	0.46	MICH	139.65	MONT	20.47
26	NEBR	91.88	CONN	16.43	CONN	0.43	ARK	128.61	ALAS	19.92
27	PA	89.99	MASS	16.24	MD	0.41	DC	127.00	PA	19.60
28	TEX	88.54	NJ	14.96	MO	0.41	MONT	126.96	WYO	18.64
29	FLA	87.30	IOWA	14.93	WYO	0.37	MINN	122.00	MISS	15.52
30	WIS	85.56	MONT	14.49	MICH	0.36	IOWA	120.85	KY	14.49
31	ME	82.75	VA	14.25	CAL	0.35	SD	118.73	MINN	14.40
32	MONT	75.78	LA	13.91	WIS	0.32	NM	115.00	MD	14.20
33	DC	75.08	NH	13.81	TEX	0.26	NJ	114.45	LA	13.20
34	LA	74.85	WYO	13.68	GA	0.25	WVA	113.11	MO	12.75
35	INDI	73.88	UTAH	13.50	ME	0.22	RI	107.66	NC	12.30
36	ARK	73.69	MD	13.08	DEL	0.20	ND	106.85	ARK	11.87
37	NC	73.32	NY	13.05	NM	0.19	MD	106.65	KANS	11.30
38	IDA	72.67	HAWA	12.95	ALAS	0.17	NC	101.38	NM	10.75
39	NY	72.46	WVA	12.72	OKLA	0.14	NY	100.91	VT	10.64
40	MISS	69.34	MINN	12.69	MISS	0.14	PA	100.04	CONN	10.59
41	NJ	68.93	KANS	12.43	ARK	0.13	TEX	83.46	VA	10.15
42	IOWA	61.58	ND	12.34	ARIZ	0.13	ALAS	80.63	IOWA	9.82
43	RI	60.86	ARIZ	11.93	SD	0.12	DEL	80.33	NY	9.80
44	WYO	60.78	OKLA	10.35	NEV	0.11	CONN	80.13	WIS	8.89
45	NH	59.07	COLO	10.33	IDA	0.11	FLA	77.55	NH	7.87
46	MASS	57.62	NM	9.77	HAWA	0.10	HAWA	67.90	ME	7.57
47	DEL	51.67	DC	8.98	KANS	0.09	NH	67.09	RI	6.01
48	MD	45.18	NEBR	8.97	FLA	0.05	SC	66.99	SD	5.91
49	CONN	31.03	TEX	8.38	LA	0.05	ME	64.79	MASS	4.00
50	SC	30.38	SD	7.93	NC	0.04	MASS	52.55	ND	2.38
51	VT	26.92	FLA	6.94	SC	0.01	VT	51.15	WVA	1.50

TABLE A-2.   FAMILY STRESSORS, 1982

Rank	Illegitimate Births per 1 K Pop. State	STR8R	Infant Deaths per 1 K Births State	STR9R	Fetal Deaths per 1 K Births State	STR10R	Divorces per 1 K Pop. State	STR6R	Abortions per 100 K Pop. State	STR7R
1	DC	9.55	DC	21.90	GA	13.80	NEV	13.90	DC	4,573.48
2	MISS	6.98	SC	15.40	MISS	13.30	ALAS	8.30	NEV	1,134.40
3	LA	6.04	MISS	15.20	SC	12.80	WYO	7.80	CAL	1,075.96
4	NM	5.90	ALA	14.10	VA	12.30	OKLA	7.50	NY	1,039.90
5	ALAS	5.70	NC	13.80	DC	11.90	ARIZ	7.10	HAWA	916.75
6	GA	5.28	TENN	13.50	NY	11.20	INDI	7.10	NJ	822.29
7	SC	5.00	ILL	13.30	HAWA	11.10	NM	7.00	COLO	819.87
8	MD	5.00	LA	13.00	ALA	11.00	FLA	6.90	RI	815.32
9	CAL	4.72	FLA	12.80	PA	10.20	ARK	6.90	MD	814.84
10	ARIZ	4.71	ND	12.70	LA	10.10	IDA	6.60	WASH	798.18
11	ILL	4.71	NY	12.60	FLA	10.10	TEX	6.60	CONN	741.52
12	DEL	4.57	GA	12.50	NC	10.10	WASH	6.50	FLA	734.57
13	ALA	4.54	MO	12.50	WVA	10.10	ALA	6.40	MASS	718.02
14	HAWA	4.45	VA	12.10	COLO	9.90	TENN	6.40	VT	713.46
15	NY	4.44	NEV	11.90	MD	9.00	OREG	6.20	MICH	704.22
16	FLA	4.11	UTAH	11.90	DEL	9.00	MONT	5.80	TEX	689.43
17	ARK	4.08	DEL	11.80	RI	9.00	GA	5.70	GA	680.94
18	TENN	3.79	ALAS	11.70	KY	8.90	COLO	5.60	DEL	645.00
19	MO	3.66	MICH	11.70	ILL	8.80	CAL	5.60	VA	635.80
20	OHIO	3.65	OKLA	11.40	MO	8.50	MO	5.50	OREG	612.82
21	VA	3.63	KY	11.40	NEBR	8.50	UTAH	5.40	KANS	599.92
22	NC	3.63	INDI	11.30	OHIO	8.30	DC	5.40	NH	590.72
23	SD	3.58	TEX	11.10	NJ	8.30	DEL	5.30	ILL	574.39
24	NJ	3.56	RI	11.00	TEX	8.30	KANS	5.30	OHIO	570.31
25	TEX	3.52	WVA	11.00	WYO	8.30	NH	5.30	TENN	560.21
26	INDI	3.32	NJ	10.90	TENN	8.20	WVA	5.30	ND	552.45
27	MONT	3.31	OREG	10.80	KANS	8.20	MISS	5.20	ARIZ	547.56
28	OKLA	3.25	MASS	10.60	INDI	8.10	VT	5.10	NM	546.45
29	PA	3.23	OHIO	10.50	ARIZ	8.00	ME	5.10	PA	539.27
30	COLO	3.21	NEBR	10.40	OKLA	7.90	OHIO	5.00	MONT	525.47
31	MICH	3.12	MD	10.30	NM	7.80	NC	4.90	LA	509.13
32	KY	3.11	CONN	10.10	SD	7.80	VA	4.80	ALA	505.58
33	CONN	3.08	ARIZ	10.00	NEV	7.80	KY	4.60	SC	500.31
34	OREG	3.08	COLO	10.00	VT	7.80	ILL	4.40	ND	498.51
35	WIS	2.98	NM	9.90	CAL	7.70	SC	4.30	ME	481.51
36	WASH	2.95	CAL	9.90	ALAS	7.60	HAWA	4.30	MINN	460.31
37	NEV	2.92	ARK	9.90	CONN	7.60	MICH	4.20	ALAS ·	434.68
38	VT	2.87	KANS	9.70	MASS	7.60	NEBR	4.10	WIS	429.50
39	KANS	2.77	WASH	9.50	WIS	7.30	NJ	3.90	NEBR	414.10
40	NEBR	2.76	MINN	9.40	WASH	7.20	IOWA	3.80	MO	400.24
41	ME	2.72	PA	9.30	ME	7.10	RI	3.80	OKLA	392.76
42	UTAH	2.67	ME	9.20	IDA	7.10	LA	3.70	IDA	309.11
43	MASS	2.66	HAWA	8.90	ARK	7.00	SD	3.70	KY	293.18
44	WYO	2.66	IOWA	8.90	MICH	6.90	WIS	3.60	ARK	288.69
45	MINN	2.58	IDA	8.60	ND	6.90	MASS	3.60	INDI	286.03
46	RI	2.57	NH	8.60	NH	6.90	MINN	3.50	IOWA	283.11
47	ND	2.53	SD	8.40	UTAH	6.60	MD	3.50	UTAH	266.07
48	WVA	2.53	WIS	7.80	MONT	6.40	NY	3.50	SD	255.04
49	IDA	2.38	VT	7.80	OREG	6.40	CONN	3.40	MISS	214.26
50	NH	2.29	MONT	7.40	IOWA	6.40	ND	3.30	WYO	200.00
51	IOWA	2.21	WYO	6.30	MINN	6.30	PA	3.20	WVA	174.40

TABLE A-3.　COMMUNITY STRESSORS, 1982

	State Resident Less than 5 Yrs (% of Adult Pop.)		New Houses Authorized per 1 K Pop.		New Welfare Cases per 100 K Pop.		High School Dropouts per 100 K Pop.		Disaster Assistance per 100 K Pop.	
Rank	State	STR12R	State	STR13R	State	STR14R	State	STR15R	State	STR11R
1	NEV	31.50	ALAS	18.47	WIS	1,554.08	LA	806.50	DC	71.41
2	ALAS	29.10	TEX	13.11	MICH	1,514.67	SC	682.92	CONN	63.08
3	WYO	28.30	ARIZ	12.63	VT	1,480.00	DC	666.13	INDI	54.09
4	ARIZ	23.90	COLO	10.36	WVA	1,454.61	NY	665.69	ME	53.17
5	COLO	20.60	FLA	9.91	MINN	1,318.42	MISS	652.32	OHIO	50.09
6	IDA	20.00	NEV	9.23	DC	1,217.41	GA	650.01	PA	46.24
7	FLA	19.60	OKLA	8.88	CAL	1,151.04	ALA	648.99	MASS	44.11
8	NH	18.50	GA	6.85	ME	1,144.54	NC	592.92	MO	40.93
9	NM	17.40	NM	6.29	DEL	1,136.83	TEX	548.58	TEX	40.72
10	HAWA	16.90	HAWA	5.72	NY	1,104.21	MASS	532.39	WVA	39.42
11	OREG	16.90	WYO	5.69	ALAS	1,087.16	KY	526.18	MICH	37.64
12	DC	16.60	SC	5.58	KY	1,044.23	MICH	489.23	NEV	37.47
13	WASH	16.20	NC	5.50	WASH	989.97	VA	473.70	KY	35.36
14	UTAH	16.00	VA	5.45	OHIO	988.58	FLA	467.14	ALA	35.82
15	MONT	15.00	DEL	5.00	MISS	960.62	TENN	461.45	OKLA	34.48
16	VT	14.30	MD	4.92	MO	957.24	IDA	459.37	ILL	33.04
17	VA	13.90	UTAH	4.77	PA	952.98	NM	441.33	NJ	31.53
18	OKLA	13.70	NH	4.75	GA	948.43	MD	430.92	MD	31.06
19	DEL	13.30	LA	4.63	MD	938.97	NH	385.44	ALAS	29.73
20	ND	12.70	MINN	4.55	ILL	933.95	ME	383.98	IOWA	29.07
21	KANS	12.60	VT	4.23	IOWA	911.01	CAL	373.79	SC	28.55
22	ARK	12.40	ND	4.17	SD	899.14	ARK	364.02	VT	26.73
23	SC	11.50	WASH	4.12	OREG	878.45	RI	343.13	KANS	26.13
24	GA	11.50	KANS	3.57	UTAH	871.87	NJ	338.02	HAWA	25.38
25	SD	11.10	CAL	3.44	IDA	847.19	PA	331.98	RI	25.08
26	TEX	11.00	CONN	3.29	NM	844.04	INDI	327.20	GA	24.63
27	ME	10.80	TENN	3.18	HAWA	833.20	MO	322.44	MISS	24.54
28	TENN	10.60	NJ	2.87	LA	825.38	OREG	314.06	CAL	24.03
29	NEBR	10.50	OREG	2.81	TENN	823.65	WYO	308.82	VA	23.57
30	MD	10.40	ARK	2.73	RI	806.72	OKLA	291.15	ND	23.21
31	NC	9.80	ME	2.73	NJ	805.39	VT	281.73	DEL	22.67
32	MO	9.40	RI	2.73	KANS	786.12	HAWA	280.94	LA	21.13
33	CONN	9.30	MASS	2.68	MASS	767.82	ARIZ	279.73	OREG	20.43
34	MISS	9.20	WIS	2.59	FLA	759.14	WVA	273.79	FLA	19.41
35	KY	9.00	IDA	2.56	COLO	749.25	COLO	259.64	WASH	18.85
36	ALA	8.90	MONT	2.48	MONT	742.86	CONN	246.90	NH	18.67
37	RI	8.70	MISS	2.42	ALA	740.01	DEL	240.50	TENN	18.44
38	WVA	8.60	MO	2.33	SC	727.00	WASH	221.28	ARIZ	18.23
39	CAL	8.50	INDI	2.28	OKLA	688.92	NEV	200.11	WIS	14.23
40	LA	8.40	NEBR	2.27	ARK	668.31	KANS	192.94	MINN	14.01
41	IOWA	7.90	ALA	2.21	NH	651.27	SD	179.68	ARK	13.70
42	NJ	7.80	KY	2.03	VA	642.13	MONT	178.63	COLO	12.31
43	INDI	7.60	PA	1.87	INDI	635.57	NEBR	169.73	IDA	12.08
44	MINN	7.30	IOWA	1.82	WYO	615.29	ND	161.31	SD	11.96
45	MASS	7.00	SD	1.73	ARIZ	601.21	IOWA	160.82	NEBR	11.64
46	WIS	6.70	ILL	1.66	CONN	588.90	ILL	156.44	MONT	11.55
47	ILL	6.10	MICH	1.56	NC	576.23	ALAS	146.40	NY	10.75
48	OHIO	5.70	OHIO	1.54	ND	569.20	UTAH	119.54	NC	9.99
49	PA	5.20	NY	1.42	NEV	566.97	OHIO	87.94	NM	8.92
50	MICH	5.10	WVA	0.92	TEX	546.52	MINN	77.06	WYO	4.12
51	NY	3.80	DC	0.64	NEBR	420.20	WIS	21.85	UTAH	2.48

TABLE A-4. PERCENTAGE OF CHANGE IN ECONOMIC STRESSORS, 1976–1982

Rank	Business Failures per 1 Million Pop.		Initial Unemployment Claims		Workers on Strike per 100K Adults		Personal Bankruptcies per 100K Pop.		Mortgage Foreclosures per 100K Pop.	
	State	STR1P	State	STR2P	State	STR3P	State	STR4P	State	STR5P
1	WYO	60,684.31	SC	133.37	NH	356.06	DC	269.78	SD	1948.32
2	HAWA	12,889.17	WYO	132.48	ND	301.30	SC	233.14	IDA	1645.15
3	RI	1,310.44	MISS	126.35	MINN	178.78	MD	182.26	MONT	1456.18
4	WVA	1,077.87	TENN	124.03	MONT	170.27	UTAH	131.64	ND	1424.05
5	NM	990.65	NC	106.59	VT	136.41	TEX	118.69	UTAH	809.98
6	ND	925.53	VA	96.14	COLO	80.22	NJ	111.76	WYO	799.55
7	COLO	815.69	IOWA	95.79	DC	66.63	SD	104.06	NEBR	287.99
8	KANS	623.77	KANS	89.33	UTAH	32.75	PA	99.96	RI	281.39
9	SD	507.20	ALA	82.34	NEBR	−2.38	MISS	63.56	OREG	215.51
10	NC	481.11	OHIO	78.83	RI	−14.51	WASH	63.34	ALAS	200.79
11	UTAH	474.53	WIS	64.68	ILL	−25.45	ND	62.23	WASH	175.56
12	LA	404.40	INDI	64.49	TEX	−37.58	ARK	59.82	DC	163.26
13	DEL	401.17	KY	64.44	PA	−41.33	TENN	55.78	KANS	146.67
14	MISS	380.09	GA	62.88	WASH	−43.66	RI	55.77	ALA	146.11
15	MO	343.93	LA	62.80	MD	−45.16	MICH	54.19	HAWA	139.94
16	OREG	330.60	TEX	55.52	OREG	−45.18	WIS	52.26	NEV	132.55
17	KY	315.53	IDA	54.38	WYO	−52.78	OHIO	50.16	MICH	126.68
18	NEV	297.32	UTAH	40.20	MASS	−56.16	CAL	45.25	NM	102.46
19	ALA	257.66	MINN	40.04	CONN	−56.21	DEL	42.81	INDI	99.71
20	TENN	244.04	ILL	38.28	WVA	−58.17	LL	40.81	ME	87.34
21	ME	240.53	MICH	37.81	GA	−58.70	GA	38.24	TENN	72.48
22	ARIZ	233.21	ARK	37.25	NJ	−59.30	IDA	31.13	KY	69.20
23	MONT	217.00	SD	33.88	NY	−59.40	ALA	28.40	MD	63.65
24	NEBR	203.60	OKLA	33.87	VA	−60.67	OREG	28.39	PA	57.97
25	INDI	199.01	ND	28.68	TENN	−61.52	NY	26.08	WIS	53.03
26	VA	192.77	NEBR	25.13	CAL	−66.53	NC	24.20	OHIO	44.51
27	ARK	187.80	PA	24.03	WIS	−68.44	INDI	23.85	IOWA	40.81
28	FLA	182.74	OREG	22.82	MISS	−69.08	ALAS	18.88	ARK	11.17
29	ALAS	177.66	MD	22.65	ALA	−72.90	MINN	18.38	ILL	10.21
30	OHIO	172.65	MO	22.25	DEL	−73.33	OKLA	16.72	NJ	10.08
31	SC	170.37	MASS	20.54	ARK	−75.51	WYO	16.63	NY	5.53
32	IOWA	163.76	DEL	19.57	OKLA	−75.84	LA	13.35	CAL	5.29
33	DC	163.53	WVA	16.32	KY	−77.76	IOWA	11.60	ARIZ	−2.84
34	TEX	163.24	HAWA	16.16	MO	−78.38	HAWA	10.38	COLO	−4.64
35	OKLA	153.20	VT	15.89	INDI	−79.38	FLA	10.31	FLA	−8.70
36	CAL	150.42	CAL	14.96	OHIO	−79.38	MONT	10.15	DEL	−10.73
37	WASH	146.32	COLO	10.53	ME	−80.22	COLO	9.03	VA	−12.33
38	WIS	127.96	ARIZ	10.38	IOWA	−80.82	NEV	7.66	CONN	−13.90
39	GA	115.95	MONT	9.18	FLA	−81.45	VA	7.37	MINN	−17.24
40	MICH	111.22	NM	4.50	HAWA	−81.64	NEBR	6.86	TEX	−20.64
41	ILL	109.97	NM	1.96	NH	−84.10	MO	6.64	NC	−21.64
42	PA	104.11	RI	−0.27	SD	−86.10	KY	6.07	MO	−23.89
43	MINN	67.05	NJ	−1.55	LA	−87.40	ARIZ	3.37	WVA	−26.06
44	IDA	43.79	DC	−7.64	ARIZ	−88.29	WVA	1.25	NH	−26.53
45	NY	27.84	WASH	−9.43	IDA	−88.45	CONN	0.83	SC	−33.97
46	NH	5.56	CONN	−14.47	MICH	−89.41	NH	−6.47	VT	−34.92
47	MASS	−7.29	NY	−14.88	NC	−90.36	NM	−10.38	OKLA	−35.61
48	CONN	−21.37	FLA	−18.71	KANS	−90.50	KANS	−11.77	LA	−44.32
49	NJ	−23.39	ME	−23.20	SC	−91.85	MASS	−14.14	GA	−45.75
50	VT	−28.80	ALAS	−27.85	ALAS	−96.44	VT	−37.69	MISS	−67.09
51	MD	−32.17	NEV	−30.81	NEV	−97.98	ME	−56.62	MASS	−69.20

TABLE A-5. PERCENTAGE OF CHANGE IN FAMILY STRESSORS, 1976–1982

Rank	Illegitimate Births per 1 K Pop.		Infant Deaths per 1 K Births		Fetal Deaths per 1 K Births		Divorces per 1 K Pop.		Abortions per 100 K Pop.	
	State	STR8P	State	STR9P	State	STR10P	State	STR6P	State	STR7P
1	NM	180.98	UTAH	0.85	ME	31.48	NJ	30.00	MISS	79.50
2	UTAH	105.33	ND	−5.61	VT	26.98	VT	27.50	RI	77.24
3	CAL	88.82	DEL	−9.23	MD	6.71	MASS	24.14	MONT	72.16
4	HAWA	80.81	DC	−10.61	NEBR	5.70	DC	22.73	ARK	70.88
5	ALAS	69.08	MASS	−12.55	ALAS	3.05	INDI	20.34	ND	62.93
6	VT	68.64	NEV	−13.14	IDA	1.43	NY	16.67	NEV	58.18
7	MONT	65.60	OREG	−14.67	NH	−0.13	SC	16.22	SC	57.09
8	NH	55.41	FLA	−14.99	NY	−1.41	VA	14.29	ALA	55.35
9	NY	53.20	TENN	−15.88	NEV	−2.50	ND	13.79	ME	53.62
10	COLO	51.01	ME	−16.36	GA	−3.55	WIS	12.50	IDA	47.09
11	WIS	48.44	MO	−18.09	WVA	−6.72	LA	12.12	INDI	45.11
12	NEBR	48.31	HAWA	−19.55	FLA	−6.97	NC	11.36	VT	41.19
13	WYO	46.93	CAL	−20.40	OHIO	−7.04	SD	8.82	WVA	40.22
14	CONN	46.78	ILL	−20.58	ARIZ	−7.25	RI	8.57	NH	39.89
15	ME	46.18	SC	−20.94	CONN	−8.49	WVA	8.16	MD	39.46
16	WASH	46.01	NY	−21.19	LA	−8.66	UTAH	8.00	CONN	36.26
17	ARIZ	43.67	GA	−21.56	SC	−9.11	NEBR	7.89	NJ	32.64
18	MINN	43.47	NC	−22.05	ALA	−9.25	WYO	6.85	LA	30.59
19	OREG	43.23	INDI	−22.30	VA	−9.75	MO	3.77	ARIZ	29.70
20	MD	42.78	RI	−22.44	NM	−12.00	PA	3.23	MO	27.01
21	PA	40.01	COLO	−22.93	WIS	−12.45	TEX	3.13	DEL	22.61
22	MASS	40.01	KY	−22.97	SD	−13.33	TENN	0.00	SD	22.42
23	IOWA	39.33	MICH	−23.02	WASH	−13.47	MISS	0.00	WIS	21.61
24	KANS	38.21	VA	−25.70	NJ	−13.58	MINN	0.00	TEX	19.94
25	RI	37.05	NEBR	−26.37	WYO	−14.56	NH	0.00	MICH	19.53
26	ND	36.42	NH	−26.67	OKLA	−15.43	IOWA	0.00	NC	19.12
27	SD	35.73	LA	−26.85	MASS	−15.56	ALAS	−1.19	NEBR	16.82
28	OHIO	35.13	NJ	−27.01	PA	−15.76	ME	−1.92	IOWA	14.54
29	FLA	32.13	ALAS	−27.44	INDI	−15.99	KY	−2.13	VA	11.42
30	NJ	32.09	CONN	−28.00	CAL	−16.16	ALA	−3.03	COLO	11.35
31	INDI	31.36	ALA	−28.51	HAWA	−17.40	OKLA	−3.85	FLA	8.85
32	OKLA	30.54	MISS	−29.26	MO	−17.51	IDA	−4.35	CAL	7.96
33	VA	29.55	OHIO	−29.91	ILL	−17.85	ILL	−4.35	UTAH	5.82
34	MO	26.22	TEX	−30.68	MISS	−17.95	KANS	−5.36	OKLA	5.30
35	GA	22.81	OKLA	−31.19	KANS	−18.00	DEL	−5.36	MASS	5.04
36	DEL	22.70	KANS	−31.83	NC	−18.60	FLA	−8.00	MINN	4.38
37	WVA	21.75	MINN	−31.92	UTAH	−18.95	OHIO	−9.09	GA	3.26
38	NEV	21.50	WVA	−33.82	COLO	−20.72	MONT	−9.37	PA	1.41
39	TEX	20.64	WASH	−34.61	MONT	−20.76	GA	−9.52	OHIO	0.75
40	ILL	20.01	ARIZ	−34.96	KY	−20.79	CAL	−9.68	NM	0.34
41	KY	19.92	IDA	−35.59	IOWA	−22.09	OREG	−10.14	DC	0.17
42	TENN	19.21	VT	−35.76	TEX	−22.15	NM	−10.26	NY	−0.07
43	IDA	18.87	NM	−36.13	DEL	−22.58	MD	−10.26	HAWA	−2.78
44	MISS	18.12	ARK	−36.37	MICH	−28.20	CONN	−10.53	OREG	−6.80
45	NC	15.79	IOWA	−37.18	MINN	−28.32	MICH	−10.64	KANS	−9.07
46	ARK	14.29	WIS	−37.64	OREG	−28.66	WASH	−13.33	WASH	−10.70
47	SC	13.79	PA	−39.82	ND	−31.62	ARIZ	−15.48	ILL	−11.95
48	LA	13.20	MD	−40.08	RI	−33.11	COLO	−17.65	KY	−13.53
49	ALA	12.33	SD	−49.35	ARK	−34.25	NEV	−17.75	WYO	−17.36
50	DC	9.22	MONT	−53.75	TENN	−34.52	HAWA	−18.87	TENN	−22.98
51	MICH	9.03	WYO	−63.85	DC	−55.09	ARK	−20.69	ALAS	−42.98

TABLE A-6. PERCENTAGE OF CHANGE IN COMMUNITY STRESSORS, 1976–1982

Rank	State Resident Less than 5 Yrs (% of adult pop.)		New Houses Authorized per 1 K Pop.		New Welfare Cases per 100 K Pop.		High School Dropouts per 100 K Pop.		Disaster Assistance per 100 K Pop.	
	State	STR12P	State	STR13P	State	STR14P	State	STR15P	State	STR11P
1	WYO	23.04	ALAS	67.98	WIS	62.90	MASS	14.46	ALAS	366.22
2	SD	9.90	TEX	67.37	MINN	53.32	IDA	10.73	ME	222.68
3	NC	6.52	OKLA	67.14	MICH	42.73	LA	4.27	COLO	176.44
4	SC	5.50	GA	51.95	ALAS	25.19	NY	2.54	INDI	156.81
5	KY	3.45	FLA	26.11	DC	23.80	TENN	−1.64	CAL	156.20
6	ND	2.42	VT	25.87	WVA	18.50	ALA	−6.24	ARIZ	143.84
7	KANS	1.61	NC	15.75	ILL	11.66	ARIZ	−8.70	OHIO	123.12
8	MO	0.00	ARIZ	14.18	IOWA	11.61	MICH	−11.16	IOWA	122.80
9	MONT	−1.32	DEL	11.92	MISS	8.75	NH	−11.91	WYO	121.18
10	NH	−1.60	COLO	9.65	ND	7.31	WYO	−19.03	KY	114.45
11	OHIO	−1.72	LA	6.55	MO	5.28	TEX	−19.36	SC	111.46
12	WASH	−1.82	WVA	−1.68	SD	3.16	CAL	−19.43	MO	80.04
13	IDA	−4.31	SC	−2.06	DEL	2.44	COLO	−20.70	RI	77.49
14	VT	−4.67	NY	−12.17	ME	0.86	PA	−22.68	HAWA	72.31
15	OKLA	−4.86	MISS	−12.53	NH	−2.21	SC	−23.72	NEV	66.82
16	TENN	−7.02	NM	−14.56	NY	−2.84	VA	−23.73	GA	62.56
17	MICH	−7.27	MASS	−21.75	NJ	−3.21	NJ	−24.44	NC	59.57
18	WVA	−7.53	CONN	−22.78	GA	−3.39	FLA	−24.86	NEBR	53.46
19	UTAH	−9.09	ME	−23.16	VT	−3.49	GA	−25.33	DC	51.33
20	IOWA	−9.20	MD	−23.42	TENN	−6.05	MD	−27.08	CONN	49.42
21	GA	−9.45	MINN	−27.26	INDI	−7.40	KY	−27.76	MICH	43.30
22	WIS	−10.67	NH	−27.74	LA	−7.88	NM	−27.80	TEX	42.81
23	NEV	−10.76	TENN	−28.03	VA	−8.20	HAWA	−29.47	NM	41.21
24	OREG	−11.05	ARK	−28.90	ALA	−9.26	WASH	−30.42	NH	33.81
25	INDI	−11.63	VA	−30.21	ARIZ	−11.35	OREG	−32.44	KANS	31.72
26	DC	−11.70	NJ	−31.25	HAWA	−11.35	MO	−32.50	WIS	29.25
27	RI	−12.12	HAWA	−39.63	NM	−11.82	MISS	−33.41	VT	27.93
28	MISS	−13.21	KY	−42.95	FLA	−11.87	VT	−34.10	MD	24.19
29	PA	−13.33	RI	−45.02	IDA	−11.88	ME	−34.28	SD	23.64
30	NM	−14.71	KANS	−46.75	TEX	−11.93	NC	−34.38	DEL	23.17
31	CONN	−15.45	PA	−48.45	MD	−13.72	ARK	−34.46	LA	17.42
32	ARK	−16.22	MO	−50.36	WYO	−14.28	DC	−36.41	MASS	13.65
33	LA	−16.83	WYO	−52.82	PA	−14.40	INDI	−38.30	ILL	13.53
34	ME	−17.56	ND	−53.81	OHIO	−15.70	RI	−39.66	OREG	−1.43
35	COLO	−17.93	ALA	−54.04	CONN	−15.71	NEV	−41.13	WVA	−8.33
36	HAWA	−18.75	INDI	−56.82	OKLA	−17.14	OKLA	−41.66	MONT	−9.16
37	DEL	−18.90	NEV	−58.31	KY	−17.19	NEBR	−45.91	VA	−13.37
38	NEBR	−19.23	MONT	−60.20	UTAH	−19.09	CONN	−48.20	FLA	−21.43
39	ILL	−19.74	NEBR	−62.96	MASS	−21.71	IOWA	−48.70	PA	−22.10
40	ALA	−19.82	WIS	−63.13	MONT	−23.26	KANS	−48.81	ARK	−26.31
41	MINN	−20.65	CAL	−66.41	NC	−24.58	MONT	−51.81	WASH	−38.69
42	VA	−22.35	OHIO	−66.52	SC	−22.58	ND	−53.21	MISS	−46.73
43	TEX	−23.61	UTAH	−67.96	WASH	−25.29	SD	−53.43	NJ	−47.82
44	MASS	−23.91	WASH	−68.37	RI	−26.20	WVA	−56.18	OKLA	−49.13
45	NJ	−25.00	MICH	−68.41	NEBR	−28.33	UTAH	−60.14	ND	−50.97
46	FLA	−25.48	ILL	−68.78	ARK	−28.65	DEL	−64.09	MINN	−53.18
47	ARIZ	−26.46	IOWA	−73.44	KANS	−30.41	MINN	−69.73	ALA	−60.24
48	ALAS	−29.02	SD	−74.76	CAL	−38.07	ILL	−72.16	UTAH	−76.13
49	MD	−31.13	IDA	−74.98	OREG	−42.27	ALAS	−80.26	TENN	−80.67
50	NY	−35.59	OREG	−75.66	COLO	−47.81	OHIO	−82.92	NY	−83.30
51	CAL	−37.50	DC	−79.61	NEV	−48.31	WIS	−107.69	IDA	−96.07

TABLE A-7. ECONOMIC, FAMILY, AND COMMUNITY STRESS SUBINDEXES IN RANK ORDER BY STATE

Rank	State	Economic Index	State	Family Index	State	Community Index
1	NEV	96.64	DC	100.00	ALAS	100.00
2	WASH	96.18	MISS	85.58	DC	100.00
3	OREG	88.44	GA	81.91	TEX	82.31
4	TENN	87.26	SC	77.94	NEV	77.08
5	MICH	82.04	ALA	74.89	FLA	76.50
6	ALA	76.22	FLA	73.19	ARIZ	75.97
7	IDA	72.98	NEV	72.63	GA	72.82
8	CAL	71.23	NY	70.07	VT	71.30
9	ARIZ	68.87	ALAS	68.99	ME	71.18
10	COLO	68.60	VA	64.52	MICH	66.25
11	UTAH	66.84	LA	64.49	SC	64.74
12	ILL	66.82	NM	62.22	COLO	63.18
13	OHIO	66.01	CAL	61.62	LA	61.41
14	IND	63.76	TENN	60.61	OKLA	60.72
15	PA	63.73	NC	60.37	KY	57.87
16	GA	60.87	DEL	59.59	WVA	57.74
17	MINN	59.87	HAWA	59.56	MD	56.82
18	WVA	58.60	ILL	58.39	NM	55.43
19	KY	57.61	ARIZ	57.33	HAWA	55.00
20	ALAS	53.04	TEX	56.33	MISS	54.92
21	MONT	51.34	COLO	55.57	DEL	53.75
22	RI	47.36	MD	53.35	ALA	52.89
23	OK	46.74	OKLA	51.50	MASS	51.46
24	NC	45.93	MO	50.25	IDA	51.41
25	MISS	45.87	INDI	48.00	VA	50.58
26	MO	45.62	NJ	46.94	NH	48.80
27	WIS	45.21	WASH	46.80	CAL	48.77
28	DC	44.91	OHIO	45.31	CONN	48.38
29	VA	44.33	RI	43.79	MO	48.33
30	KANS	42.27	ARK	43.25	WYO	47.39
31	SC	41.62	OREG	42.88	WASH	46.82
32	NH	37.68	MICH	40.66	OREG	45.72
33	ARK	37.63	KANS	39.93	PA	43.30
34	NJ	37.58	WVA	39.21	INDI	41.96
35	ND	37.17	KY	38.93	TENN	40.04
36	NEBR	36.82	PA	37.36	NY	38.60
37	WYO	35.35	CONN	35.45	NC	37.84
38	NM	34.44	VT	35.20	NJ	35.67
39	ME	32.46	MASS	35.03	KANS	34.23
40	LA	32.21	NEBR	33.28	OHIO	33.93
41	HAWA	31.68	UTAH	32.98	MINN	33.53
42	IOWA	31.68	ND	31.64	RI	32.69
43	DEL	31.43	WYO	31.54	WIS	31.05
44	NY	29.51	ME	30.69	ARK	27.30
45	VT	28.01	MONT	30.24	UTAH	27.13
46	MD	26.76	IDA	29.81	IOWA	25.19
47	MASS	25.97	NH	29.36	ILL	24.82
48	SD	25.34	SD	23.81	ND	24.27
49	CONN	25.26	WIS	20.70	MONT	22.50
50	TEX	25.05	MINN	20.07	SD	19.37
51	FLA	21.15	IOWA	14.18	NEBR	0.00

APPENDIX B

Data Sources

CHAPTER 2

A. Population Estimates by Age, 1982

    Estimates of the Population of States by Age: July 1, 1981–1983, U.S. Bureau of the Census, Current Population Reports, Series P-25, no. 951. These estimates were used as denominators to compute the rates for this chapter.

B. Economic Stressors

    Business failures per 1 million population, 1982

        Statistical Abstract of the United States, 1985, Washington, D.C.: U.S. Government Printing Office, p. 519.

    Unemployment claims per 100*K* adults aged 18 and over, 1982

        World Almanac and Book of Facts, 1984, New York: Newspaper Enterprise Association, p. 67.

    Striking workers per 100*K* adults aged 18 and over, 1981

        Handbook of Labor Statistics (Bulletin 2175). 1981. Washington, D.C.: Bureau of Labor Statistics, U.S. Department of Labor. This bulletin, containing the most recent statistics collected, is the latest publication of these data.

    Bankruptcy cases per 100*K* population, 1982

        Administrative Office of the United States Courts. *Annual Report of the Director.* Washington, D.C.: U.S. Government Printing Office, 1983, pp. 418–419.

    Mortgage foreclosures per 100*K* population, 1982

        Mortgage Bankers Association of America. *National Delinquency Survey,* Washington, D.C.: Mortgage Bankers Association of America, 1982.

C. Family Stressors

    Divorces per 1*K* population, 1982

        Monthly Vital Statistics Report, August 1983, Washington, D.C.: U.S. Government Printing Office, p. 14.

    Abortions per 100*K* population, 1982

        Abortion Services in the United States, Each State and Metropolitan Area, 1981–1982. New York: Alan Guttmacher Institute, pp. 77–81.

    Illegitimate births per 100*K* population aged 14 and over, 1982

        Monthly Vital Statistics Report, August 1983, Washington, D.C.: U.S. Government Printing Office, p. 29.

Infant deaths per 1*K* live births, 1982

> *Monthly Vital Statistics Report,* August 1983, Washington, D.C.: U.S. Government Printing Office, p. 13.

Fetal deaths per 1*K* live births, 1982

> Unpublished data provided by Arthur Horn, Vital Statistics Office, Statistical Resources Branch, Division of Vital Statistics, 3700 Eastwest Highway, Hyattsville, Md. 20782.

D. Community Stressors

Disasters assistance per 100*K* population, 1982

> American National Red Cross. *Summary of Disaster Services Activities by Area and State, 1981–1982,* Washington, D.C.: American Red Cross Disaster Services.

Percentage of population residing in state less than 5 years, 1980

> *Statistical Abstract of the United States,* 1985, Washington, D.C.: U.S. Government Printing Office, p. 16.

New housing units per 1*K* population, 1982

> *Statistical Abstract of the United States,* 1984, Washington, D.C.: U.S. Government Printing Office, 1984, p. 743.

New welfare recipients per 100*K* population, 1982

> *Quarterly Public Assistance Statistics, 1982,* U.S. Department of Health and Human Services, Social Security Administration, Office of Research, Statistics, and International Policy.

New disabled awards—unpublished

> *SSI Remics—1982.* This is the "Revised Management Information Counts System" and is recognizable as a reference. Information was provided by Art Kahn, Social Security Administration, Baltimore, Md. We were referred to him by Louise Segal, editor of *Monthly Vital Statistics.*

High school dropouts per 100*K* population, 1982

> *Common Core of Data, National Center for Education Statistics, 1981,* pp. 6–7, and the *Historical Report, 1986,* Center for Statistics, U.S. Department of Education, Office of Educational Research and Improvement, pp. 4–7. Data was provided by Norman Brandt.

CHAPTER 3

Packs of Cigarettes per Capita

> Tobacco Institute. 1982. *The Tax Burden on Tobacco.* Tobacco Institute Historical Compilation 17. Table 11, pp. 26–29. Washington, D.C.: The Tobacco Institute.

Percentage of Smokers

> See methods section of this chapter.

Measure of Status Integration

> Computed by the authors following the method recommended by Gibbs and Martin (1967).

Smoking-Related Mortality Measures

> See methods section of this chapter; and Colby, Linsky, and Straus (1994).

CHAPTER 4

Restrictive Norm Index

> See methods section of this chapter; and Linsky, Colby, and Straus (1986).

Death Rates from Cirrhosis, Alcoholism, and Alcoholic Psychosis

> See methods section of this chapter.

Consumption of Alcohol

See methods section of this chapter.

CHAPTER 5

Subjective Stress
  See methods section of this chapter; and Straus and Gelles (1990).
Perceived Stress Index
  See methods section of this chapter; and Straus and Gelles (1990).
Suicidal Thoughts
  See methods section of this chapter; and Straus and Gelles (1990).

CHAPTER 6

Homicide Rates by Relationship of Victim and Offender and by Weapon
  The homicide rates specified according to relationship of victim to offender and type of weapon
  were calculated by Kirk R. Williams using a data tape of the Supplemental Homicide Reports,
  provided by the Uniform Crime Reporting division of the Federal Bureau of Investigation. The
  methods used are described in Williams and Flewelling (1987, 1988).

CHAPTER 7

Frequency of Drunkenness
  Aggregated from the National Family Violence Survey described in chapter 5.
Heavy Drinking
  Aggregated from the National Family Violence Survey described in chapter 5.

CHAPTER 8

Homicide Rates
  See data source for chapter 6.

CHAPTER 9

Weapon-Specific Homicide
  See data source for chapter 6.
Gun Magazine Circulation
  The data on copies of *Guns and Ammo* and *Shooting Times* sold in each state are for 1979 and include both newsstand and subscription sales. The sales data were obtained from the Audit Bureau of Circulation and then converted to a rate per $100K$ population. See Baron and Straus
  (1989) for further information.

CHAPTER 10

Rape Rates
  See methods section of this chapter.
Gender Equality Index
  See methods section of this chapter; and Sugarman and Straus (1989).
Sex Magazine Readership
  See methods section of this chapter; and Baron and Straus (1987, 1989).
Social Control Index
  See methods section of this chapter; and Baron and Straus (1987, 1989).

REFERENCES

Albrecht, S. L., B. A. Chadwick, and D. S. Alcorn. 1977. "Religiosity and Deviance: Application of an Attitude-Behavior Contingent Consistency Model." *Journal for the Scientific Study of Religion*, 16:263–274.

Aneshensel, C. S. 1992. "Social Stress: Theory and Research." *Annual Review of Sociology*, 18:15–38.

Aneshensel, C. S., L. I. Pearlin, and R. H. Schuler. 1993. "Stress, Role Captivity, and the Cessation of Caregiving." *Journal of Health and Social Behavior*, 34:54–70.

Arieti, S. 1959. "Manic Depressive Psychosis." In *American Handbook of Psychiatry*, vol. 2, edited by S. Arieti. New York: Basic.

Avison, W., and D. D. McAlpine. 1992. "Gender Differences in Symptoms of Depression among Adolescents." *Journal of Health and Social Behavior*, 33:77–96.

Bachman-Prehn, R., A. S. Linsky, and M. A. Straus. 1988. "Homicide of Family Members, Acquaintances, and Strangers, and State-to-State Differences in Social Stress, Social Control and Social Norms." Paper presented at the meeting of the American Sociological Association, Atlanta.

Bales, R. F. 1946. "Cultural Differences in Rates of Alcoholism." *Quarterly Journal of Studies on Alcohol*, 6:480–499.

Ball-Rokeach, S. J. 1973. "Values and Violence: A Test of the Subculture of Violence Thesis." *American Sociological Review*, 38:736–749.

Barnett, R. C., L. Biener, and G. K. Baruch, eds. 1987. *Gender and Stress*. New York: Free Press.

Baron, L., and M. A. Straus. 1987. "Four Theories of Rape: A Macrosociological Analysis." *Social Problems*, 34:467–488.

——. 1988. "Cultural and Economic Sources of Homicide in the United States." *Sociological Quarterly*, 29:371–390.

——. 1989. *Four Theories of Rape in American Society*. New Haven: Yale University Press.

Baron, L., M. A. Straus, and D. Jaffee. 1988. "Legitimate Violence, Violent Attitudes, and Rape: A Test of the Cultural Spillover Theory." In *Human Sexual Aggression: Current Perspectives*, edited by R. A. Prentky and V. L. Quinsey. Annals of the New York Academy of Science, vol. 528.

Berkowitz, L. 1962. *Aggression: A Social Psychological Analysis*. New York: McGraw-Hill.

——. 1989. "The Frustration-Aggression Hypothesis: An Examination and Reformulation." *Psychological Bulletin*, 106:59–73.

——. 1993. *Aggression: Its Causes, Consequences, and Control*. New York: McGraw-Hill.

Bieliauskas, L. A. 1982. *Stress and Its Relationship to Health and Illness*. Boulder: Westview Press.

Blau, J. R., and P. M. Blau. 1982. "Metropolitan Structure and Violent Crime." *American Sociological Review*, 47:114–129.

Blau, P., and R. Golden. 1986. "Metropolitan Structure and Criminal Violence." *Sociological Quarterly*, 27:15–26.

Blum, R. 1981. "Violence, Alcohol, and Setting: An Unexplored Nexus." In *Drinking and Crime*, edited by J. Collins. New York: Guilford Press.

Boor, M. 1980. "Relationship between Unemployment Rates and Suicide Rates in Eight Countries." *Psychological Reports*, 47:1095–1101.

Bourque, L. B. 1989. *Defining Rape*. Durham: Duke University Press.

Brenner, M. H. 1973. *Mental Illness and the Economy*. Cambridge: Harvard University Press.

———. 1976. "The Impact of Social and Industrial Changes on Psychopathology: A View of Stress from the Standpoint of Macrosocietal Trends." In *Society, Stress, and Disease*, edited by L. Levi. Oxford: Oxford University Press.

———. 1977. "Health Costs and Benefits of Economic Policy." *International Journal of Health Services*, 7:581–623.

———. 1980. "The Influence of Economic Stress on Criminal Aggression." In *Colloquium on Stress and Crime*, vol. 2, edited by M. Molof. McLean, Va.: Mitre Corp.

Brown, R. M. 1979. "The American Vigilante Tradition." In *Violence in America: Historical and Comparative Perspectives*, edited by H. D. Graham and T. R. Gurr. Beverly Hills: Sage.

Browne, A., and K. Williams. 1989. "Exploring the Effect of Resource Availability and the Likelihood of Female-Perpetrated Homicides." *Law and Society Review*, 23:75–94.

Brunswick, A. F., and P. A. Messeri. 1984. "Origins of Cigarette Smoking in Academic Achievement, Stress and Social Expectations: Does Gender Make a Difference?" *Journal of Early Adolescence*, 4:353–370.

Bureau of the Census. 1984. *County and City Data Book, 1983*. Washington, D.C.: U.S. Government Printing Office.

———. 1986. *State and Metropolitan Area Data Book, 1986*. Washington, D.C.: U.S. Department of Commerce.

———. 1987. *State and Metropolitan Data Book*. Washington, D.C.: U.S. Government Printing Office.

Burke, P. J. 1991. "Identity Processes and Social Stress." *American Sociological Review*, 56:836–847.

Burr, R. G. 1984."Smoking among U.S. Navy Enlisted Men: Some Contributing Factors." *Psychological Reports*, 54:287–294.

Cahalan, D. 1970. *Problem Drinkers*. San Francisco: Josey Bass.

Cannon, W. B. 1963. *Wisdom of the Body*. New York: Norton.

Catalano, R., and C. D. Dooley. 1977. "Economic Predictors of Depressed Mood and Stressful Life Events in a Metropolitan Community." *Journal of Health and Social Behavior*, 18:292–307.

Cavan, R. S. 1928. *Suicide*. Chicago: University of Chicago Press.

Centers for Disease Control. 1984. "Behavioral Risk Factor Surveillance, 1981–1983." *Mortality and Morbidity Weekly Report*, vol. 33, no. 1ss–3ss.

———. 1989a. "Behavioral Risk Factor Surveillance." *Mortality and Morbidity Weekly Report*, vol. 38, July 28.

———. 1989b. "Behavioral Risk Factor Surveillance." *Mortality and Morbidity Weekly Report*, vol. 38, August 18.

Chafetz, M. 1971. Introduction to *First Special Report to the U.S. Congress on Alcohol and Health*. Washington, D.C.: National Institute on Alcohol Abuse and Alcoholism.

Coddington, R. D. 1972. "The Significance and Life Events as Etiological Factors in the Diseases of Children." *Journal of Psychosomatic Research*, 16:7–18.

Colby, J. P., Jr. 1985. *Status Integration and Alcohol Problems in the United States*. Ph.D. diss., University of New Hampshire.

Colby, J. P., Jr., Arnold Linsky, and Murray Straus. 1994. "Social Stress and State-to-State Differences in Smoking and Smoking-Related Mortality in the United States." *Social Science and Medicine*, 38:373–381.

Coleman, D. H., and M. A. Straus. 1983. "Alcohol Abuse and Family Violence." In *Alcohol, Drug Abuse and Aggression,* edited by E. Gottheil, K. A. Druley, T. E. Skolada, and H. M. Waxman. Springfield, Ill.: C. C. Thomas.

Collins, J. J., Jr., ed. 1981. *Drinking and Crime.* New York: Guilford Press.

Collins, R., and S. Coltrane. 1991. *Sociology of Marriage and the Family: Gender, Love, and Property,* 3d ed. Chicago: Nelson-Hall.

Commission on Obscenity and Pornography. 1970. *The Report of the Commission on Obscenity and Pornography.* New York: Bantam.

Conger, R. D., F. O. Lorenz, G. H. Elder, Jr., R. Simons, and X. Ge. 1993. "Husband and Wife Differences in Response to Undesirable Life Events." *Journal of Health and Social Behavior,* 34:71–87.

Conway, T. L., R. R. Vickers, H. W. Ward, and R. H. Rahe. 1981. "Occupational Stress and Variation in Cigarette, Coffee and Alcohol Consumption." *Journal of Health and Social Behavior,* 22:156–165.

Crutchfield, R. D., M. R. Geerken, and W. R. Gove. 1982. "Crime Rate and Social Integration: The Impact of Metropolitan Mobility." *Criminology,* 20:467–478.

Curtis, L. A. 1975. *Violence, Race, and Culture.* Lexington, Mass.: Lexington Books.

Davis, K. E., and G. N. Braucht. 1973. "Exposure to Pornography, Character, and Sexual Deviance: A Retrospective Survey." *Journal of Social Issues,* 29:3, 183–196.

DeFronzo, J. 1983. "Economic Assistance to Impoverished Americans: Relationship to Incidence of Crime." *Criminology,* 21:119–136.

Distilled Spirits Council. 1983. *Summary of State Laws and Regulations Relating to Distilled Spirits.* Washington, D.C.: Distilled Spirits Council.

Dixon, J., and A. Lizotte. 1987. "Gun Ownership and the Southern Subculture of Violence." *American Journal of Sociology,* 93:383–405.

Dodge, D. L., and W. T. Martin. 1970. *Social Stress and Chronic Illness: Mortality Patterns in Industrial Society.* Notre Dame: University of Notre Dame Press.

Dohrenwend, B. S., and B. P. Dohrenwend, eds. 1974. *Stressful Life Events: Their Nature and Effects.* New York: Wiley.

——. 1981. *Stressful Life Events and Their Contexts.* New York: Wiley.

Dohrenwend, B. S., L. Kranoff, A. R. Askenasy, and B. P. Dohrenwend. 1978. "Exemplification of a Method for Scaling Life Events: The PERI Life Events Scale. *Journal of Health and Social Behavior,* 19:205–229.

Dollard, J., L. W. Doob, N. E. Mowrer, and R. R. Sears. 1939. *Frustration and Aggression.* New Haven: Yale University Press.

Donnerstein, E. 1984. "Pornography: Its Effect on Violence against Women." In *Pornography and Sexual Aggression,* edited by N. M. Malamuth and E. Donnerstein. New York: Academic Press.

Durkheim, E. [1897] 1951. *Suicide: A Study in Sociology.* Translated by J. A. Spaulding and G. Simpson, with an introduction by G. Simpson. New York: Free Press.

——. [1912] 1954. *The Elementary Forms of Religious Life.* Glencoe, Ill.: Free Press.

Eaton, J. W., and R. J. Weil. 1955. *Culture and Mental Disorders.* Glencoe, Ill.: Free Press.

Elliott, G. R., and C. Eisdorfer, eds. 1982. *Stress and Human Health: Analysis and Implications of Research.* New York: Springer.

Ensel, W. E., and N. Lin. 1991. "The Life-Stress Paradigm and Psychological Distress." *Journal of Health and Social Behavior,* 32:321–341.

Erikson, K. T. 1966. *Wayward Puritans: A Study in the Sociology of Deviance.* New York: Wiley.

Erlanger, H. S. 1975. "Is There a Subculture of Violence in the South?" *Journal of Criminal Law and Criminology,* 66:483–490.

Faris, R. E. L. 1955. *Social Disorganization.* 2d ed. New York: Ronald Press.

Farrington, K. 1980. "Stress and Family Violence." In *The Social Causes of Husband-Wife Violence,* edited by M. A. Straus and G. T. Hotaling. Minneapolis: University of Minnesota Press.

——. 1986. "The Application of Stress Theory to the Study of Family Violence: Principles,

Problems and Prospects." *Journal of Family Violence,* 1:131–147.

Fenwick, R., and M. Tausig. 1990. "The Political Economy of Stress." Third International Conference on Social Stress Research, London.

Fuchs, V. R. 1974. *Who Shall Live?* New York: Basic.

Gallup, G. 1978. "More Americans Drink and They're Drinking More." *Boston Globe,* July 2, C1.

Gastil, R. D. 1971. "Homicide and a Regional Culture of Violence." *American Sociological Review,* 36:412–427.

Gelles, R. J., and M. A. Straus. 1979. "Determinants of Violence in the Family: Toward a Theoretical Integration." In *Contemporary Theories about the Family,* edited by W. R. Burr, R. Hill, F. I. Nye, and I. L. Reiss. New York: Free Press.

———. 1988. *Intimate Violence.* New York: Simon and Schuster.

Gerard, C. 1993. "Age, Gender and Suicide: A Cross-National Analysis." *American Sociological Review,* 58:553–574.

Gersten, J. C., T. S. Langner, J. G. Eisenberg, and L. Orzek. 1974. "Child Behavior and Life Events: Undesirable Change or Change Per Se." In *Stressful Life Events: Their Nature and Effects,* edited by B. S. Dohrenwend and B. P. Dohrenwend. New York: Wiley.

Gibbs, J. P., and W. T. Martin. 1964. *Status Integration and Suicide: A Sociological Study.* Eugene: University of Oregon.

Glaser, D. 1971. "Frontiers and the Ecology of Deviance." In *Social Deviance,* chap. 2. Chicago: Markham.

Globetti, G. 1978. "Prohibition Norms and Teenage Drinking." In *Drinking: Alcohol in American Society,* edited by J. Ewing and B. Rouse. Chicago: Nelson-Hall.

Goldstein, M. C., H. S. Kant, and J. J. Hartman. 1974. *Pornography and Sexual Deviance.* Berkeley: University of California Press.

Gore, S. 1978 "The Effects of Social Support in Moderating the Health Consequences of Unemployment." *Journal of Health and Social Behavior,* 19:157–165.

Gore, S., and M. E. Colten. 1991. "Gender, Stress and Distress: Social-Relational Influences." In *The Social Contex of Coping,* edited by J. Eckenrode. New York: Plenum Press.

Gottman, J. M. 1979. *Marital Interaction: Experimental Investigations.* New York: Academic Press.

Gove, W. R., M. Hughes, and M. Geerken. 1985. "Are Uniform Crime Reports a Valid Indicator of the Index Crimes? An Affirmative Answer with Minor Qualifications." *Criminology,* 23:451–491.

Gusfield, J. R. 1963. *Symbolic Crusade: Status Politics and the American Temperance Movement.* Urbana: University of Illinois Press.

Hackney, S. 1969. "Southern Violence." *American Historical Review,* 74:906–925.

Harlow, L. L., M. D. Newcomb, and P. M. Bentler. 1986. "Depression, Self-Derogation, Substance Use and Suicide Ideation: Lack of Purpose in Life as a Mediational Factor." *Journal of Clinical Psychology,* 42:5–21.

Hatch, M. C., S. Wallenstein, J. Beyea, J. W. Nieves, and M. Susser. 1991. "Cancer Rates after the Three Mile Island Nuclear Accident and Proximity of Residence to the Plant." *American Journal of Public Health,* 81:719–723.

Henry, A. F., and J. F. Short. 1954. *Suicide and Homicide.* Glencoe, Ill: Free Press.

Hindelang, M. J. 1974. "The Uniform Crime Reports Revisited." *Journal of Criminal Justice,* 2:1–17.

Hirschi, T. 1969. *Causes of Delinquency.* Berkeley: University of California Press.

Hirschi, T., and R. Stark. 1969. "Hellfire and Delinquency." *Social Problems,* 17:202–213.

Holmes, T. H., and M. Masuda. 1974. "Life Change and Illness Susceptibility." In *Stressful Life Events: Their Nature and Effects,* edited by B. S. Dohrenwend and B. P. Dohrenwend. New York: Wiley.

Holmes, T. H., and R. H. Rahe. 1967. "The Social Readjustment Rating Scale." *Journal of Psychosomatic Research,* 2:213–218.

Hovland, C., and R. Sears. 1940. "Minor Studies in Aggression: VI. Correlation of Lynchings with Economic Indexes." *Journal of Psychology,* 9:301–310.

Huff-Corzine, L., J. Corzine, and D. Moore. 1986. "Southern Exposure: Deciphering the South's Influence on Homicide Rates." *Social Forces,* 64:906–924.

Humphrey, J. A., and S. Palmer. 1986. "Stressful Life Events and Criminal Homicide." *Omega,* 17:299–308.

Hyman, M. M., M. A. Zimmermann, C. Gurioli, and A. Helrich. 1980. *Drinkers, Drinking and Alcohol-Related Mortality and Hospitalizations.* New Brunswick: Rutgers Center for Alcohol Studies.

Janerich, D. T. 1991. "Can Stress Cause Cancer?" *American Journal of Public Health,* 81: 687–688.

Johnson, D., P. Picard, and B. Quinn, eds. 1984. *Churches and Church Membership in the United States.* Washington, D.C.: Glenmary Research Center.

Kantor, G., and M. A. Straus. 1987. "The Drunken Bum Theory of Wife Beating." *Social Problems,* 34:213–226.

Kaplan, H. B., ed. 1983. *Psychosocial Stress: Trends in Theory and Research.* New York: Academic Press.

Keith, C. 1990. "Disturbances of Conduct Following Stress." In *Stressors and Adjustment Disorders,* edited by K. D. Noshpitz and R. D. Coddington. New York: Wiley.

Kessler, R. C., and J. D. MacLeod. 1984. "Sex Differences in Vulnerability to Undesirable Life Events." *American Sociological Review,* 49:620–631.

Klein, H. 1991. "Cultural Determinants of Alcohol Use in the United States." In *Society Culture and Drinking Patterns Reexamined,* edited by D. J. Pittman and H. R. White. New Brunswick: Rutgers Center for Alcohol Studies.

Kobrin, F. E., and G. E. Hendershot. 1977. "Do Family Ties Reduce Mortality? Evidence from the United States, 1966–68." *Journal of Marriage and the Family,* 33:373–377.

Kovacs, M., A. T. Beck, and A. Weissman. 1975. "Hopelessness: An Indicator of Suicidal Risk." *Suicide,* 5:98–103.

Lafferty, N. A., J. Holden, and E. Klein. 1980. "Norm Qualities and Alcoholism." *International Journal of Social Psychiatry,* 26: 159–165.

Landau, S. F. 1984. "Trends in Violence and Aggression: A Cross-Cultural Analysis." *International Journal of Comparative Sociology,* 25:133–158.

——. 1988. "The Relationship between Objective and Subjective Social Stress Indicators: Some Israelli Findings." *European Sociological Review,* 4:In Press.

——. 1989. "The Effect of Objective Social Stress Factors on Subjective Perception of Well-Being and Social Solidarity: The Israeli Case." *Human Relations,* 42:487–508.

Landau, S. F., and A. Raveh. 1987. "Stress Factors, Social Support, and Violence in Israeli Society: A Quantitative Analysis." *Aggressive Behavior,* 13:67–85.

Landau, S. F., and G. Rahav. 1989. "Suicide and Attempted Suicide: Their Relation to Subjective Stress Indicators." *Genetic, Social and General Psychology Monographs,* 115:273–294.

Lang, A. R., D. J. Gaeskner, V. J. Adesso, and G. A. Marlott. 1975. "Effects of Alcohol on Aggression in Male Social Drinkers." *Journal of Abnormal Psychology,* 84:508–518.

Larsen, D., and B. Abu-Laban. 1968. "Norm Qualities and Deviant Drinking Behavior." *Social Problems,* 15:41–450.

Lazarus, R. S. 1966. *Psychological Stress and the Coping Process.* New York: McGraw-Hill.

Lazarus, R. S., and S. Folkman. 1984. *Stress, Appraisal and Coping.* New York: Springer.

Lennon, M. C., and S. Rosenfield. 1992. "Women and Mental Health: The Interaction of Job and Family Conditions." *Journal of Health and Social Behavior,* 33:316–327.

Levi, L., ed. 1976. *Society, Stress and Disease.* Oxford: Oxford University Press.

Lin, N., W. M. Ensel, R. S. Simeone, and W. Kuo. 1979. "Social Support, Stressful Life Events and Illness: A Model and Empirical Test." *Journal of Health and Social Behavior,* 20:108–119.

Lindenthal, J. J., J. K. Myers, and J. P. Pepper. 1972. "Smoking, Psychological Status and

Stress." *Social Science and Medicine,* 6:583–591.

Linsky, A. S. 1965. "Religious Differences in Lay Attitudes and Knowledge on Alcoholism and Its Treatment." *Journal for the Scientific Study of Religion,* 5:41–50.

———. 1969. "Community Structure and Depressive Disorders." *Social Problems,* 17:120–131.

Linsky, A. S., R. Bachman-Prehn, and M. A. Straus. 1989. "Objective and Subjective Stress and the Suicide Continuum." Paper presented at the meeting of the American Sociological Association, San Francisco.

Linsky, A. S., J. P. Colby, and M. A. Straus. 1986a. "Drinking Norms and Alcohol-Related Problems in the United States." *Journal for the Study of Alcohol,* 47:384–393.

———. 1986b. "Social Stress, Smoking Behavior and Respiratory Cancer: A Macro-Social Analysis." Paper presented at the Second National Conference on Social Stress Research, Durham: University of New Hampshire.

———. 1987. "Social Stress, Normative Constraints, and Alcohol Problems in American States." *Social Science and Medicine,* 24:875–883.

Linsky, A. S., and M. A. Straus. 1981. "Social Stress in the United States: Some Preliminary Findings." Paper presented at the annual meeting of the Society for the Study of Social Problems, Toronto.

———. 1986. *Social Stress in the United States: Links to Regional Patterns in Crime and Illness.* Dover, Mass.: Auburn House.

Linsky, A. S., M. A. Straus, and R. Bachman-Prehn. 1988a. "Social Stress, Legitimate Violence, and Gun Availability: Links to Weapon-Specific Homicides." Paper presented at the annual meeting of the Society for the Study of Social Problems, Atlanta.

———. 1988b. "Cultural Context, Social Stress and the Drinking Violence Connection." Paper presented at the Tenth Congress of the International Society of Criminology, Hamburg, Germany.

Linsky, A. S., M. A. Straus, and J. P. Colby. 1985. "Stressful Events, Stressful Conditions, and Alcohol Problems in the United States: A Partial Test of the Bales' Theory of Alcoholism." *Journal of Studies on Alcohol,* 46:72–80.

Loftin, C., and R. H. Hill. 1974. "Regional Subculture and Homicide: An Examination of the Gastil-Hackney Thesis." *American Sociological Review,* 39:714–724.

MacAndrew, C., and R. B. Edgerton. 1969. *Drunken Comportment.* Chicago: Aldine.

Markle, G. E., and R. J. Troyer. 1979. "Smoke Gets in Your Eyes: Cigarette Smoking as Deviant Behavior." *Social Problems,* 26:611–625.

Masuda, M., D. L. Cutler, L. Hein, and T. H. Holmes. 1978. "Life Events and Prisoners." *Psychosomatic Medicine,* 40:236–261.

Masuda, M., and T. H. Holmes. 1978. "Life Events: Perceptions and Frequencies." *Psychosomatic Medicine,* 40:236–261.

Mathews, K. A., and D. C. Glass. 1981. "Type-A Behavior, Stressful Life Events and Coronary Heart Disease." In *Stressful Life Events and Their Contexts,* edited by B. S. Dohrenwend and B. P. Dohrenwend. New York: Prodist.

Mawson, A. 1987. *Transient Criminality: A Model of Stress-Induced Crime.* New York: Praeger.

Mechanic, D. 1976. "Stress, Illness and Illness Behavior." *Journal of Human Stress,* 2:2–6.

Menzel, H. 1950. "Comments on Robinson's Ecological Correlations and the Behavior of Individuals." *American Sociological Review,* 15:674.

Merton, R. S. 1957. *Social Theory and Social Structure,* rev. ed. Glencoe, Ill: Free Press.

Messner, S. F. 1983. "Regional and Racial Effects on the Urban Homicide Rate: The Subculture of Violence Revisited." *American Journal of Sociology,* 88:997–1007.

Mizruchi, E. H., and R. Perrucci. 1962. "Norm Qualities and Differential Effects of Deviant Behavior: An Exploratory Analysis." *American Social Review,* 27:391–399.

Molof, M. J., ed. 1980. *Colloquium on Stress and Crime,* vol. 2. McLean, Va.: Mitre Corp.

Mueller, C. W. 1983. "Environmental Stressors and Aggressive Behavior." In *Aggression:*

Theoretical and Empirical Reviews, vol. 2, edited by R. G. Green and E. I. Donnerstein. New York: Academic Press.

National Office of Vital Statistics. 1977. *Vital Statistics of the United States, 1975–77*. Washington, D.C.: U.S. Government Printing Office.

National Office of Vital Statistics. 1985. *Vital Statistics of the United States, 1983*. Washington, D.C.: U.S. Government Printing Office.

Newton, G. D., and F. E. Zimring. 1969. *Firearms and Violence in American Life: A Staff Report to the National Commission on the Causes and Prevention of Violence*. Washington D.C.: U.S. Government Printing Office.

Nicholls, L. L. 1976. "Tourism and Crime." *Annals of Tourism Research*, 3:176–182.

O'Connor, J. F., and A. J. Lizotte. 1978. "The Southern Subculture of Violence Thesis and Patterns of Gun Ownership." *Social Problems*, 25:420–429.

Ost, J., and M. A. Straus. 1980. "The Medical Affluence Index: A New Tool for Research in Medical Sociology." Paper presented at the second conference on Clinical Applications of the Social Sciences to Health, University of Illinois.

Parker, S., and R. J. Kleiner. 1969. *Mental Illness in the Urban Negro Community: A Pointed Inquiry into Goal-Striving and Stress in a Climate of Limited Opportunity*. New York: Free Press.

Paykel, E. S., B. A. Prusoff, and J. Myers. 1975. "Suicide Attempts and Recent Life Events: A Controlled Comparison." *Archives of General Psychiatry*, 32:327–35.

Paykel, E. S., B. A. Prusoff, and E. H. Uhlenhuth. 1971. "Scaling of Life Events." *Archives of General Psychiatry*, 25:340–347.

Pearce, P. L. 1982. *The Social Psychology of Tourist Behavior*. New York: Pergamon.

Pearlin, L. I., and C. Aneshensel. 1986. "Coping and Social Supports: Their Function and Applications." In *Applications of Social Science to Clinical Medicine and Health*, edited by L. H. Aiken and D. Mechanic. New Brunswick: Rutgers University Press.

Pearlin, L. I., M. A. Lieberman, E. Menaghan, and J. T. Mullan. 1981. "The Stress Process." *Journal of Health and Social Behavior*, 22:337–356.

Petrich, J., and C. Hart. 1980. "Arrest and Life Change Magnitude." In *Colloquium on Stress and Crime*, vol. 2, edited by M. Molof. McLean, Va.: Mitre Corp.

Pittman, D. J. 1967. "International Overtones: Social and Cultural Factors in Drinking Patterns, Pathological and Nonpathological." In *Alcoholism*, edited by D. J. Pittman. New York: Harper and Row.

Plass, P. S., and M. A. Straus. 1987. "Intra-Family Homicide in the United States: Incidence, Trends, and Differences by Region, Race, and Gender." Paper presented at the Third National Family Violence Research Conference, University of New Hampshire, Durham.

Rabkin, J. G., and E. L. Streuning. 1976. "Life Events, Stress and Illness." *Science*, 194:1013–1020.

Raush, H. L., W. A. Barry, R. K. Hertel, and M. A. Swain. 1974. *Communication, Conflict, and Marriage*. San Francisco: Jossey-Bass.

Reckless, W. C. 1973. *The Crime Problem*, 5th ed. Englewood Cliffs, N.J.: Prentice-Hall.

Rhodes, A. L., and A. J. Reiss, Jr. 1970. "The 'Religious Factor' and Delinquent Behavior." *Journal of Research in Crime and Delinquency*, 7:83–98.

Robinson, W. S. 1950. Ecological Correlations and the Behavior of Individuals. *American Sociological Review*, 15:(June)351–357.

Room, R. 1976. "Ambivalence as a Sociological Explanation: The Case of Cultural Explanations of Alcohol Problems." *American Sociological Association*, 41:1047–1065.

——. 1978. "Evaluating the Effects of Drinking Laws on Drinking." In *Drinking: Alcohol in American Society*. edited by J. A. Ewing and B. A. Rouse. Chicago: Nelson-Hall.

Ross, C. E., and J. Mirowski II. 1979. "A Comparison of Life Event Weighting Schemes: Change, Undesirability and Effect-Proportional Indices." *Journal of Health and Social Behavior*, 20:166–177.

Russell, D. E. H. 1975. *The Politics of Rape:*

The Victim's Perspective. New York: Stein and Day.

——. 1984. *Sexual Exploitation: Rape, Child Sexual Abuse, and Workplace Harrassment.* Beverly Hills: Sage.

Schachter, S., B. Silverstein, L. T. Kozlowski, C. P. Herman, and B. Liebling. 1984. "Effects of Stress on Cigarette Smoking and Urinary pH." *Journal of Experimental Psychology: General,* 106:24–30.

Schachter, S., B. Silverstein, and D. Perlick. 1977. "Psychological and Pharmacological Explanations of Smoking under Stress." *Journal of Experimental Psychology: General,* 106:31–40.

Schlesinger, L. B., and E. Revitch. 1980. "Stress, Violence and Crime." In *Handbook on Stress and Anxiety,* edited by I. L. Kutash and L. B. Schlesinger. San Francisco: Jossey-Bass.

Selye, H. 1966. *The Stress of Life.* New York: McGraw-Hill.

——. 1980. "The Stress Concept Today." In *Handbook on Stress and Anxiety,* edited by I. L. Kutash and L. B. Schlesinger. San Francisco: Jossey-Bass.

Shryock, H. S., and J. Siegel. 1976. *Studies in Population: The Methods and Materials of Demography.* New York: Academic Press.

Simon, R. W. 1991. "Parental Role Strains, Salience of Parental Identity, and Gender Differences in Psychological Distress." *Journal of Health and Social Behavior,* 33:25–35.

Skolnick, J. H. 1958. "Religious Affiliations and Drinking Behavior." *Quarterly Journal of Studies on Alcoholism,* 19:452–470.

Smith, M. D., and R. Parker. 1980. "Type of Homicide and Variation in Regional Rates." *Social Forces,* 59:136–147.

Snyder, C. R. 1958. *Alcohol and the Jews: A Cultural Study of Drinking and Sobriety.* Monograph 1. New Brunswick: Rutgers Center of Alcohol Studies.

Sorenson, S. B., J. A. Stein, J. M. Siegel, J. M. Golding, and M. A. Burnam. 1987. "The Prevalence of Adult Sexual Assault: The Los Angeles Epidemiologic Catchment Area Project." *American Journal of Epidemiology,* 126:1154–1164.

Stark, R., D. P. Doyle, and L. Kent. 1980. "Rediscovering Moral Communities: Church Membership and Crime." In *Understanding Crime: Current Theory and Research,* edited by T. Hirschi and M. Gottfredson. Beverly Hills: Sage.

Steinberg, L. D., R. Catalano, and D. Dooley. 1981. "Economic Antecedents of Child Abuse and Neglect." *Child Development,* 52:975–985.

Straus, J., and M. A. Straus. 1953. "Suicide, Homicide and Social Structure in Ceylon." *American Journal of Sociology,* 58:461–69.

Straus, M. A. 1974a. "Leveling, Civility and Violence in the Family." *Journal of Marriage and the Family,* 36:13–29.

——. 1974b. "Leveling, Civility and Marital Violence in a National Sample of American Families." In *Forensic Psychology and Psychiatry,* edited by F. Wright, C. Bahn, and R. W. Rieber. New York: New York Academy of Sciences.

——. 1980a. "The ZP Scale: A Percentaged Z Score Scale." Durham: Family Research Laboratory, University of New Hampshire.

——. 1980b. "Social Stress and Marital Violence in a National Sample of American Families." *Annals of the New York Academy of Sciences,* 347:229–250. Also in *Forensic Psychology and Psychiatry,* edited by F. Wright, C. Bahn, and R. W. Rieber. New York: New York Academy of Sciences.

——. 1980c. "Stress and Child Abuse." In *The Battered Child,* 3d ed., edited by C. H. Kempe and R. F. Helfer. Chicago: University of Chicago Press.

——. 1985a. "The Index of Legitimate Violence." Durham: Family Research Laboratory, University of New Hampshire.

——. 1985b. "The Validity of U.S. States as Units for Sociological Research." Paper presented at the annual meeting of the American Sociological Association, Washington, D.C.

——. 1988. "Primary Group Characteristics and Intra-Family Homicide." Paper presented at the Third National Family Violence Research Conference, University of New Hampshire, Durham.

Straus, M. A., and R. J. Gelles. 1990. *Physical Violence in American Families: Risk Factors and Adaptations to Violence in 8,145 Families.* New Brunswick, N.J.: Transaction Publishers.

Straus, M. A., and G. T. Hotaling, eds. 1980. *The Social Causes of Husband-Wife Violence.* Minneapolis: University of Minnesota Press.

Straus, M. A., and G. Kaufman Kantor. 1987. "Stress and Child Abuse." In *The Battered Child*, 4th ed. edited by R. E. Helfer and R. S. Kempe. Chicago: University of Chicago Press.

Straus, M. A., A. S. Linsky, and R. Bachman-Prehn. 1989. "Change in the Stressfulness of Life in American States and Regions from 1976 to 1982." *Social Indicators Research,* 19:229–257.

Straus, M. A., and K. R. Williams. 1987. "Homicide Victimization and Offense Rates by Age, Gender, Race, Relation of Victim to Offender, Weapon Used, and Circumstances, for the United States, 1976–79 and 1980–84." Typescript.

———. 1988. "Disaggregated Homicide Victimization and Offense Rates for the United States, 1976–79 and 1980–84." Typescript.

Straus, R., and Bacon, S. 1953. *Drinking in College.* New Haven: Yale University Press.

Stull, D. 1975. "Hologeistic Studies of Drinking: A Critique." *Drinking and Drug Practices Surveyor,* 10:4–10.

Sugarman, D. B., and M. A. Straus. 1989. "Gender Equality in American States and Regions." *Social Indicators Research,* 20:229–270.

Tagliacozzo, R., and S. Vaughn. 1982. "Stress and Smoking in Hospital Nurses." *American Journal of Public Health,* 72:441–448.

Thoits, P. 1981. "Undesirable Life Events and Distress." *American Sociological Review,* 46:97–109.

———. 1983a. "Dimensions of Life Events That Influence Psychological Distress: An Evaluation and Synthesis of the Literature." In *Psychosocial Stress: Trends in Theory and Research,* edited by H. Kaplan. New York: Academic Press.

———. 1983b. "Multiple Identities and Psycho-

logical Well-Being." *American Sociological Review,* 48:174–187.

———. 1991. "Gender Differences in Coping with Emotional Distress." In *The Social Context of Coping,* edited by J. Eckenrode. New York: Plenum Press.

Turner, R. J. 1981. "Experienced Social Support as a Contingency in Emotional Well-Being." *Journal of Health and Social Behavior,* 22:357–367.

———. 1983. "Direct, Indirect, and Moderating Effects of Social Support on Psychological Distress and Associated Conditions." In *Psychosocial Stress: Trends in Theory and Research,* edited by H. B. Kaplan. New York: Academic Press.

Turner, R. J., and W. R. Avison. 1992. "Innovations in the Measurement of Stress: Crisis Theory and the Significance of Event Resolution." *Journal of Health and Social Behavior,* 33:36–50.

U.S. Department of Justice. 1981. *Sourcebook of Criminal Justice Statistics.* Washington D.C.: Bureau of Justice Statistics.

———. 1985a. *Uniform Crime Reports: Crime in the United States.* Washington, D.C.: U.S. Government Printing Office.

———. 1985b. *Sourcebook of Criminal Justice Statistics, 1984.* Washington, D.C.: U.S. Government Printing Office.

Ullman, A. D. 1968. "Sociocultural Backgrounds of Alcoholism." *The Annals of the American Academy of Political and Social Science,* 135:48–54.

Umberson, D., C. B. Wortman, and R. C. Kessler. 1992. "Widowhood and Depression: Explaining Long-Term Gender Differences in Vulnerability." *Journal of Health and Social Behavior,* 33:10–24.

Warheit, G. J. 1979. "Life Events, Coping, Stress and Depression Symptomatology." *American Journal of Psychiatry,* 136:502–511.

Wheaton, B. 1985. "Models for the Stress-Buffering Functions of Coping Resources." *Journal of Health and Social Behavior,* 26:352–364.

Whitehead, P. C., and C. Harvey. 1974. "Explaining Alcoholism: An Empirical Test and

Reformulation." *Journal of Health and Social Behavior,* 15:57–65.

Wilkins, L. 1980. "Remarks." In *Colloquium on Stress and Crime,* vol. 1, edited by M. J. Molof. McLean, Va.: Mitre Corp.

Wilkinson, K. P. 1984. "A Research Note on Homicide and Rurality." *Social Forces,* 10:25–51.

Williams, K. R. 1984. "Economic Sources of Homicide: Reestimating the Effects of Poverty and Inequality." *American Sociological Review,* 49:283–289.

Williams, K., and R. Flewelling. 1987. "Family, Acquaintance and Stranger Homicide: Alternative Procedures for Rate Calculations." *Criminology,* 25:543–560.

——. 1988. "The Social Production of Criminal Homicide: A Comparative Study of Disaggregated Rates in American Cities." *American Sociological Review,* 53:421–431.

Wolfgang, M., and F. Ferracuti. 1967. *The Subculture of Violence: Toward an Integrated Theory in Criminology.* London: Tavistock.

Wright, J. D., P. H. Rossi, and K. Daly. 1983. *Under the Gun: Weapons, Crimes, and Violence in America.* New York: Aldine.

Yllo, K., and M. A. Straus. 1984. "The Impact of Structural Inequality and Sexist Family Norms on Rates of Wife-Beating." *International Journal of Comparative Social Welfare,* 1:16–29.

INDEX

Abu-Laban, B., 55
Acquaintance homicide, 126
African-Americans: homicide and, 124–126; lynching of, 14; weapon-specific homicide and, 134–136
Aggression: individual-level *vs.* social system–level analysis, 9–11; research on, 8–9; social stress and, 10–11, 157–161; theories of, 7–8. *See also under specific forms, e.g.,* Homicide, Violence, *etc.*
Alcoholism: ambivalence hypothesis of, 64–65; Bales's theory of, 54–55, 61, 67–69; disinhibition theory and, 163; indicators of, 17, 59; inoculation hypothesis of, 64–65; in Ireland, 13; normative controls and, 61–63; in preliterate societies, 56; Restrictive Alcohol Norms, Index of, 56–59, 62–63, 103; social-control approach to, 64; stress and, 59–61, 159; in United States, 13–14
Ambivalence hypothesis of alcoholism, 64–65
Aneshensel, C. S., 80
Anomie theory of deviant behavior, 8, 157, 171

Bacon, S., 64
Bales, R. F., 54–55, 61, 67–69, 101
Baron, L., 104–105, 119, 121
Behavioral Risk Factor Surveys, 43, 65–66
Berkowitz, L., 14, 144–145
Blum, R., 100
Blunt instruments, homicide rates by, 136
Brenner, M. H., 10
Burr, R. G., 42

Cancer. *See* Lung cancer
Catalano, R., 9
Change in social stress, 37–38: events approach, 35–36; frequency approach, 36–37; historical context of, 24–26; methodological issues, 35–37; at national level, 26–29; percentage of, 33–35; ranking of states and regions, 30–33; at regional level, 29–35; scoring method, 33n3
Chronic obstructive pulmonary disease, 45–47
Chronic stress, 169–171
Chronic Stress Index, 169–170
Church membership, homicide and, 121
Cognitive model of stress, 79
Comparative Homicide File, 83–85
Control theory of homicide, 116–117, 121–122
Conway, T. L., 42
Coping with changes, stressfulness of, 5
Cotton price, lynching of African-Americans and, 14
Cultural context: of rape, 144–145, 152–153, 163–164; of social stress, 11–14; of stress, 5–6; of violence, 104, 106–111, 145
Cultural theory of homicide, 115
Cultural-spillover theory of violence, 145

Daly, K., 141
Depression, in Hutterites, 12
Deviant behavior, anomie theory of, 8
Disease, stress and, 41–42
Disinhibition theory, 163
Divorce, homicide and, 123

First published 2009 AD
© Angela Moore 2009 AD

Published by The Squeeze Press.
8A Market Place, Glastonbury, Somerset

British Library Cataloguing in Publication Data
Moore, A.
In Love With Venus

A CIP catalogue record for this beautiful book
is available from the British Library.

ISBN10   1 906069 02 6
ISBN13   978 1 906069 02 5

Printed on Forestry Stewardship Council approved
paper from sustainably managed forests.

Printed and bound in Great Britain
by Henry Ling Ltd.
Dorset, UK.

the
SQUEEZE
PRESS

in love with
Venus

★

a touch of astronomy
can change your life forever

ANGELA MOORE

to the Lover
in all of us

Special thanks to Nick Kollerstrom for his
enormous help with this book, also to Suzi Steer,
John Martineau, Alex Trenoweth (for help with
Chapter 8), Keith Critchlow, Robin Heath,
Scott Olsen, Jake Ewen, Michael Schneider,
Matt Tweed, Geoff Stray, Daud Sutton, Stephen
Parsons, Usama Shehadeh and Ian Roskruge.

Copyright owners - thanks for your kindnesses.
Venuses overleaf and on pg 88 by Burne Jones.
Venus on page 68 by Bougereau.

It's time the secret is out!

Chapter 1

Her Perfect Motion

here is one planet which weaves out its dance around us in perfect beauty, harmony and proportion. Understanding its motions can change your perception of the universe. This most beautiful secret of our solar system is sometimes overlooked by astronomers. They can be so keen on their high-tech gear, their hard facts and their distant objects that they are often impervious to the marvelous significance of beautiful things really close to them. In this book we will be exploring something a bit more permanent, which can reveal something good and true about the kind of world we live in. Modern astronomy is largely fascinated with things which are invisible to the naked eye, objects which only ultra-powerful telescopes can discern. The journey you are about to take, however, is more old-fashioned.

For a start it is *sensible* astronomy, it concerns the way things look like from here, as perceived by our senses, and secondly it deals with what astronomy used to be about: ideas of beauty, proportion and harmony. Ideas perfectly expressed by Venus!

In these pages we will meet the Greek idea of *Cosmos*, a proportion in the total scale of things; an affirmation that the totality, the whole, *has beauty*. Before the fifth century BCE the Greek word *Kosmos* meant 'adornment' or 'pretty', as in lipstick being 'cosmetic' - it's actually the same word. We are going to try to re-access that ancient meaning by looking at the perfect pattern that one planet weaves around us.

The word *'universe'*, or uni-verse means 'turning as one,' but Venus draws attention to herself in a unique way. She, alone in the solar system, spins on her own axis in the opposite rotation to all the other planets. Everything else in the solar system moves and spins 'uni-verse,' turning-as-one, except for Venus! Perhaps we should con-verse a little on this subject (Latin *verso*, to turn).

The planets all travel the same way around the Sun in their orbits, and they all revolve, or spin on their own axes, in the same direction too. All except Venus, who spins the other way as she goes (see the diagram opposite), and, as we shall see, thus setting

up graceful patterns in space and time that are both musical and geometrical in their essence.

You may not realise it but the way you perceive the cosmos greatly affects your outlook on love, life and happiness. If you believe the universe and our solar system are essentially random, you will tend to see life in that way too. Tuning into the beauty that is going on all around you can awaken you to a higher order, give you an anchor to a certainty of amazing wonder, and effect subtle alignments in your psyche which can literally change your life.

It's time to throw away the stale old bread we've all been feeding on and try on some new ideas. It will be challenging at times, but fun at others, and well worth the effort.

Portia, in Shakespeare's *The Merchant of Venice* says:

"The man that hath no music in himself, Nor is not mov'd with concord of sweet sounds, Is fit for treasons, stratagems and spoils; The motions of his spirit are dull as night, And his affections dark as Erebus: Let no such man be trusted."

Some astronomers could mull over this stern judgment. Scientists study complex systems - so here's another one. Let's try to understand that beauty and proportion can be, just occasionally, part of the design of things. I know what some experts say, that the surface of Venus resembles a tortured, hellish landscape, with acid rain and bone-crushing pressure. Well maybe, but let's begin with what's visible, shall we? Science, *scientia*, means 'knowledge', and in this book we are going to look at what we know about the patterns in space and time made by our neighbours in the solar system, beautiful and lovely harmonies and proportions which Venus manifests more perfectly than any other planet.

Nowadays, as the night skies fade from our view due to light-pollution, little more than the Moon, Plough, Venus and Jupiter remain visible to most of us, so many people are emotionally starved of the *meaning* of the night sky. Bright lights accompany us until bed-time, so the rods in our eyes hardly get used (these are the parts of the retina used for night vision, and they adapt, if you give them half an hour, to the silvery tones of a moonlight scene, our own hi-biotech night vision). We were never meant to live like this and we can't honestly hope to find satisfaction in it. Let's start by trying to honour the planet Venus, as she appears in the night sky - swinging between her magnificent dualities of *Hesperus* the Evening Star and *Lucifer* the Morning Star, the one which dies down into the sunset at dusk in the East and the other (for the early-riser) arising boldly before dawn in the West.

In June 2004 there was a transit of Venus (when Venus passed over the face of the Sun). It was an event that no person then living had ever seen. It fell on a specific date and zodiac degree (see Appendix 1, p121), and, get this, both four years earlier and four years later, Venus had and will have the *same* zodiac degree on the *same* date. In fact, in *four* years Venus conjuncts the Sun *five* times, alternating in front and behind. Er, how does that happen? Some African polyrhythms can help, or try some music in 5:4 time to put you in the mood, Dave Brubeck's 'Take Five,' or the 3rd movement of Tchaikovsky's *Pathetique* symphony.

Venus tablets from almost four thousand years ago (*opposite*)

7

honour its ten appearances and disappearances per eight years, one of the first calendrical experiences of the human race. Can you see how the 5:4 rhythm echoes in that pattern? These tablets were found in Chaldea (Iraq) and are one of the earliest astronomical texts - before that there were just eclipse records and omen texts. They were inscribed centuries before any twelvefold division of the heavens appeared in Greece or Babylon. Chapter 10 looks at this.

There will be a few surprises in this text, perhaps new harmonies you haven't heard of before. Women are often judged by their proportions, and it's time to realise that the planet associated with love and beauty, our closest neighbour, our planetary partner, manifests such overwhelmingly, gorgeous, jaw-droppingly beautiful proportions that you can't help but be in love with her.

Every year books are published about "The Big Secret", "The Insights of the Cult of X", "The Lost Papers of Hubris", "The Key to Everlasting Happiness" and so on. But actually the biggest secret of all is very simple. It's Venus, Love and Beauty manifest, Goddess of Love. She's the Key, and in these pages you are going to learn about her and realise that you should have been told long ago.

If you haven't heard much about any of this before, it's partly because the rotation rates of Mercury and Venus (their spins on their own axes) were only discovered in the 1960s, so astronomers haven't had long to chew it over. But, there's more to it than that: they don't seem to be really interested. Planets are singing and dancing together in beautifully proportioned patterns to primal geometries and harmonies, but few scientists can tell you about it, because most don't even know. There's no programme on television, and no-one to talk with about it. Perhaps it's because there's no explanation, or possibly even because it can be intense being in love. Love changes everything. And falling in love with Venus can change your life.

In more superstitious times it used to be considered unlucky to dance around 'widdershins,' anticlockwise, the way the solar system actually revolves, uni-verse, turning-as-one. Find a friend and turn round with them, *con-verse*, turn together, perhaps as our Moon revolves, facing ever earthwards, holding hands and spinning round, or try both turning on the spot. Now try doing both at once. As the conversation grows so it can deepen.

Astronomy today is all big bangs, star factories, meteors, extreme events and black holes. Where's the magic gone? Has everyone forgotten the harmony of the spheres? The food of love?

Planets can make love too!

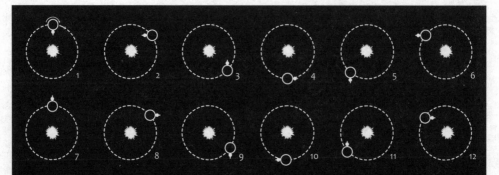

We have drawn a bobble on the surface of Mercury.
In 1 the bobble is pointing towards the Sun. Midday for the bobble on Mercury.
One Mercury day (whole sequence) is equal to two of its years (1-7 and 7 on to 1),
during which time it rotates on its own axis three times (1-5, 5-9 and 9 on to 1).
Try it with a teacup at home!

Chapter 2

The Merry Waltz of Mercury

*I*t's hard to know where to begin, but let's start with the first planet: Mercury; and some first principles. Also the first numbers, 1, 2 and 3. For Mercury manifests the most simple harmonies possible. While Venus' motion is like a grand symphony, where we can only hope to experience one part or another at a time, little Mercury performs a simple and merry 1-2-3 waltz all by itself. Let's assume that you are refusing point-blank to believe anything about harmony and proportion in the solar system. See if Mercury can initiate you, Mercury the magician, the trickster.

Imagine living on a planet where the stars all go round exactly three times in the sky, every day ... and the Sun passes through the stars exactly twice, in the same day. *Mercury spins three times on its axis in two of its years, in one Mercury day.* This is rather mind-wrenching, so look at the step by step examples opposite, practice with some teacups and give yourself a year or so to mull it over - seriously.

Way back in the 1950s it was all so simple: Isaac Asimov wrote his classic *I, Robot* about a bunch of robots that went to Mercury. The first planet was permanently locked into facing ever sunward (scientists all agreed). The robots in the story noted how Mercury's 'terminator,' the day/night boundary, was forever fixed upon its surface. This was because whenever astronomers looked at Mercury's surface through their telescopes (which they could only do in one part of its orbit when furthest from the Sun) they always saw the same side facing them. Mercury had them well tricked.

There are three key time measurements we need to introduce here: *day, year* and *axial rotation period*. This is a kind of dry run for when we come to Venus, where things get more complicated. Don't worry! It won't hurt a bit.

For us on Earth, the axial rotation period, or the time it takes for a star to rise again, is called the *sidereal day* - think of it as a *star-day*. It more or less coincides with our *sun-day*, or day, the time it takes for the Sun to be due south again, only less a few minutes. Our *year* is how long it takes to go round the Sun.

You can see that Mercurius has done very well indeed to cleverly come up with its beautiful threefold harmony, 3:1, between its rotation against the stars and its rotation against the Sun. But

Mercury has some other incredible tricks up its sleeve, tricks stranger than fiction.

On Mercury, Asimov's robots would have witnessed a weirder and far more wondrous and beautiful pattern than they ever expected: Standing on the surface of Mercury they would have seen the Sun rise, then climb up into the meridian, stop, turn back, set, then rise again before tracking right across the sky. Mercury's rock-and-roll sunrise! The reason for this is Mercury's highly elliptical orbit and the considerable acceleration it experiences in its orbit when it is closer to the Sun, when it moves much faster.

The same face of Mercury always faces sunward every alternate perihelion (when it is nearest to the Sun, from *peri*, near and *Helios*, Sun). It is thereby manifesting an incredibly strange relation to the Sun, nothing like what scientists had surmised, much more like a dance. If that wasn't enough, it also subtly manages to point Earthwards at key moments, so that when it is briefly visible to Earth it is usually manifesting the same side or face to human telescopes. You can see here that the celestial dance of tiny Mercury is one of interconnection and linkage, as it relates to both Sun and Earth. This makes certain astronomers very uncomfortable.

So, why don't astronomy books tend to mention the

lovely and charming 1-2-3 dance with which tiny Mercury goes a-whirling round the Sun? It's simple, beautiful and harmonic. You would have thought it would be taught in school as an example of beauty in the universe. But, like most of what you are going to read in this book, it's not. You can barely find a mention of it anywhere. Why not? Perhaps it's because the reason it happens is not understood, and simple things which look easy and are not understood can make scientists look a little silly. And we can't have that can we, so perhaps it's better not to mention them.

Let's turn now to an Earth-centred diagram by geometer and architect Keith Critchlow showing how Mercury's three 'loops' in the sky form a triangle. One should not start something, say astrologers, when Mercury is 'retrograde.' Well the loops in this figure show how it does this three times in a year. By 'retrograde' we just mean moving backwards against the stars, as seen from Earth, for a while.

The diagram is a view from above that shows several retrograde loops, which occur during its 'inferior conjunctions' with the Sun. We'll meet inferior conjunctions later on. These important events happen when Mercury or Venus are situated between us and the Sun, also the time when they come closest to Earth.

Mercury and Venus's mean orbits are accurately defined every time

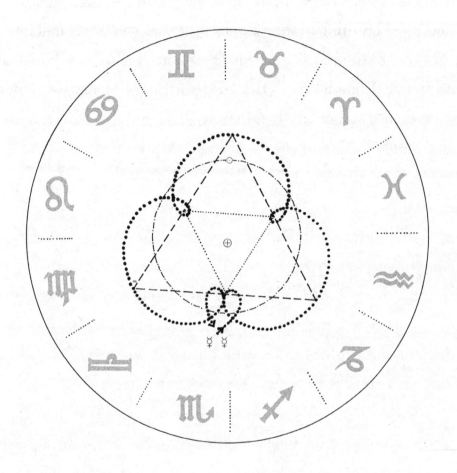

you push three coins together. See John Martineau's diagram below which fits to 99.9%. A 'mean' orbit is a kind of average. Imagine a planet's wobbly orbit creating a thick spherical 'shell' over millions of years - the mean orbit is the simple version, shell reduced to circle. This simple diagram echoes the 1-2-3 rhythm of Mercury's motion, but exists in space, rather than in time.

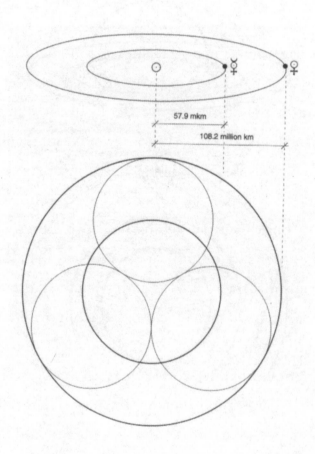

57.9 mkm

108.2 million km

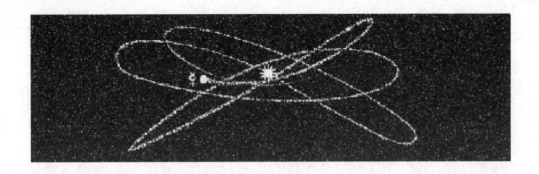

Now let's move to an image (*above*) that looks completely different, a diagram inspired by Steiner astronomer Joachim Schultz. It shows Mercury's precise motion over a year (as seen from Earth looking towards the Sun). Mercury looks like it is buzzing around the Sun like a demented bee. I mean, where is it going?

By now you are probably feeling confused, because of the several different points of view that we have taken. We started off from a robot on Mercury watching its sunrise, then we computed the key ratios, then looked at the loops of its retrograde motion, and now have seen what the view of its path from the Earth would be like if we could see it moving about close to the Sun (which we can't). Is your brain stretching nicely? Good. Cosmology does involve us in taking different viewpoints, and there is no one correct view. What matters here, what is important, are the perfect harmonies.

'Resonance,' the astronomers say. It's caused by resonance.

Resonance happens when you put a tuning-fork onto a grand piano, and then suddenly hear the note grow louder. It's a transfer of energy between two systems oscillating at the same frequency. But the two systems can also oscillate at simple integer ratios, for example an octave. This is still resonance. So how is this relevant to astronomy? It's relevant because astronomers generally agree that the 'lock' between Mercury's day and its solar orbit in a 2:3 ratio is somehow produced by resonance. They have to agree because there's no other solution in sight.

For ages astronomers said the same thing about the Moon, which keeps its same face forever facing the Earth so that no Earth-bound telescope has ever seen 'the dark side of the Moon'. This is caused by 'resonance,' they explained, adding 'spin-orbit coupling', and what could one say to that? There's probably a bulge on the Moon, and Earth's gravity thereby holds it facing Earthwards. This is important because both Venus and Mercury 'face' earthwards under different conditions, so let's try and get a focus on this.

Luna revolves by herself every twenty-seven days. Her same side always faces us so the Moon's orbit-period and axial rotation are totally synchronised, they are locked in together. Is this due to Earth's gravitational pull upon her? When they went out to visit the Moon in the 1960s, they found that she did indeed have a large bulge, a huge one in fact, but it was on the wrong side - on the far side, away from Earth. Then they discovered that there was some extra-dense something beneath the huge frozen lava seas of Luna that existed only on the Earthward side, no-one knew why, and so the whole argument as to why it faced earthward now came to hinge upon some rather peculiar dense subterranean masses, an arcane secret of Luna's past that no-one was ever likely to de-crypt.

A further problem was that Luna is so far away that she isn't really held by the Earth, instead sojourning round with us like a companion planet, pulled at least twice as strongly by the Sun as by Earth. Anyone wishing to explain why Luna faces earthwards has to begin by assuming that she was once much closer to us, with a stronger gravitational pull.

So we have an explanation vaguely based upon resonance and gravity-theory, and one might well expect it to apply more forcefully to Mercury. If the latter was once semi-molten (so the argument goes) then tides from the Sun's mighty pull would soon have damped out any independent rotation it might have had, to make it end up facing ever Sunwards.

What do you think?

Chapter 3

The Dance of Venus

The most beautiful pattern in the heavens, for anyone living on Earth (so all of us), has to be the double pentagram made by Venus. This is a design woven around Earth by the Goddess of Love, our closest planetary neighbour, and takes the form of a five-fold design danced around us every eight years (or 99 moons).

The double pentagram is formed in space and perfectly proportioned by Venus' meetings with the Sun as she orbits it. In the diagram shown opposite Earth is in the centre. Follow the pattern of positions of Venus and the Sun (V and S), starting at the top where Venus (V1) is behind the Sun (S1) and then see how 292 days later Venus (V2) is in front of the Sun (S2), and then 292 days later is (V3) behind the Sun (S3) again, four fifths of the way around from the last time. And so on.

Venus is furthest from Earth when she is the far side of the Sun (her *superior* conjunctions), and nearest to Earth when she is between Earth and the Sun (her *inferior* conjunctions). Every eight years Venus weaves out a pentagram of superior conjunctions and another pentagram of inferior conjunctions. These two pentagrams are in synch with each other so that whenever Venus is between us and the Sun, closest to the Earth, four years later to the day she will again meet the Sun, on the far side, *at the same point in the zodiac.* The zodiac is punctuated by this fivefold pattern.

Venus alternates in these celestial meetings, inferior and superior, ten per eight years (*shown opposite*). These nice old words actually allude to her going behind the Sun when far away from us (the idea that 'superior' was 'above' the Sun) then coming close and growing brighter as she swings in nearer to become 'inferior'. Slowly these pentagrams in the sky revolve round against the stars, once per twelve centuries. One of them is six times larger than the other, more or less. You may notice that, as we saw with the Mercury-rhythms, astronomy books do not describe this marvellous double-pentagram, and neither does it seem to have been known to the ancients. These new examples of harmony are being discovered in our own lifetime. The table below shows how these two pentagrams pan out in time, to give repeats every four years - *same degree, same day.* So the Venus-pentagrams give four-

Aries	Capricorn	Scorpio	Leo	Gemini
30.3.01	15.1.02	31.10.02	17.8.03	8.6.04
R: 9½°	25°	R: 8°	24°	R,T: 18°
30.3.05	14.1.06	28.10.06	18.8.07	8.6.08
9½°	R: 23½°	4½°	R: 25°	18°

yearly structures in time. How closely in synch are they? Well, in terms of a child's birthday, each four years it gets a 'Venus-return' as one of its 'many happy returns,' i.e., it comes back to the same position in the sky, and by twenty-four years of age this has moved a little out of synch, the 'return' being six degrees away.

For comparison, Luna manages much higher precision. Every nineteen years at your birthday the Sun and Moon arrive in the same position in the zodiac and in the sky as when you were born, and that will keep going right through your life (on

23

your 38th and 57th birthdays). But then, Sol and Luna are more concerned with the measuring of time anyway.

The famous Earth-centred Venus heart-and-rose mandala shown below first appeared in the early 1980s and was produced by home computer programs. Weirdly it seems to have been of little or no interest before computers were able to draw it. The version opposite is Sun-centred, and is created by drawing a straight line every day between the positions of Earth and Venus. These

diagrams work well because Earth and Venus have nearly circular orbits, and thirteen Venusian years is eight Earth years, this rhythm creating the symmetry of the harmonic difference, which is fivefold. Earth comes just three percent closer to the Sun in midwinter than it does in midsummer, and Venus' distance changes even less - it has the most perfectly circular orbit of any in the solar system.

In contrast, the inmost planet, Mercury, has a very elliptical orbit, as does Pluto, the outermost planet. Earth and Venus rejoice

together in their near-perfect circularity, unusual in the solar system. That's why we can broadly ignore the elliptical motions.

If you just saw the Moon's path, it would look like a circle - we only notice it being elliptical because Earth's isn't quite in the centre. Let's call that a fifteen percent eccentricity - the Moon comes fifteen percent closer to us at perigee (*peri* = near, *geo* = earth, near to earth) than apogee (*apo* = far). Earth has three percent - we're that much closer at perihelion than at aphelion. Venus is even less, more like one percent. Neptune's orbit is the only other having a comparable circularity to that of Venus. Why is Venus' orbit so beautifully circular? Nobody really knows.

Isaac Newton saw the nearly-perfect circularity of planetary orbits as evidence of the 'divine arm' that set the whole show a-rolling at the start; otherwise, he said, they would all have highly eccentric orbits like the comets. That is a tempting argument, which has grown a lot stronger since 1997 when astronomers started checking out other solar systems on distant stars. What have they found so far? Mostly large planets with highly eccentric orbits!

Some people wonder whether the neatly set out arrangement of our solar system, i.e., roughly circular orbits nearly in the same plane, might be the result of a creative process involving harmony rather than chaos, proportion rather than chance. It could be that the techniques used to discover distant solar systems only find very wobbly ones. There might be more peaceful solar systems like ours out there, we just can't see them yet. Plato viewed the planets as divine on account of the mathematical beauty of their circular motions, and saw circles as being the most perfect shape.

A recent paper by two British astronomers who checked out resonances in the solar system concluded that there were more there than should exist by chance. A helpful example of resonance occurs between Jupiter and the asteroid belt: mighty Jupiter has caused the asteroids to concentrate in certain orbit-periods that are simple fractions of its own. Also, conversely, there are some gaps in asteroid belt orbits that have been evacuated by Jupiter. Then, as we saw earlier, there is a possible resonance argument concerning Mercury and the Sun. We'll return later to the question of whether it can likewise be applied to Venus, but suffice it to say that the full beautiful picture painted for you in this book is not yet understood. Even slightly.

A small group can have fun whirling around and weaving out the dance of Venus. The diagram overleaf shows how to speed up and slow down. The spacing of the dots indicates the speed, over one single 'heart.' Five of these comprise the total 'rose' that is woven.

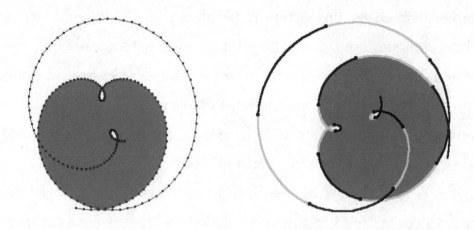

While coming in close to the centre one slows right down, then speeds up around the outside. The second diagram shows how far Venus goes in equal intervals, so indicates just how much dancers slow down and speed up as they move around. It's difficult - in fact, it's very hard, few people manage it! When farthest outside at each loop one passes by the 'superior conjunction,' so another dancer could play the fixed speed circular path of the Sun with Venus orbiting at arms length. As we saw with Mercury, Venus draws closest to Earth while at its inferior conjunction when it is retrograde. It moves retrograde less than any other planet, a mere seven percent of the time, so only one in 14 people are born with Venus retrograde.

Earlier we saw how these motions made the two sky-pentagrams, but now we have a different picture showing the geocentric motion. Again we have an image not known to the ancients - a new experience. People like to experience it, because it's a mandala, which means that it promotes our wholeness, our integral experience, which we all need. We don't just want abstract diagrams. This picture is in relation to us, pointing towards the Earth. It shows something special about the pattern of interlinkage between Venus and Earth. Dancing the path of Venus can help you understand how things look like from here. How our closest planetary neighbour actually moves in space around us.

Earth weaves the same pattern around Venus as Venus does around the Earth (shown on page 24), so the picture from Venus would look exactly the same. Venusians would experience the dance of Earth as the same fivefold flower! Even just taking the heliocentric orbits, which means sun-centred, if you start off with Venus and Earth both together (a Sun-Venus conjunction) and join up a line every day between them you will end up with a similar five-fold pattern (shown on page 25). How does this happen? Can you see why yet?

We've now seen the same rose-pattern in three different ways: centred on the Earth, centred on Venus, and centred on the Sun. It turns up more or less the same under these three different perspectives. If you don't get it straight away, don't worry, it's not easy, it took me some time before it all made sense. Keep thinking about it, keep seeing it, and do the dance. You'll feel better afterwards.

And have some fun. If a train of half a dozen or so perform the dance together it can look great as the dancers interweave around the loops. There are also two different moods one can get into during performances: of motherly, caring concern when slowing right down and coming nearest to the Earth, then of ecstatic abandon when whirling round more quickly amidst the stars, furthest away.

Let's conclude with the words of the 'first poetess' Enheduanna (we come back to her in Chapter 10) concerning the Venus-deity Inanna of Sumeria, composed over four thousand years ago:

And She goes out
White-sparked, radiant
In the dark vault of evening's sky
Star-steps in the street
Through the Gate of Wonder.

Chapter 4

The Divine Proportion

*P*erfection isn't an easy concept, I admit. One is often habituated to chaos and violence in the modern world. Just look at the headlines. Can you imagine a news feature: "VENUS IS ASTONISHINGLY BEAUTIFUL, GASP SCIENTISTS" ?

What is beauty anyway? Why is it important? Let's start off by looking at the pentagram and the golden ratio present in pentagrams, known as phi, or Ø. This is a proportion found all over the plant and biological world, and in the dance of Venus.

The golden ratio is the only way to divide a line so that the whole and parts are related to each other in the same way. It divides a line into a large part and a small part, so that

Large Part / Small Part = Whole / Large Part = 1.61803399...

$$\emptyset = 1 + \cfrac{1}{1 + \cfrac{1}{1 + \cfrac{1}{1 + \cfrac{1}{1 + \cfrac{1}{1 + \cfrac{1}{1 + \cfrac{1}{1 + \cfrac{1}{1 + \cdots}}}}}}}}$$

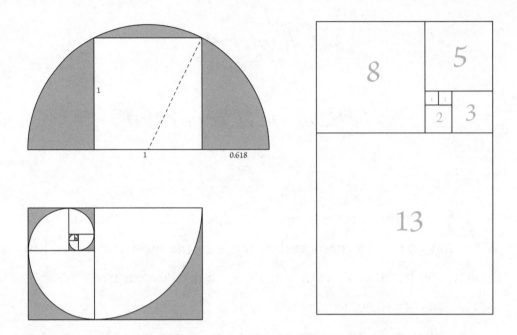

The idea of perfection in the golden ratio comes from the special way in which it so perfectly reflects back on itself. A square added or removed from a golden rectangle simply creates another golden rectangle. We can construct phi by fitting a square into a semi-circle (*above*). A studio window built on this design might help you see things in divine proportion. Pi comes from 'squaring the circle,' but phi comes from a square in half a circle! The golden ratio is also found in pentagrams, and all regular five-fold forms.

The golden section is very beautiful. Let's look at Botticelli's

Renaissance masterpiece, *The Birth of Venus* (*below*). Check out your height, then measure how high your navel is from the floor. Dividing one of these by the other should, with a bit of luck, bring you close to 1.618 (or 0.618 - as they are reciprocals), because an adult's navel divides their height in the golden ratio.

Botticelli focuses the entire attention of the viewer on to the navel of the goddess, also the golden height of the horizon which divides the painting in golden proportion vertically. It's so exact he must have done it deliberately. Notice too how he uses golden grid to delineate other key elements of the painting.

The next thing we are going to look at is the Fibonacci series. which is a series of numbers whose adjacent terms form ratios that move ever nearer to the golden section without ever quite getting there. The sequence is 1, 1, 2, 3, 5, 8, 13, 21, 34, 55 et cetera, with each term the sum of the two previous ones. So five plus three equals eight, and 5/8 is closer to 0.618033989 than 3/5, and 8/13 is even closer. See the whirling squares on the previous page for a visual diagram of the same thing.

Now, the really strange thing is that the majority of plants on Earth use Fibonacci numbers in their spirals, and not other numbers. A Fibonacci-buff can pick up a pineapple and show you its 5:8:13 ratios, woven between its spiral whorls going five in one direction,

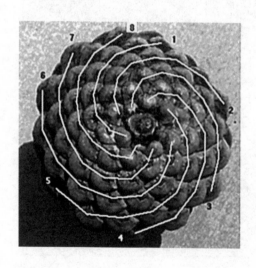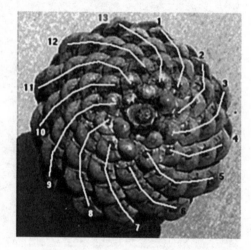

eight in the other and thirteen vertically. Most pine cones show a similar pattern, either 5:8 or 8:13. Sunflowers use higher Fibonacci ratios, in the number of spirals coming out from the centre of the flower, often 34 and 55 clockwise and anticlockwise spirals. You can even count Fibonacci numbers spiralling in the petals of roses! But, get this, it turns out that apart from huge flowers like sunflowers, most plants on Earth just use the numbers 5, 8 and 13! And, if you remember, these are the numbers of Venus, for Venus draws her pentagram in the sky around Earth every 8 years, which is 13 of her own Venusian years: 5, 8 and 13 again! As above, so below! How could it possibly be that the numbers written in the sky around Earth by our closest planetary neighbour, the Goddess of Love, are the same numbers that are used by most plants on Earth? And how could it possibly be that no one told you that before? I mean, wow!

Addition and multiplication also strangely come together in the golden section series. Taking the sequence 1, Ø, Ø², Ø³, etc. where Ø phi is the golden ratio, each one is the sum of the two previous ones, just like the Fibonacci series. The facade of the Parthenon was built in this ratio and many people think it is a perfect example of fine architecture. Before it was blown up by the Turks it would have looked quite good as a temple to Athena. In

fact, The name 'phi' was chosen for the golden section in the 20th century in honour of the ancient Greek sculptor Phidias, who was involved in decorating the Parthenon.

Pentagrams aren't often found rocks or crystals but they burgeon in living things and sea-creatures, and it turns out there are several ways in which phi can be found in a pentagram. How's that? The pentagram is the only figure made entirely of golden ratios - all its sides are 'golden' to the others. Was that why witches were burnt at the stake for using it? Somehow it had a supernatural significance. Christians like their four-sided Cross and Jews their six-sided Star of

David, but women wearing five-fold pentagrams, they must be trouble! Look at the diagram below. All of the relationships are golden. You can even guess the ratios, as they have to be 0.618, 1, 1.618 or 2.618. Easy when you know how. The one-tenth division is the angle used by DNA, as its spiral turns once per ten steps, so the 'molecule of life' is also continually expressing the golden proportion.

When you have got a sense of how the different pentagram sides reverberate to the divine proportion, then we can move on.

Next we are going to compare two years, those of Earth and Venus. Their ratio spells phi to within one percent. Taking the Venus synodic period (how long it takes to be behind the Sun again) of 19 months and comparing this to the Earth year, gives us phi to

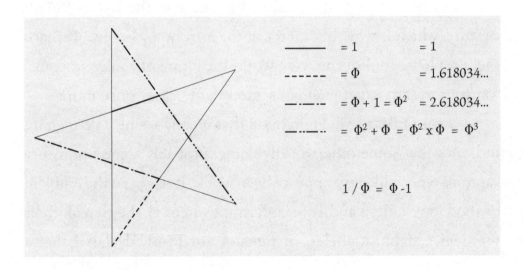

$$\underline{\qquad\qquad} = 1 \qquad\qquad = 1$$

$$\text{------} = \Phi \qquad\qquad = 1.618034...$$

$$\text{--- -- } = \Phi + 1 = \Phi^2 \quad = 2.618034...$$

$$\text{--- -- } = \Phi^2 + \Phi = \Phi^2 \times \Phi = \Phi^3$$

$$1 / \Phi = \Phi - 1$$

half a percent. So, Venus the planet of love, beauty and harmony once again expresses its connection with Earth; just as it did a bit earlier when we saw how the same part of Venus' surface always pointed earthwards at each nearest approach. What's more, Venus's celestial music is deeply oriented towards Earth, that is to say it can only be heard from a geocentric viewpoint, from Earth.

We were reminded of the golden ratio by the starry pentagrams which Venus inscribes around Earth each eight years, and now it has turned up as a pattern in time. This is mostly new research. Astrosophist Hazel Straker first described the double pentagrams, and archaeoastronomer Robin Heath first described golden ratios in the orbit-periods. It seems that the divine harmonies of Venus only started to be apprehended by humanity in the late twentieth century, which is why they aren't in the astronomy books. Perhaps the 'prophetic soul of the wide world dreaming of things to come' wants us to start experiencing harmony and beauty once more.

Fans of Buffy will apprehend that merely seeing a pentagram indicates that some otherworldly being, probably some unsavoury vampire-type, is likely to appear. Even worse, it has been the emblem of the US, Chinese and Russian armies wherever they wreak their mayhem. Mephistopheles, in the story of Faust, declared that a pentagram on the wall 'causes me pain,' so what the devil was going on? For these reasons let's stress that the double-pentagram is the true emblem of Venus. Nevertheless, there is something creative about the pentagram, as if something unexpected may appear. I like the phrase 'the irregular and vital beauty of the pentagram' - from the New York architect Claude Bragnon.

We can improve on the golden ratio by using the Fibonacci series. The patterns in time we looked at earlier are more closely equal to these ratios:

Venus' synodic cycle : Earth's year = 8/5, to within 0.08%
Earth year : Venus' year = 13/8, to within 0.03%.

So that's how the years of Venus and Earth form lovely steps in the Fibonacci sequence. Steps which relate to the golden ratio. 5, 8 and 13, also the most common numbers used by plants all around us. A pattern in heaven as on Earth.

Five is also the favourite number of petals for flowering plants on Earth. The flowers of all edible fruits, like apples and pears, have five petals. Eight and thirteen reappear in music as the octave in the seven-note and twelve-notes scales.

Chapter 5

Music of Venus

We've looked at the 5:8 ratio, and now we come to Venus' last and most subtle rhythm of 12:13. That's the final one she uses for her complete symphony. I have to warn you that it is a bit tricky. It happens within the eight-year period, as she weaves out the heart-and-rose mandala. To do this we have to focus on her axial rotation period. We've seen how the geometry of Venus indicates a strong relationship with the Earth. Well, here she proves her affection again through the synodic period.

Synodos is a Greek word meaning 'meeting', and the 584 day synodic period of Venus tells us how long it takes for her to grow into the bright Evening star, or pass behind the Sun. It's an experiential interval between us and her. Venus' synodic period is one-fifth of eight years. Earth and Venus come closest, so that she shines most brightly, each synodic cycle. The period covers two Sun-Venus conjunctions, superior and inferior. Like the lunar cycle, Venus grows into her period of glory and then fades away, sinking further each day into the dusky turquoise of the sunset. Some say that this disappearance pertains to old Babylonian legends of the goddess Ishtar descending into the underworld.

Now to even stranger things. Venus revolves on her own axis relative to the stars twelve times per those same eight Earth-years. When you are by yourself, just spin around. That's your personal rotation in space. If you move round with somebody else then that is more like an orbit, you are both moving round a centre. Venus' own rotation period of 243 days is two-thirds of an Earth-year, slower than any other planet - and she spins in the opposite direction. Incredibly, what all of this means is that in the five synodic periods of the complete rose-pattern she divides space into five, goes eight times round the Earth, revolves twelve times in her own space and goes thirteen times round the Sun. That is the amazing symphonic whole.

Venus experiences 5.001 of her days per synodic period. A 'day' means how often a Venusian would see the Sun rise. We saw how in the last chapter, performing the Venus-dance, one comes to face the centre four times per 'heart,' i.e. per synodic period. And the centre of that dance is Earth. This means that there is a lovely

4:5 rhythm that a Venusian would experience, in the interval of sunrises and earthrises. From Venus one would see four earthrises and five sunrises per synodic period - rising in the west. Wow!

Is this an example of resonance? There is a well-forgotten report from a meteorology department, mouldering away in some dusty old volume, by an Australian called Mr Bigg. He discerned that each time Venus draws nearest to us, Earth's magnetic field becomes subdued. Venus is then nearer to us than any other planet ever comes. No-one is sure how Earth's magnetic field is actually produced. It varies in a lively manner from day to day and reverses at intervals through geological epochs - but Mr Bigg's discovery that it somehow quietened down as Venus draws near suggests the inferior conjunctions have a *geophysical* effect. This report appeared shortly before astronomers managed in 1967 to penetrate the dense clouds clouding Venus's surface from our prying eyes, to detect for the first time ever her own rotation in space. It was a few years earlier they had detected that of Mercury.

You see the same part of Venus's surface faces earthwards *both* at superior *and* at inferior conjunctions - that's ten times per eight years. So, cast your mind back to the Venus-dance. We had to face earthwards four times per heart, which works out at twenty

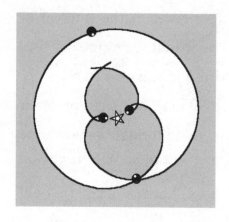 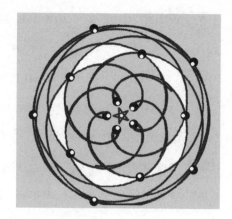

times in all as we wheel eight times around against the stars.

Try to feel it, feel the music of Venus. Here's a nice picture of one part of her dance, showing the positions where her same side faces earthwards. Remember she is spinning around the Sun and Earth one way, but spinning on her own axis the other way.

'Resonance' the astronomers said. But resonance can only happen if a physical transfer of energy takes place. For example we've all heard of how tidal forces are created by the Moon and how this slows down Earth's rotation and pushes the Moon further away (don't worry, its only by centimetres per year). So a transfer of energy and momentum is taking place and so we can just about believe that this could account for Luna's lovely face facing ever earthwards. Convinced?

The back and front of the Moon are completely different. The side facing us is a surreal dreamscape with huge, dark once-molten lava seas, with long silvery rays a-shimmering and strange sinuous rilles meandering about as if they were once river valleys (which they never were). The back of the Moon is quite uninteresting. It has chains of mountains and no lava seas, and looks like the back of someone's head. Lunar poetry might hardly have existed if the front of Luna resembled its behind. We saw in Chapter 2 a possible physical explanation as to why the Moon is locked into facing ever earthwards. It involved gravity and resonance.

Then we saw how with Mercury astronomers are happy to have resonance accounting for the 2:3 music between it and the Sun. Neither you (I guess) nor I can handle the equations of its elliptical orbit, so we have to take their word that their interaction produces such a result.

But Venus? It stretches credulity. What about a 'Passing Biff'? Astronomers sometimes say Venus might have received a 'biff' by some passing comet or whatever to have knocked it into its reverse-rotation mode. The modern theory about how the solar system was formed by a 'pestilent congregation of vapours', as Hamlet mused to himself (with man as the mere 'quintessence of dust'), has everything revolving the same way as coalesces and cools down. But Venus' axis of rotation is fairly vertical: it doesn't look as if its been knocked about. Secondly, Venus has a more perfectly circular orbit than any other known planet, hardly what you'd expect after a big knock. Thirdly, does its orbit diverge from the plane of the ecliptic as one might expect from a bump? No. And fourthly, were its beautifully strange rotation due to impact, would one expect it to be revolving more slowly than anything else in the solar system? One can hardly have the rather musical-harmonic ratios of 12:13 and 5:4 resulting from a collision with a comet!

In fact, not only will a cometary impact not work, but resonance won't work either. Venus is fairly spherical, it has no great bulge anywhere, so Earth's pull can't have gotten a grip on it to alter its rotation, and there is no tidal means whereby a lock could have been established onto its rotation to slow it down or speed it up. So it seems that a dance is going on that physics can't currently account for. The astronomer Kepler wrote about *Harmonices Mundi* the 'Harmonies of the World' and, unfashionable though this may be today, Venus seems to be showing us just this.

Venus' axial rotation demonstrates *quantum relationships*. Let's go through them again: first there is the 2:3 ratio of its axial rotation

period to Earth's year (99.8%); then there are the five Venus-days per synodic cycle (99.98%) and the four 'Earth-days' per synodic cycle (99.96%), and finally there is the 13:12 ratio between its axial rotation and year (99.8%). German researcher Hartmut Warm's diagrams above shows some of the patterns made by perpendicular lines drawn from the same spot on the surface of Venus over time as she passes by the Earth. It has required exact calibration of the Venus-rotation by space-equipment in the last two decades to obtain the evidence for these awesomely precise, interlocking synchronies.

Every eight years the Venus-pentagrams shift around by some two degrees. The two pentagrams of Venus revolve majestically against the stars, *exactly* once per twelve centuries (to 99.9%, or 1199 years). We have earlier come across the number twelve, in connection with Venus' rotation against the stars. The next chapter looks at the effect of this twelve-century period, after which the slowly rotating Venus-pentagram repeats.

These numbers can sound so bewildering. So put your feet up on the verandah, listen to the rustling of the trees, sip some elderflower cordial, and mull over them. That special number, the lynchpin of Venus' symphony, her axial rotation period which gives her such majestic slowness of spin, is the *fifth power* of three:

$$3 \times 3 \times 3 \times 3 \times 3 = 243$$

Mars spins on its own axis once a day, much like Earth, and Jupiter twice, so how did Venus get to have this special rotation period, six hundred times slower than Jupiter? We've already suggested an answer in terms of the elegance of the dance that a ballet dancer performs, to give perfect poise and grace to her motion (Chapter 3), but you may not have been very happy with that.

However, compare Venus with the Moon to see the mystery

deepen. The Moon revolves once in space against the stars every twenty-seven days, which is the *third power* of three. We don't see that axial rotation because Luna always faces us, revolving around Earth in the same period. These powers-of-three numbers seem to be required for the (apparently) vitally important business of facing earthwards: for one side of the Moon is always shown to us, and one side of Venus likewise always faces earthwards at her closest approaches.

A woman goes through nine mo(o)nths, nine meetings of the Sun and Moon, during pregnancy. These measure out (*mensuration, menstruation,* from *mens,* Latin, 'a month') the period of gestation.

So this is probably a good moment to ponder how it is that Venus revolves *nine times more slowly* on her own axis in space than our Moon.

Demurely, she has always concealed this, so no-one knew about it, right through history, until just recently!

> *O body swayed to music, O brightening glance,*
> *How can we know the dancer from the dance?*
>
> W.B.Yeats

Chapter 6

Rainbows and Glories

If you thought things couldn't get stranger, think again. We have already seen how Earth and Venus draw a beautiful five-fold flower in space over eight years (which is thirteen Venus years), and have drawn attention to the fact that these numbers 5, 8 and 13 are the same ones used by almost all plant life on Earth. That in itself is something magical, something beautiful, and something so strange that scientists mostly avoid mentioning it. 5, 8 and 13. As above, so below. You are an example of 5:8:13 phyllotaxis. You have five fingers on four appendages, and you have five teeth in each quarter of your mouth as a child. When you grow up your five milk teeth in each quarter fall out and are replaced by eight adult teeth, which means that you have thirteen teeth in each quarter over your lifetime.

There is also another odd fact you should be aware of. A harmony so strange and fascinating it will make you high and put a smile on your face every time you think about it. It is a correlation so mysterious and lovely that it can only ever lie outside the bounds of science. Evidence for an almost holographic order in the entire system of things, it was discovered in 2009 by English geometer John Martineau and this is how it works:

Have you ever seen a Sun dog? They are rainbow spots which

appear to the left and right of the Sun. Sun dogs are caused by small ice-crystals high in the atmosphere and appear most often in the winter, although you can see them any time of year. And do keep an eye out for them! Once you start looking for them you should see them fairly regularly - vertical rainbow spots in thin cloud, on calm afternoons. Sun dogs appear 22 degrees left and 22 degrees right of the Sun from your viewpoint.

Sun dogs are in fact only the first elements to appear of a full 22 degree ice halo (the circle opposite), a thin rainbow circle around the Sun. Occasionally, a second larger ice halo appears outside the first at 46 degrees from the Sun, with a moon-like crown, like the symbol for Mercury. See the whole formation in Flammarion's old plate on the previous page. This full form is called a 'glory'. They are very rare.

So what you may ask? Well get this: Ready? *When you look at a glory you are also looking at the sizes of the spheres of the inner two planets' mean orbits around the Sun, precisely drawn in light.*

What? How can that be? Well Mercury's mean orbit appears from Earth at 21.8° from the Sun, and the inner halo occurs from 21.5° for the red band to 22.4° for the blue band. So the bright rainbow spots we call Sun dogs and the entire inner ice halo is none other than a huge rainbow drawing of the sphere of Mercury's mean orbit around the Sun, drawn so you can see where Mercury lives.

If that doesn't give you goosebumps, nothing ever will. "A coincidence" you may protest. But, amazingly, Venus proves there is almost a rule here, because *the outer 46° ice halo is a precise depiction of Venus's sphere around the Sun.* Venus has a very circular orbit and if you could see it as a sphere in the sky the outer ice halo is how big it would appear to us on Earth. Drawn as a rainbow circle. Exactly.

Why? Well, seen from Earth, the sphere of Venus' mean orbit would appear as a circle 46.3° around the Sun, bang in the middle of the 46° outer ice halo. The thickness of the thin rainbow circle even shows you the amount of wobble in the system! That outer ice halo is where Venus lives, that's the bubble whose surface she moves over. And the inner halo is the bubble of Mercury average orbit.

Jon Oldroyd's fisheye photograph opposite shows not only a full glory, but also an exact snapshot of the mean orbital bubbles of the two inner planets. If Mercury and Venus travelled in circles round the Sun on the surface of bubbles or spheres, that's how big those bubbles would look like from Earth. Sun dogs and glories are circles of light precisely superimposed on to something that is actually happening there. The two fit perfectly. It's a perfect picture.

Now, one rainbow circle fitting one orbit from Earth's viewpoint is one thing. But two ice halos round the Sun fitting two planets' average orbits is much much weirder. We are into uncharted territory. A glimpse of higher reality? What can one make of it?

There's icing too: The two inner planets, Mercury and Venus, orbit the Sun *inside* our orbit, so, looking at the Sun we can imagine seeing their full orbits. But the next planet out (after Earth) is Mars, and its orbit is *outside* ours, it goes behind us. How might we visualise that? Well, turn around, put your back to the Sun, and look at an ordinary rainbow like the one above. By the way, did you know you always see the same rainbow? The same size of circle? Point one arm at the centre of the circle of a rainbow (often below the horizon) and another at the rainbow itself, and you will always make the same angle, 41 degrees). It turns out *a primary rainbow is how big the sphere*

of Earth's orbit looks like from Mars. Strange and beautiful, or what? So the orbital spheres of all three nearby planets can be *experienced*, as rainbow circles for us on Earth. And they have been, by most life on Earth, ever since there were coloured skins and eyes to see light.

This is a coincidence between orbits, light and the optics of water. Look at the diagram below and see if you can understand what's going on. You're the dot in the middle, either looking towards the Sun with ice haloes (on the right), or you have your back to the Sun, and are looking at rainbows (on the left).

The solar system jumps into three dimensions, a hologram, in front of you. Recorded in the structures of water. Amazing!

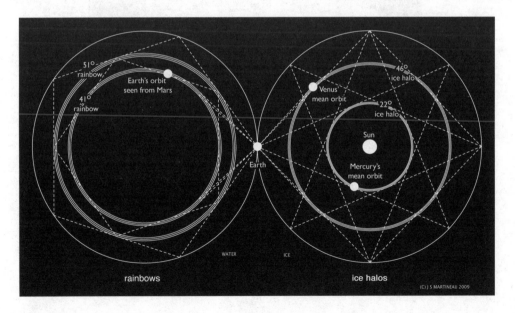

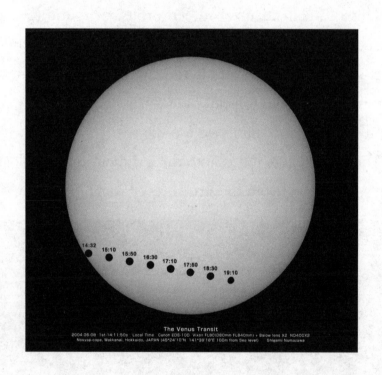

The Venus Transit
2004.06.08 1st-14:11:50s Local Time Canon EOS-10D Vixen FL80(D80mm FL640mm) + Balow lens X2 ND400X2
Nosyap-cape, Wakkanai, Hokkaido, JAPAN (45°24'10"N 141°39'18"E 100m from Sea level)   Shigemi Numazawa

Chapter 7

Sojourn Across the Sun

*E*very now and then Venus does something very special indeed. Silhouetted against the Sun, she can appear in the daytime as a tiny spot that moves across its face (*opposite*). No living person had ever seen this when it happened in the summer of 2004.

When objects pass *directly* in front of the Sun astronomers speak of a transit. When the Sun is blocked we call it an eclipse.

Understanding eclipses and transits requires us to understand *nodes, and* the nodes of Venus are where her orbital path cuts that of the Sun. These nodes move very very slowly. Think of Venus' orbit through the stars as making a plane. And make another plane for the Earth-Sun orbit. These two planes intersect to make a line that rotates very very slowly in space. Meanwhile, the eight-year Venus pentagram takes 1200 years for a full rotation, and every time one of its five corners meets this barely moving node-axis, transits occur.

A transit can only happen at an inferior conjunction when

Venus is Sun-side and near a node, i.e. close to the ecliptic. Venus transits come in pairs eight years apart, currently around June 8th, and at the opposite end of the year around December 8th, as the Sun crosses the Venus-node.

The Venus pentagram revolves in space once every twelve centuries, one-fifth of which is 240 years, but, due to the very slow rotation of the Venus-nodes, the actual interval is 243 years (remember that number?). Over this time, four Venus-transits happen, two in June and two in December. You can see from the picture opposite how transits at 243-year intervals have more or less identical paths across the Sun, more or less on the same days of the year!

Transits have only been seen since the 17th century, after telescopes were invented and Kepler's astronomy was published. This was the first time that observations and theories were accurate enough to discover the planetary nodes. In Paris in 1631, Pierre Gassendi was the first person to witness a transit of Mercury, then in Britain in 1639 the young Jeremiah Horrocks cleverly predicted and saw the first-ever Venus-transit, somewhere outside Manchester.

The tiny size of these planets against the Sun staggered everyone. People for the first time could directly apprehend the vast scale of the solar system. Horrocks asked his friend William Crabtree to watch

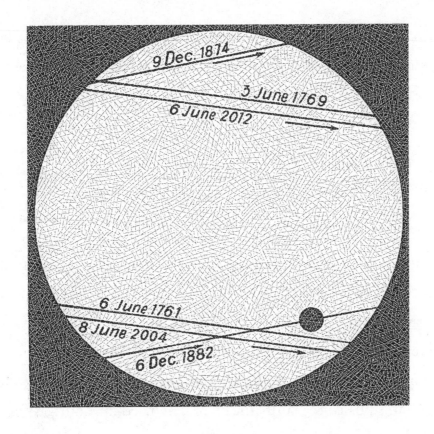

the Venus-transit, and recorded his friend's thrill:

> "Rap't in contemplation he stood, motionless, scarce trusting his
> senses, through excess of joy."

Crabtree and Horrocks both died young, but their work,
which only just and partially survived the ravages of the English

civil war, kick-started British astronomy. Horrocks' account kept breaking out into verse. Of future transits of Venus, he wrote:

'Thy return
Posterity shall witness; years must roll
Away, but then at length the splendid sight
Again shall greet our distant children's eyes.'

In another famous Venusian adventure, Captain Cook set out from Portsmouth harbour in 1768 to observe the Venus-transit on Tahiti predicted for 1769. He discovered beautiful Hawaii on the way, part of a gruelling eight month journey to find an island a mere twenty miles across. Captain Cook was a superb navigator; he found his latitude from the midday Sun, and his longitude from the Moon's position against the stars. He used an hourglass and a knotted rope to tell his speed. The crew ate sauerkraut, which kept them free from the dreaded scurvy.

Upon finally reaching Tahiti, the ship's young naturalist Joseph Banks wrote in his diary that it was 'the truest picture of an arcadia that the imagination can form.'

On the day of the Venus-transit, the king of the island, called Tarróa, plus his sister, Nuna, joined them for breakfast. Later that day, Banks' diary records, there was a visit by 'three handsome women.' Banks added little about the observation of the actual transit. Venus had struck again.

Philos. Trans. Vol. LXI. Tab XIV. p. 410.

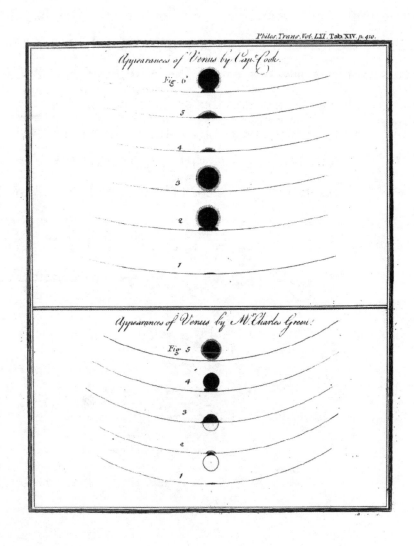

So how do Venus transits work? The diagram below shows how the pentagram of Venus-Sun conjunctions is woven every eight years, for both inferior (Sun-Venus-Earth) and superior (Venus-Sun-Earth) conjunctions. Amazing don't you think? The 19° Gemini conjunctions define the node-axis of Venus, where the plane of Earth's orbit cuts the plane of Venus' orbit. The two orbit-planes are tilted by three degrees to each other, and that's where they intersect. A transit therefore moved across the face of the Sun, on 8th June 2004.

Of distinctly less interest is the fact that on 8th June 2008 there was an 'occultation', as Venus passed directly *behind* the Sun.

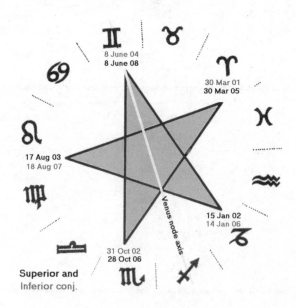

Of course, no-one saw it. This is very similar to how a lunar eclipse can happen two weeks either side of a solar eclipse.

These events happen every eight years, and carry on in eight-year chains that span at least half a century, with the two Venus-transits in the middle of this long chain. Thus there will be another occultation in 2016, then in 2024 etc., so the occultations are four years apart from the transits. Due to perspective and parallax it's quite easy for Venus to pass behind the Sun, whereas it needs some quite exact positioning for it to appear in front at inferior conjunction. One of these events takes far longer then the other, owing to the different directions in which they are moving: the occultation takes two days, in contrast with the mere five hours of the transit.

As the pentagram slowly revolves, another pair of transits will happen at the other end of the Venus-node, some 120 years later. If two pairs of Venus-transits turn up every 243 years, does that period ring a bell? Why yes, it's our friend the axial rotation period. So we have a day-for-a-year concordance going on here. How close is it?

Venus transit cycle = 243.00 Earth - years,
Venus axial rotation period = 243.018 Earth - days.

a bizarre agreement to within several parts per million. And we saw earlier how 243 isn't just any number, it's the *fifth* power of three, or 3 x 3 x 3: So what does all this mean? It must mean *something*. One can express this in terms of days: there are 365.24 days in a year here on Earth, and Venus spins 365.23 times in its transit-cycle. What on Earth is going on? The most recent and up-to-date radar orbital satellite data have been used here, to show the incredible precision with which Venus and Earth are dancing.

The finely tuned synchronies so cleverly woven by Venus are also mirrored in cycles and eerie number games involving Luna which we shall come to in chapter 13.

What all these relationships have in common is that there is absolutely no reason (that anyone can discern) why they should exist. They just happen to be there, in the machinery of things. They are an embarrassment to current physics. Some have long been of central importance for astronomy, for the preparing of calendars or for predicting eclipses; and yet they are, so to speak, just coincidences. And as though to suggest what might be going on, that beauty and harmony might be principles whose influences go beyond the laws of physics, only the two traditionally 'feminine' planets, the Moon and Venus, produce so many excellent harmonies.

Women. Beauty. Harmony. Mysterious beings outside the understanding of modern science. And note the way in which that magical number five keeps turning up, in great sky-pentagrams, in the proportions of orbits, as the five-to-one Venus-day ratio, or the fifth power of the number three.

Five, the number of biological life, seems to point towards the very *quintessence* of Venus.

French commemorative medal of 1874 Venus Transit

Chapter 8

The Evening and Morning Star

"*Venus is not to be seen at all times, and to those who are not acquainted with her movement she seems to come and go as she pleases. For months altogether the Star of Evening is hidden from mortal eyes.*

It is a beautiful clear evening, the Sun has just set, and in the golden glory of the western sky a beauteous gem is seen to glitter. A few weeks later the Queen of Beauty has risen higher above the horizon and rides, an even more brilliant object in the sky, long after the shades of night have descended. She only occasionally attains her full splendour, but at such times she outshines even Sirius more than twenty times. Then again she draws near the Sun and remains lost to view for many months, until she enters upon a new cycle of changes after an interval of a year and seven months."

So wrote the American astronomer, Mary Proctor in 1928. Today, if you are fortunate enough to dwell away from the city's neon glare, you may like to note the dates when you can first espy Venus in

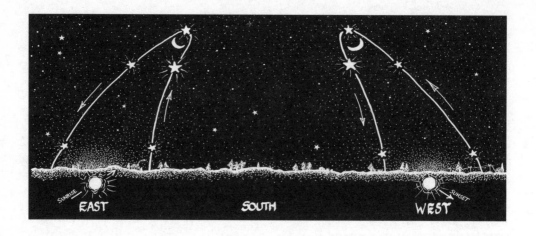

the evening or morning sky, and then when, months later, she fades away. There are 263 days between these, and this also happens to be the average period of human gestation, from conception to birth. The rose-and-heart mandala that we saw earlier doesn't indicate when Venus appears and disappears, it simply maps out its *perfect* blueprint of sidereal motion, *sidera* being the Greek word for stars, i.e. Venus' motion against the stars. In this chapter we are going to be less concerned with Venus' position against the zodiac and stars, more with how we experience her against our local horizon. In Robin Heath's illustration above we can see how the possible positions of Venus just before sunrise and just after sunset form a pair of horns.

The Greeks of Homer's day hadn't twigged that the Evening Star, which they called *Hesperus*, and the bright star of the morning, which they called *Phosphorus*, were one and the same (four centuries later they made the connection). The Romans likewise used two different words, *Lucifer* and *Vespers*, for Venus, as the Morning and Evening star.

The diagram below depicts the synodic cycle (of conjunctions) as a circle, as it cycles through time. Venus' period of maximum brilliance arrives a month or so *after* she has risen to her highest in the sky, and several weeks *before* she swiftly fades away. This is the perfect time for that enchanting breakfast or evening party you were meaning to organise. Sitting out on the grass or on the balcony and viewing Venus together as she slowly rises or sinks can be a beautiful social experience. Plan ahead for it, or, if that week isn't convenient, find from Table 2 (page 122) a time when the thin crescent moon (waning or waxing) conjuncts the Morning or Evening Star. It's a lovely sight in the sky. Some would argue it's *the* loveliest sight in the night sky.

A – Vanishes as Morning Star
B - Emerges as Evening Star
C - Rises highest in the sky, ('greatest elongation')
D - Most Brilliant
E - Retrograde Station
F - Disappears
G - Inferior Conjunction
H – Reappears as Morning Star, moving retrograde

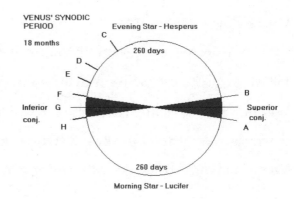

VENUS' SYNODIC PERIOD

18 months

Evening Star - Hesperus

260 days

Inferior conj.

Superior conj.

260 days

Morning Star - Lucifer

In antiquity the character of the Morning Star was like Nike the goddess of war, as if she were more brave and bold when appearing in advance of the Sun. Boldly glittering as herald of the dawn, she had the connotation of getting up and striding forth into the world, while the Evening Star was Aphrodite, the seductive love-goddess, whose sinking down into the sunset put people more in mind of going to bed. Her first reappearance as Morning Star (called a 'heliacal rising') was honoured as a good omen.

When Venus re-emerges from the other side of the Sun as Lucifer, bright Star of the Morning, she is 'retrograde'. Her faster orbital period than Earth's means that each day she seems to move slowly backwards against the stars. She moves at her slowest against the zodiac at her disappearance and reappearance. All in all, Venus' retrograde motion lasts for forty days, during which she backtracks over 15-18° of an arc. See if you can visualise the dance sequence of her celestial ballet.

After her reappearance Venus becomes stationary, and stops moving backwards in the zodiac, then she starts to move forward, becoming most brilliant, before climbing to her highest into the pre-dawn sky. Why not romantically climb up a hill every 19 months, at Venus' maximal brilliance as Evening Star, or else in a more strident fashion to greet the reappearance of the Morning Star.

Now let's return to the period of human gestation mentioned earlier, because this also closely relates to nine cycles of the Moon. Nine Moons. The Sun and Moon meet in the sky nine times from conception to birth, giving us 266 days, and Venus is visible, on average for a period of 263 days. Exactly between the two is the statistically average period of human gestation.

Thus, amazingly, the two traditionally feminine planets harmonise with the duration of human pregnancy. This was not always understood. In the nineteenth century, nurses reckoned that pregancy lasted forty weeks (280 days), way off, this popular value alluding more to the date of the last period a woman recalled having had, i.e. before the conception. Don't mention sex!

To impress your friends try predicting some of these cycles, starting off with some of the dates of solar conjunctions given in Chapter 3. Subtract six weeks from an inferior conjunction date to get the week or so of maximal brightness of the Evening Star. Check your predictions against a 'Venus diary' on the web (e.g. www.astro.com/swisseph/ae/venus1999.pdf, which gives all of the relevant dates, year by year).

So how did Lucifer get painted so black? The story is a sorry one. The Greek word for the Morning Star, 'phosphorus', makes its appearance in a bible text in the third century BC called the *Septuagint*, a Greek translation of Hebrew books, made in Alexandria, probably at the great and newly-established library there. Its *Book of Isaiah* (14:12) has the immortal line,

How thou art fallen from Heaven O Lucifer, Son of the Morning!

Or at least that is the King James' version of it - see Gustave Doré's engraving opposite. Lucifer is the Latin translation of the Greek 'phosphorus', both of which had the dual meanings, 'bearer of light' and 'Venus, the Morning Star'. The Hebrew text from which this Septuagint translation was made, from either the seventh or 8th century BC, goes:

"How have you fallen from heaven O Helel, son of Shahar! How art thou cut down to the ground, which didst weaken the nations."

Helel and Shahar being obscure Canaanite deities. Shahar was a dawn-god, so does that mean that his son would be Venus, the Morning Star? Isaiah was having a tirade against the King of Babylon, who would, he affirmed, be descending into the Realm of Hades. It's clear that the text sounds a lot more exciting using Phosphorus/Lucifer rather than Helel.

The lovely meaning of the Latin Lucifer was extolled by Roman poets:

"Aurora watchful in the reddening dawn, threw wide her crimson doors and rose-filled halls; the stars took flight, in marshalled order set by Lucifer who left his station last."

Ovid, Metamorphoses 2.112

and:

And now Aurora, rising from her Mygdonian resting-place, had scattered the cold shadows from the high heaven, and, shaking the dew-drops from her hair, blushed deep in the sun's pursuing beams; toward her through the clouds, rosy Lucifer turns his late fires, and with slow steed leaves an alien world, until the fiery father's orb be full replenished and he forbid his sister to usurp his rays."

Statius, Thebaid 2.134

Later, when the New Testament was composed, praise of the new Saviour compared him with the Morning Star:

"I, Jesus have sent my angel to give you this testimony for the churches. I am the root and the offspring of David, and the bright Morning Star."

That last quote is taken from the Book of Revelation, written about 95 AD. Here the words *ho Aster, ho Lampos, ho Proinos* are used (Gk, *orthrinos*). Finally, in what was probably the last book of the New Testament to be composed we find '... until that day dawns and the Morning Star [Phosphorus] rises in your hearts' (*Second Letter of Peter*, 1:19)

All in all there are three references to the Morning Star in the New Testament, and they either allude to Jesus or to the Holy Spirit. To quote from a recent book, *Satan a Biography*, the Morning Star Lucifer 'is a consistently positive image and one that is solidly associated with Jesus the Messiah.' (p.167). So it wasn't just the pentagram that ended up with a twisted reputation in uneducated modern times. Jesus as Venus did too. How did that happen?

How did it come to pass that once the Old and New Testaments were put together, the Greek word *Phosphorus* could allude both to the Saviour, Jesus, and to a being who was soon due to be dramatically re-cast as the Lord of Hell?

Well, one of the early culprits seems to have been Origen of Alexandria (185 – c.250), who wove together the story of Lucifer and the fallen angels cast from heaven. He contrasted what he declared was the spiritual meaning of certain texts with their literal meaning.

Then in the fourth century the *Vulgate* - a Latin translation of the Bible by Jerome, which was to be Europe's standard Bible for over a thousand years - used the word 'Lucifer' for the Isaiah passage.

Strike a match, and watch the phosphorus burn. From Dante to Jagger and the Rolling Stones, a tiny translation error triggered off the powerful image of a fallen Ruler of the Underworld. In fact modern Bible translations don't even use the word Lucifer in the Isaiah text, Venus has been banished all together.

Pentagrams need not be scary. Instead, reader, you fivefold being with five appendages sticking out from your torso, and five fingers and thumbs at the end of four of them, I wish upon you the blessing of the Second Letter of Peter:

That the Morning Star may rise in your hearts.

> 'She walks in beauty, like the night
> Of cloudless climes and starry skies;
> And all that's best of dark and light
> Meet in her aspect and her eyes:
> Thus mellow'd to that tender light
> Which heaven to gaudy day denies.'
>
> Lord Byron

Chapter 9

Quantum Symmetries

We have seen how the golden ratio turns up mysteriously in the unfolding of the pentagram and also in the motions of Venus. We now turn to a geometry that uses the square of that ratio. The circle around a pentagram, and a smaller one drawn where its arms cross, are in that ratio. Don't take my word for it, try drawing a pentagram and comparing the diameters of these two circles, outside and inside: they should give you the ratio 2.618.

In the early 1990s a young British geometer, John Martineau, started looking for ways to understand the solar system in simple geometrical and harmonic terms. Starting with Mercury, what he found was a simple pattern that fitted both the orbits and relative sizes. The mean orbits of Mercury and Earth fit the pentagram pattern, to around 99%, and then doing the same with their relative sizes gave him a much closer fit (99.8%). These proportions are as the square of the golden ratio. A diagram is shown overleaf:

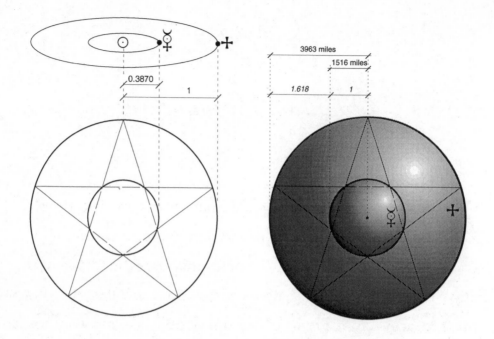

Interestingly an eight-pointed star, or octagram, defines the same
ratio (see page 86), so a pair octagrams could be used instead of the
pentagrams above. Five and eight again. A similar geometry gives us,
oddly enough, Earth's mean orbital radius, as compared with Venus'
- look at the diagram opposite left. Venus' orbit is very nearly circular,
so this makes a good approximation - it works to within 99.9%.

We might try re-phrasing what we have just found: taking
the average radius of Venus' orbit, as it goes round the Sun, and
dividing this by the difference between that of Earth and Venus,

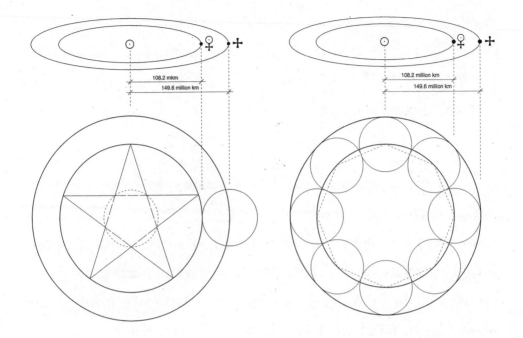

gives us one plus the golden ratio, i.e., 2.618. One could say that there is no 'reason' why this symmetry should exist, it certainly does not follow on from anything we learnt in Chapter Four.

Our next Martineau symmetry gives us an even higher order of precision. Putting eight circles touching each other around the Venus-orbit, gives Earth's orbit, and that is to an awesome 99.99%, or one part in ten thousand! As before we are using the mean orbits which are perfect circles. Our designs here are fivefold and eightfold, these being fundamental numbers for the Venus-Earth music. These designs in space echo what we previously dealt with in Time. Tell me, which one of these constructions is more beautiful?

So, 'What does it mean?' Mean? Well it may help to notice something about the number of days in Venus' synodic cycle:

$$8 + 64 + 512 = 584$$

So eight, plus eight squared, plus eight cubed, gives its synodic period in days. Fancy that! In the previous chapter we looked at how *synodos* means meeting, and how the cycle of meeting and separating can be experienced as Venus appearing and then fading away from our view, as the Morning and Evening star. Astronomers would tend to see it more in terms of these diagrams, showing that moment when the two spheres have drawn together in their paths around the Sun. So this period of 584 days it isn't just any old number, it's the sum of powers of eight. This eightfold design can also be compared with the ancient symbol for Venus: an eightfold star, and in the next chapter we shall look into this.

The half Venus-cycle of five conjunctions in four years governs Olympic games and American elections. Well here's an interesting 'square' design. The symmetries we have already seen took the circular paths (the mean orbital radii) of Earth and Venus, but the ones opposite consider the slight breathing expansions and contractions

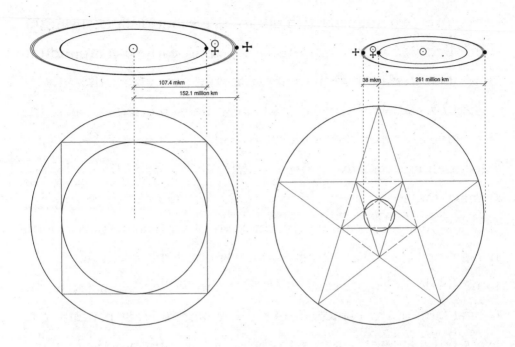

of their orbits. Here's how Mr Martineau expressed the matter:

'Marital Bliss - In which the realm of Earth & Venus is taken as a single space with a simple geometry: Earth and Venus are so very happy together that it is their whole combined space which exhibits the simplest harmony. Between Earth's greatest distance from the Sun and Venus' closest approach to the Sun lies the total realm of Earth & Venus, their home. A single square proportions this region with 99.9% accuracy. The square was generally associated with Earth, the City or the Home...'

And, when does Earth get to its greatest distance from the Sun? Luckily for us it happens each year in Early July: around the time of greatest heat we have drawn furthest away from the Sun.

Also shown beside the square on the previous page is the incredible fact that the approaches and separations of Venus and Earth define, over time, a space which can be proportioned by two pentagrams, to an astonishing accuracy of 99.99%. The drawing shows Venus in the centre, with the body of Earth's motions around her defined as $1:\emptyset^4$. Venus' motion around the Earth define the same sized 'shell'. It seems as though the hidden geometry in the orbital radii of the planets invokes their more evident patterning at every possible level - a vast synthesis of beautiful proportions and harmonies centred on beautiful Venus. The true harmony of the spheres. There is no scientific explanation for any of this to date, which is why you can only read about it in an offbeat book like this!

It is worth trying to put it all together in your mind at this point. Close your eyes and imagine the fivefold Venus rose pattern forming over eight years, or imagine watching Venus drawing an octagram around the Sun over eight years. Think of all the billions of plants on Earth using 5:8 phyllotaxis spirals. See the orbits defined by the symmetries we have just shown. Design a Venus-temple with a nice marble floor-design, synthesising your understanding so far. Read and reread this book until you understand it and are permanently bathed in the beauty of Venus.

Many of these quantum (whole number) symmetries involve the cross-sections of spheres, rather than circles, as planetary orbits are often tilted to one another. This was a view of the solar system first proposed by Kepler, whose diagram below shows the idea. He wrote about the harmonies of the world in 1618 in his *Harmonices Mundi*:

> *'Now there is need, Urania, of a grander sound, while I ascend by the harmonic stair of the celestial motions to higher things, where the true archetype of the fabric of the world is laid up and preserved.'*

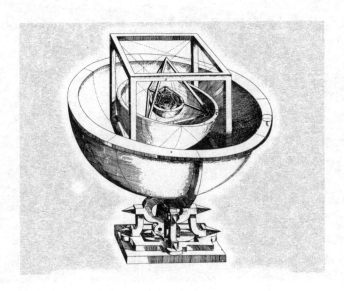

EIGHTFOLD GEOMETRY IN THE INNER SOLAR SYSTEM

Choose a calendar date when Venus passes in front of the Sun and plot Venus' position around the Sun on the same calendar date over the next eight years to get eight dots. The dots produce touching circles which space Earth and Venus' mean orbits. An octagram inside Earth's circle gives Mercury's size or orbit within the thickness of the line.

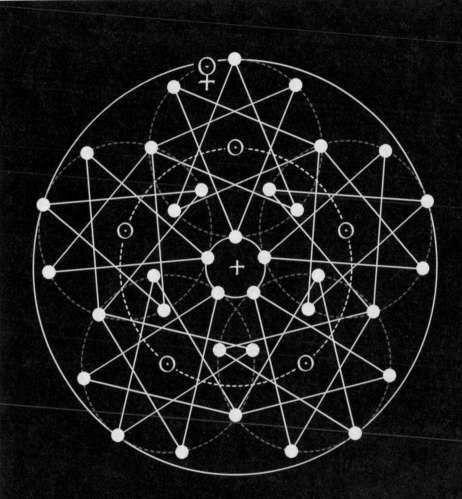

A Fivefold Pattern over Eight Years

With Earth in the centre, five calendar dates are chosen: those when Venus is
conjunct the Sun. The position of Venus relative to Earth is plotted on each
of these five dates over the eight years of the Venus rose-pattern to produce the
beautiful pentagram of octagrams above.

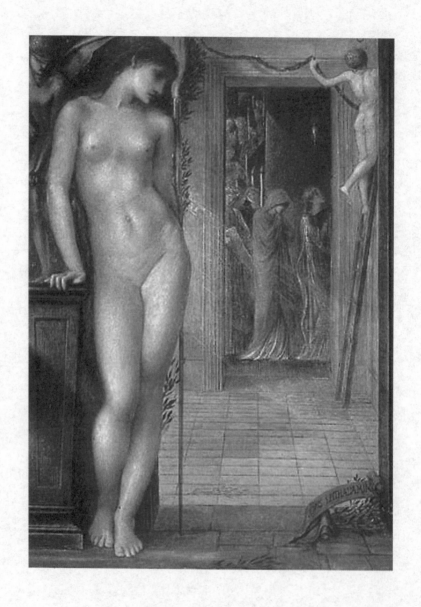

Chapter 10

From Ishtar to Aphrodite

At the end of the day, the Radiant Star,
the great Light that fills the sky,
The Lady of the Evening appears in the heavens
The people in all the lands lift their eyes to her.

Sumerian poem to Inanna

Venerate and *venereal* derive from the same root, and following their etymology takes us a long way back in time, to a love-goddess: Venus. Looking up to somebody with reverence means that we *venerate* them - whereas *venereal* issues signify trouble down there - a visit to the hospital may be called for. The words are so very opposite in their meaning, the one pertaining to spirit and the other to body, that one is hard pressed to imagine a single source for them. In antiquity they were linked to the *eight-pointed star* of Venus : Inanna! Ishtar! Aphrodite! Worshipped and adored through millennia, the first two were love-and-war goddesses, while Aphrodite, though she had some reputation for assistance in war, was really *the* love-goddess. Other planets had male and female deities, but only Venus was feminine solely.

In Appendix 1 you can read excerpts from the poems of Enheduana, from the 3rd millennium BC, when no nation except Sumeria had writing. The First Poem to Inanna is startling. If you thought Sappho was the earliest poetess, think again! *En-he-du-anna* was high Priestess of the Moon-god Nanna at Ur and the first known author to write in the first person. She lived around 2300 - 2225 BC and received her name Enheduana when ordained as a priestess of the Moon (from *en*, high priestess, *hedu*, ornament, *ana* of the sky-god). Her primal poem, her jubilant song, was to Inanna. It's hard to believe these are words from 4,300 years ago, when the pyramids were being built. The hundred or so tablets recording her

en   hé   du   an   na

incantations date from a period five centuries later, but are reckoned to be copies of earlier material. Good English translations appeared only a few years ago, but few people seem to be very interested. Appendix 1 also has an extract from a later Babylonian poem.

Below we see a Babylonian image from the 12th century BC, which is probably the earliest astronomical diagram with a discernable meaning. We can see that some serious business is going on, and hanging in the sky are three calendrical emblems, of the Sun, Moon and Venus. They seem so low, and close, to human

affairs. Two of these emblems are eightfold: The eight-pointed star was the most central and enduring image of Inanna the sky-goddess and Queen of Heaven of the ancient Sumerians, as worshiped in ancient Mesopotamia for at least four thousand years. The star represents her astral form, the morning and evening star. A tablet from the 7th century BCE also states that Ishtar of the Evening Star was female, while Ishtar of the morning star was male.

The Solar image (right of the picture) is also eightfold, because the Babylonian calendar-priests knew that the lunar months came into a rough synchrony to the year every eight years. This was an early version of the 19-year Metonic cycle, not so exact, but early enough to take the form of a Greek myth. The priests were *intercalating*, or adding in, three extra lunar months, every 8 years (each of 12 lunar months).

The Moon seems to grow then gradually shrink and vanish away before reappearing again. Standing on their ziggurats, the astronomer-priests never twigged as did the more philosophical Greeks later on that it was spherical in shape and only shone by reflected light, they lived in a more magical world. The Greeks called this 8-year period the *octaeteris*, and used it in their calendar.

In the 17th century BCE, a Venus-tablet in the library of Nineveh gives a cycle of omens with dates over an eight-year period, the omens being for the first appearance of Venus above the horizon and for the date of its last visibility, ten such events per eight years. Earlier texts are just omens around eclipses or other event. A millennium later, the Greeks halved this basic 8-year period, and started measuring out their history by these intervals, called Olympiads. The Olympic games became a pan-Hellenic four-yearly festival, when all wars and feuding had to cease. Did Venus' return to the same degree in the sky on the same day help them to do this? They wouldn't have found any recurrence of the lunar months in their four-year period, but Venus would have chimed in. If one saw the thin, crescent Moon together with Venus on some special day of the year, then eight years later they would again be together on the same day, in the same parts of their cycles, give or take a day or so. Islamic flags often show the Moon with Venus in this beautiful position, and the 99 moons it takes for the formation to reappear on roughly the same day of the year is reflected in the 99 names of Allah.

Nowadays, the Olympics chime with the leap-year and the American presidential elections, but no-one remembers the eight-year cycle that originally timed it. The Olympic games began as a foot-race over a *stade* i.e. round a stadium, scheduled by the *octaeteris* and on the 8th Full Moon of the year i.e. in July or August. There were ninety-nine moons every eight years, and the Olympics alternated between fifty and forty-nine moon intervals. In the year 776 BC the first competitions were held in Olympia in the western Peloponnesia of Greece. Long before this had become the temple city of Zeus it was dedicated to the goddess Ge. Only free Greeks could compete, provided they had not committed a murder or behaved indecently in a holy place, and they had to run naked, having trained for ten months beforehand. The competition was a sprint along a stade, a distance of about 200m. In 720 BC a longer run was added of two stades, and then gradually games were added.

In the Greek story, a beautiful maiden, Atalante, running

naked, always managed to outrun her competitors (as a child, she had been nursed in a cave by a she-bear). To win her suitors had to compete with her in a race and outrun her, but they always lost and ended up with their heads impaled, the grisly price for losing. Finally, Venus got fed up with this dire state of affairs and decided to intervene. She gave three golden apples to the suitor Hippomedes. Each time Atalante started to gain, Hippomedes would drop a golden apple, and she stooped to pick it up. Thereby Atalante lost the race, and her chastity. Experts view Atalante as an Artemis-type heroine, Artemis was goddess of the hunt and of the thin lunar crescent. The three golden apples are solar in their symbolism (gold being the Sun-metal) and represent the three months that had to be added in or 'intercalated' every eight years in order to keep the solar and lunar calendars in step. This is a lunar-solar calendar myth, with a slight touch from Venus. This ancient calendar faded in the early centuries BC, to be replaced by the more exact 19-year Metonic cycle.

Like Inanna, Aphrodite was represented by an eight-pointed star and associated with the morning and evening star. The Greeks often referred to her as a foreign goddess and as 'the Cyprian'. She had come from the Mediterranean isle of Cyprus, source of copper (latin *Cuprum*, from Kyprus) and the tall, cypress trees. Here she was worshiped from the 12th century BC until the Roman empire was Christianised in the 4th century AD. Birds were sacred to her, and she had a magic girdle that made the bearer irresistible, by 'the whispered endearments that steal the heart away, even from the thoughtful.' Her oldest temples were at Paphos on Cyprus, upon whose shore she was born in the myth, whence Bottichelli's image was derived.

By the time we get to ancient Rome, *Venerari* in Latin was a verb meaning to take an attitude of hospitality, whereby humans sought to attract the benevolence of the gods. The noun coming from it meant graciousness or charm, which became personified into a Roman goddess, Venus.

Early images of Aprodite: Left from Cyprus 6th C BC; Right from Salamis 4th C BC.

Chapter 11

The Wasp Star of the Maya

*I*n the new World, the Maya discovered some amazing gearings between the Venus cycle and other planetary calendars, many of which are so clever that they still boggle the mind today. Their astronomers used a complex mathematics involving a zero, and clocked astronomical periods reaching millennia into the past and future, even though their societies used neither wheel nor gear. In central America they built temples in the jungle, with painted pyramids aligned to the rising of the Pleiades and the spring equinox. Just four of their calendar-texts survived the Spanish missionaries, and the finest of these is called the *Dresden Codex*. Composed in the eleventh century, it describes the cycles of Venus. To the Maya, Venus was *Noh ek* or *Xux ek* - "the great star" or "the wasp star" respectively.

The 260-day Tzolkin was their template for ritual time, the all-important engine of destiny which generated astrological meanings for each day, and it was used right across central America. It counted

using base twenty (fingers and toes), plus thirteen which was the number of layers of heaven in Mayan cosmology. The Tzolkin is close to nine lunar months which is the human gestation period, and that is the main significance it still has today in Guatemala. The Tzolkin has twenty different day-signs, combined with a number 1 to 13, and this rolling sequence has continued without interruption for twenty-five centuries, still being used by the 'day-keepers' of Guatemala. Our dates have both a day of the month and a weekday, and likewise they had a 20-day 'week,' numbered in sequence 1-13.

The longer 'Calendar Round' connected the time-interval of 260 days, their Tzolkin or 'count of days,' with their 'year' of 365 days. The same day in the Tzolkin and the same day of the year would come together every 52 years. They didn't have fractions, and so their astronomy needed large numbers to keep the various cycles in synch. Once in a lifetime people experienced this, and when it came round a ceremonial 'binding of the years' took place, with communal fire-ceremonies. The lunar month and the Venus cycle had the highest importance for them, whereas, because they lived near the equator, the seasons of the year were not so important.

Amidst the huge volcanoes of Aztec and Toltec landscapes, somewhere around the 8th century BC, the 260-day calendar in its combination with the 365-day solar year was set into motion. Cuicuilco with its monumental pyramid may have the first evidence for the Calendar Round, shown by Olmec dates. The present-day Maya have a ceremony whereby one graduates to becoming an 'elder' of the community thirteen days before one's 52nd birthday. Counting the years without having any leap-years brings one just 13 days short of that birthday, you'll notice. The Maya calendar has been described as 'the gear-wheels of eternity' and no-one was able to interrupt its great cycles to reset the wheels. The number 13 keeps turning up in their scheme of things, a bit like 12 does in our calendar system.

In the Dresden codex (opposite), Kukulcan, a feathered-serpent Venus-deity, rejoices in his five different aspects. His five garbs changed with the eight-year cycle of Venus, illustrated in five decorated pages, which was their version of its eight-year period. Each of the five Venus synodic cycles was thereby perceived in a distinct manner, as Venus' path against the stars and also the local horizon recurred in this fivefold pattern. Each of these five pages focuses upon dates when the morning star first appeared, rising before dawn. Each of the five synodic cycles of Venus, over the eight-year period, is further subdivided into four intervals, of 236 days as Morning Star, eight days of disappearance at the inferior conjunction and so forth.

The Dresden Codex totted up thirteen of these eight-year cycles, reaching 104 years, or 13 x 13 Venus years, twice 52 years, which was their 'Calendar Round.' This eight-year Venus almanac thus merged into the 104-year 'Great Venus round,' called the Huehuetiliztli by the Aztecs, created when the 365-day year and the 584-day synodic period of Venus are intermeshed with the divinatory cycle of 260 days. Thirteen repetitions of the eight-year period made up this Great Round. The full planetary system is shown in Geoff Stray's amazing picture opposite.

Losing the leap-year means that Mayan 365-day 'years' followed the 8-year Venus cycle pretty exactly, because, as you'll remember, this is

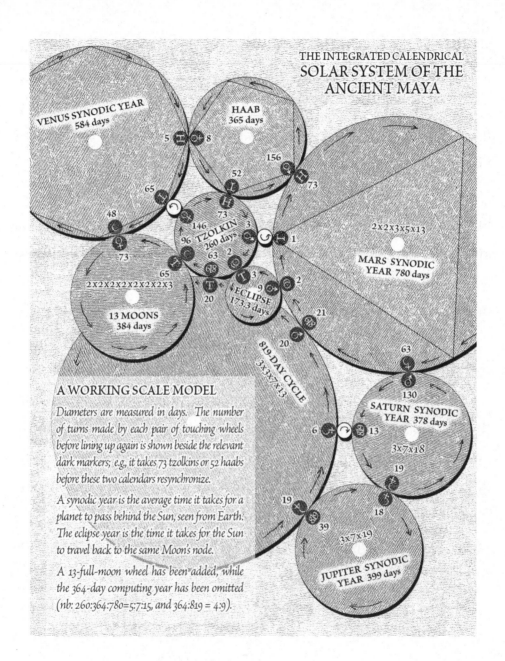

VENUS SYNODIC YEAR
584 days

HAAB
365 days

5   8

156

52

73

65

73

48

146

96   TZOLKIN
260 days

63   2

3

73

3

1

2x2x3x5x13

MARS SYNODIC
YEAR 780 days

73

65

2x2x2x2x2x2x2x3

3

9

2

13 MOONS
384 days

20

ECLIPSE
173.3 days

21

20

819-DAY CYCLE
3x3x7x13

63

A WORKING SCALE MODEL

Diameters are measured in days. The number
of turns made by each pair of touching wheels
before lining up again is shown beside the relevant
dark markers; e.g., it takes 73 tzolkins or 52 haabs
before these two calendars resynchronize.

A synodic year is the average time it takes for a
planet to pass behind the Sun, seen from Earth.
The eclipse year is the time it takes for the Sun
to travel back to the same Moon's node.

A 13-full-moon wheel has been added, while
the 364-day computing year has been omitted
(nb: 260:364:780=5:7:15, and 364:819 = 4:9).

130

SATURN SYNODIC
YEAR 378 days

3x7x18

6   13

19

19

18

3x7x19

39

JUPITER SYNODIC
YEAR 399 days

always two days short of eight years. In central Mexico, friar Toribio Motolina tells us, '...they counted the days by this star and yielded reverence and offered sacrifices to it,' and knew on what day it would reappear. Following the Venus-cycle, the Octaeteris of the ancient Greeks, is a simple way of managing a calendar.

The Dresden Codex also has tables for predicting solar and lunar eclipses, plus an ephemeris for Mars and another for Venus, and a further table of corrections which enable the Venus-table to keep time to one day in five centuries. Twice a year eclipses, solar or lunar, are likely, and an 'eclipse year' keeps in step with these 'eclipse seasons'. Four Tzolkin exactly equal three 'eclipse years' (within 0.01%), the eclipse year being 346.62 days.

Every two years and two months Mars glows very brightly in the sky and goes retrograde, the average interval for this, its synodic period, being exactly three Tzolkin, or 780 days. So the Tzolkin quantum-interval of the Maya cosmology is remarkably multi-purpose, unifying Sun, Moon, Mars and Venus.

And we should now turn briefly to Mars, for, perhaps not surprisingly, Mars is also in love with Venus.

Chapter 12

Mars in Love

Mars and Venus, our two nearest planetary neighbours, perform a particularly beautiful dance. Each grows brighter and dimmer in turn, as each approaches us and passes by. Mars takes just over two years to come close, and Venus just under. Incredibly, these two planetary neighbours of ours kiss the Earth in a 3:4 rhythm, so for every three times that Mars kisses Earth, Venus kisses us four times. The music of their synodic cycles chimes to this simple ratio to an accuracy of 99.8%. And this ratio is a common musical rhythm, much like a waltz, while in tuning harmonics it is the musical fourth, the inversion of the fifth, 3:2.

We experience this coming-closest very differently for each of our neighbours: Venus vanishes from view as it comes closest, whereas Mars grows into its brightest, glowering red in the midnight sky. Mars drew the nearest to us in the whole of human history in 2003.

Red storms rage across Mars as Mars draws nearest to the Sun.

During a Mars-storm the whole surface becomes covered with pink dust, except for its white, icy poles. Iron dust seethes up even covering the highest volcanoes of Mars, volcanos higher than any on Earth.

Mars has extreme seasons! In winter one-third of its atmosphere condenses into its frozen poles, north and south. Huge ravines recall the abundant water which once have gushed around, and which may now all be locked underground, in deep freeze. There must have once been oxygen in its atmosphere too, because of the red iron oxide covering its surface. As well as water and oxygen, there was once also plenty of carbon, now condensed as dry ice at its poles. It seems that Life tried hard to emerge on Mars.

Mars and Venus come close every 334 days, with alternate approaches on opposite sides of the Sun producing a violin-shaped pattern which spins over 32 years (below). This is Mars and Venus'

dance, like the five-fold Earth-Venus rose. Mars, like Earth, has a 24-hour day and the tilt of its axis produces its seasons over its year.

Mars has two potato-shaped, meteor-battered moons, called 'Fear' and 'Terror', *Phobos* and *Deimos*, named after the section in Homer's Iliad where Mars prepares to emerge onto the battlefield:

And he ordered Phobos and Diemos to harness his horses,
While he himself donned his sparkling armour.

There is a strange story about Mars' moons. Jonathan Swift first published *Gulliver's Travels* in 1726 under the name of Lemuel Guller as *Travels into Several Remote Nations of the World in Four Parts.* In the book reference is made to two (then undiscovered) moons of Mars. Astronomers on Laputia (a flying island), says Gulliver, have

... discovered two lesser stars, or satellites, which revolve
around Mars, whereof the innermost is distant from the center
of the primary exactly three of his diameters, and the outermost
five: the former revolves in the space of ten hours, and the latter
in twenty-one and a half.

When the two Martian moons, Phobos and Deimos, were eventually found in 1877 by Asaph Hall, their orbits turned out to be weirdly similar to those discovered by the Laputians Phobos is 6,000

km from the surface of Mars and orbits Mars in 7.7 hours, whereas Swift gave the values 13,600 km and 10 hours. Deimos averages 20,100 km from Mars and orbits in 30.3 hours; Swift gave the values 27,200 km and 21.5 hours. This has never been properly explained.

Mars and Venus also display two quite amazing and beautiful Martineau symmetries. Opposite we see the first of these. Martineau writes of this diagram:

"A dodecahedron made of spheres leaves an internal space which can be filled by another sphere. If the surrounding sphere is Mars' mean orbit, then the radius of the inner sphere matches Venus' orbit with over 99.9% accuracy. Plato hinted that the Earth had a dodecahedral structure, and the dodecahedron was associated with the fifth element of Ether. If Venus and Mars are thought of as being separated by an etheric body (the sphere dodecahedron) then we might expect Earth, whose physical orbit lies wholly in, and near the centre of, that etheric body, to play some part in this geometry. And indeed it does.

The dual of the (dotted) dodecahedron is the icosahedron, the centres of the faces of each producing the other. If, instead of a sphere dodecahedron we now hang a sphere icosahedron inside Mars' mean orbit, then the sphere-centres define the sphere of Earth's mean orbit to 99.9% accuracy. The icosahedron traditionally ruled the element of water, which by its nature and quantity uniquely characterises and facilitates the existence of biological life on Earth.

Here Earth's watery nature emanates the geometry which fixes Mar's orbit."

In a second diagram, we simply observe the fact that Mars and Venus' experience of each other can be thought of as two spheres in exactly the same 3:11 ratio as that defined by the physical sizes of the Earth and Moon, which formed between them.

Bringing us, finally, to the Moon.

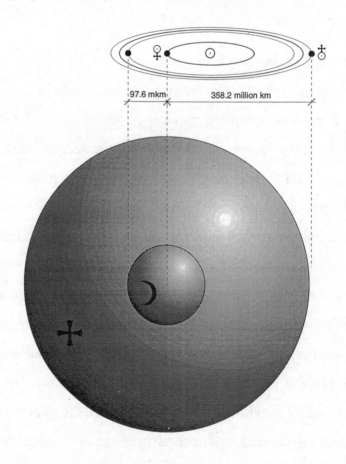

97.6 mkm

358.2 million km

Chapter 13

The Moon and Sleeping Beauty

Who doth not see the measures of the Moon?
Which thirteen times she danceth every year,
And ends her pavan thirteen times as soon
As doth her brother ...

1594 Orchestra, Sir John Davies

The Moon revolves just over thirteen times in space each year (13.37 to be more precise), whereas Venus does this much more slowly, taking eight years (thirteen Venusian years) to revolve twelve times. Luna has the *same* orbit-period as that of its rotation in space, so that it always faces towards us, whereas Venus manages an exquisite 13:12 ratio between these two. The Moon goes round against the stars thirteen times each year, thirteen times faster than the Sun, moving thirteen degrees along the zodiac for every one degree the Sun moves.

So, the number thirteen is strongly lunar as well as Venusian, which may be why some people are superstitious about it.

Thirteen full moons also make a nice number of days. A full moon occurs every 29.53 days, so there are an annoying 12.368 of them every year, but it turns out that thirteen of them (to within 99.98% accuracy) make 384 days, which is three periods of 128 days, or 3 x 128, where 128 is 2 x 2 x 2 x 2 x 2 x 2 x 2, or 2^7.

The Moon takes the shorter interval of 27.3 days to return to any given *star*. At Avebury stone circles, in England, there are 27 and 29 stones in the two inner stone circles - people have been counting these lunar rhythms for some time. Avebury's outer ring has 99 stones, possibly the 99 full moons of the 8-year Venus pentagram.

But we digress ... back to thirteen. As we saw earlier, thirteen is widely used by plants, along with five and eight. Experience this for yourself! Next spring go out and find some pussy willow. Count the buds along a stem. You will see that thirteen buds appear in a slow spiral of five turns. Exactly. Or try it with a thistle flower.

With the suppression of women's rites we lost touch with the lunar side of life and thirteen became unlucky. The Sleeping Beauty fairy-tale describes this. As the cares of the daytime ebbed away, people would gather around the storyteller, whose long memory would return with the quiet of the night-time:

"Once upon a time, there was a king who had a beautiful daughter, and he wished to invite people to a baptism-feast. There were thirteen wise women (or fairies) in the kingdom, but the king only had twelve golden plates."

And so the thirteenth fairy was not invited. Instead, after each of the twelve had given their blessings to the new child, she turned up unannounced and bestowed a curse, concerning how the princess would have to bleed on reaching her fifteenth year.

The king was a sensible fellow who liked the number twelve, because it divided by all sorts of factors, whereas thirteen was an

'irrational' prime number, ugh! As a reasonable man he wanted his daughter to remain white as a lily, he didn't want her to turn crimson with blood. He named her princess 'Aurora', a solar name, in fact that of the golden goddess of the dawn, just as the plates for his party were made of gold, the metal that used to belong to the Sun (the Latin word for gold is *aurum*). No wonder he only had twelve golden plates, expressing the way in which the lunar number thirteen had been ejected from the calendar where it should belong.

It was decreed that there were twelve months only, just as there are twelve hours in the solar day: and these were glued to the solar year, they couldn't move round any more like they used to do, when a thirteenth had to be inserted every few years to keep the year in balance. Thus the king in the story undermined the very fabric of Time, and so it stopped! Everything stopped happening as Time was suspended, until finally a brave prince arrived who was not afraid of bleeding, fighting his way through a thicket of briars (wild roses), to rescue her (shown in Walter Crane's illustration on the previous page). And so Time started up again.

But ... did they live happily ever after? Anxious faces gaze at the storyteller, as he pulls from a back-pocket two crumpled-up playing cards, a King and Queen. But they are the numbers 12

and 13 in the sequence! Shouldn't the King be 12 and the Queen 13? Personal fulfilment depends upon integration, between the feminine-lunar thirteen and the twelve of the Sun's 'golden plates.'

In the Tarot pack the Moon and the Sun are 18 and 19, and in the early 1990s British researcher Robin Heath observed the strange fact that all of the marriage numbers of the Sun, Moon and Earth can be reduced to combinations of the operation of the Golden Section around the key numbers 18 and 19. The evidence for the favour that the Sun and Moon have for 18 and 19 is further indicated both by the Metonic Cycle, which produces full moons at the same calendar dates 19 years later, and the Saros Eclipse Cycle, which results in similar eclipses repeating every 18 years.

In addition, the Moon's Nodes, the crossing points of the Solar and Lunar orbits as viewed from Earth, take 18.6 *years* to rotate once around the heavens or 18³/₅. Heath wondered if this wasn't pointing to 18 + golden section. It turns out that 18.618 *days* squared produces 346.63, a highly accurate value for the Eclipse Year in *days*, which is the length of time it takes for the Sun to return to the same Moon's node (the nodes rotate slowly in the opposite direction to the Sun, Moon, and planets). Adding 18.618 again to this produces 365.25, the number of days in a Solar Year, also 18.618 x 19.618. Then, finally, adding 18.618 *again* gives 383.87, which is 13 lunations, or the number of days between 13 full moons, also 18.618 x 20.618. Incredible don't you think? So:

Eclipse Year = 346.63 = 18.618 x 18.618 days.   +18.618 =

Solar Year = 365.25 = 18.618 x 19.618 days.   + 18.618 =

13 Moons = 383.87 = 18.618 x 20.618 days

More recently, American mathematician Benjamin Bryton, along with writer Scott Olsen, re-phrased the equation for the solar year as

Solar Year = 365.25 = 18.618 x 19.618

$$= \sum_{5,7,12} (Ø^n + Ø^{-n} + 1) = \sum_{6,8,13} (Ø^n + Ø^{-n})$$

Don't worry if you don't understand this equation. Seriously! In summary it is simply the two values of the golden section, Ø = 1.618

or 0.618, applied to the structure of the musical scale, with its 5, 7 or 12 notes depending on the resolution, or 6, 8 and 13 to include the octave. It says that the golden section applied to the structure of the musical scale gives the number of days in a year!

What is going on? And why does no scientist yet seem to be able to explain any of this? Is beauty a lost principle of science? Why are the Sun and Moon the same size in the sky anyway? Is there something we're missing? Is Venus pointing the way to a world where harmony and geometry meet as one? Where magic rules. Is that why nature is so wonderful to behold?

It seems as though Venus spreads her golden beauty to everyone close to her. All who perceive her influences fall under her spell. Everyone wants to dance the perfect dance with her.

Our lovely kissing companion, who turns everything she touches to gold. The Philosopher's Stone.

All who ever meet her fall in love with Venus.

NOTES TO CHAPTERS

Ch. 2. *Rhythmen der Sterne* Joachim Schultz, 1963. Keith Critchlow, *Time Stands Still*, 1979, p.160. John Martineau, *A Book of Coincidence* 1995.

Ch. 3. Archie Roy and M. Ovenden, 'Commensurable ...motions in the Solar System' *Monthly Notices RAS* 1954, 114, 232. Data from K.R.Laing, *Astrophysical Data: Planets & Stars*, 1991 p.41.

Ch. 4. Matila Ghyka, *The Geometry of Art and Life* 1977, Dover NY p.16 on golden ratio and human form.

Ch. 5. E.K.Bigg, 'Lunar and Planetary influences on geomagnetic disturbance' *J Geophyss Res.* 1963, 68, 4099. J.S.Lewis, 'Venus and Earth: another dynamical connection.' *Astronomy & Geophysics* Aug 1998, p.4.8. H. Warm, *Die Signatur De Spharen*, Hamburg, 2002.

Ch. 7. Mary Proctor, *The Book of the Heavens*, 1928 p.98.

Ch. 8. Robert Sullivan, *Captain Cook in the Underworld*, 2002, Auckland U. Press.

Ch. 9. *Goddesses who Rule* Ed Eliz. Benard & Beverly moon, OUP 2000, Ch. 1 Aphrodite, Ancestor of kings B Moon, Ch 4, B. Moon, *Inanna: The Star who became Queen*. 'Akkadian Hymn to Ishtar' translated by Ferris J.Stephens. *Inanna, Lady of the Largest Heart, Poems of the High Priestess Enheduanna* Betty De shong Meador 2001 U of Texas. Sections 60-73 and 143-153 of 'Queen of Countless Divine Powers.' www.angelfire.com/mi/enheduanna E.C.Krupp, *Beyond the Blue Horizon*, OUP 1991. Thomas Heath *Aristarchus of Samos*, Dover 1981 for 1913: the 8 yr cycle.

Ch. 10. G Stray, *The Mayan and other Ancient Calendars*, 2007, John Carlson, 'Venus Regulated warfare & Ritual Sacrifice in Mesoamerica', in *Astronomies and Culture* Ed C.Ruggles and N.Saunders, Colorado 1993. Anthony Aveni, *Skywatchers of Ancient Mexico*, Texas, 2001. http://members.shaw.ca/mjfinley/mainmaya.html

Ch. 11. Heather Cooper and Nigel Henbest, *Mars The Inside Story of the Red Planet*, 2001

Appendix 1

The First Poem

Inanna of ancient Sumer was a dominant goddess. When the Babylonians arrived they continued to worship her but called her Ishtar instead, who was more militaristic. Like Aphrodite much later on, Inanna would couple now and then with a mortal, so that person became king: she chose kings and this did involve ceremonially lying with them. Similar comments could be made about Ishtar: 'But thou, O Ishtar, fearsome mistress of the gods, Thou didst single me out with the glance of thine eyes.' The king acquired the powers of kingship from making love to Inanna.

According to the Sumerian myth, the Huluppu tree was planted beside the Euphrates 'in the first days when everything needed was brought into being.' But the South Wind uprooted it, and the waters of the Euphrates carried it away. Inanna appears, as one 'who walked in fear of the sky god, An,' not yet a queen because she lacked the emblems of her divine status. She rescued the tree and planted it in her garden in Uruk. But, pests invaded her tree: a snake 'who could not be charmed' made its home in the roots, and an anzu bird (part eagle and part lion) reared its young in the branches, and Lilith, a maid who was part woman and part owl, built her home in its trunk. Inanna tried to get these parasites out of her tree, but couldn't. She wept and called upon her brother the Sun, Utu, but he just turned his back on her. Then she called to Gilgamesh, who was the hero of Uruk. He arrived wearing sixty pounds of armour and a large bronze axe, with which he slew the serpent, whereupon the anzu bird and Lilith both fled. The tree became part of the institution of sacred kingship for this earliest literate civilisation, connecting the gods in heaven and their kingdom on earth.

Another story tells how the main city of Uruk acquired its wisdom. Inanna decided to pay a visit to Enki, the god of wisdom: 'I shall honour Enki, the god of wisdom, in Eridu' she said, and when she got there they had a drink together. Rather inebriated, Enki rashly shared the various decrees called *me* to Inanna which were the principles of wisdom, on all sorts of topics. When he had sobered up he regretted this, and sent various monsters to attack the departing Inanna in her Boat of heaven, but she summoned a warrior goddess companion, Ninshubur, who protected her from the monsters. When they arrived in Uruk the people line the canal rejoicing and the me were given out amidst the sounds of drums and tambourines. After Enki has given the *me* to Inanna, he then realises the next day that he doesn't have them any more! We may wish to translate *me* as technical know-how, but it could be more like, original software where one rather lacks a backup copy.

The celestial deity Inanna descended into the underworld. She prepares for this by dressing up, for example she puts on eye-shadow called 'Let him come.' She then passes through its seven gates, obliged to remove one of her seven items of sovereignty and divinity she is wearing, at each step. Finally she arrives naked before the Queen of the Dead, much-feared Erishkigal, who kills her, without a minute's hesitation, and hangs her corpse on a hook. It hangs there as a mere carcass for three days. Ninshubur laments, and seeks for aid. Enki agrees to assist, and fashions two androgynous creatures, who are able to move through the underworld planes. They take some food with them, to revive Inanna, and descend. By expressing empathy and support for Erishkigal's troubles (who is suffering from some other cause) the creatures extract from her the promise of a boon. They ask to be allowed to take Inanna's corpse, which they restore to life. A boon has to be paid, however, as the law of the underworld demands that some substitute be sent down, and Inanna's husband Dumuzi had to go instead, on account of the way he failed to lament when he heard of her death; his sentence was commuted after he bewailed his fate, so he only had to go down into the underworld for some months each year.

POEMS OF ENHEDUANA

We recall the earlier story, about the *me*. The second part has something a bit like a Moon-Venus conjunction. Notice its craggy, primordial tone:

The Great queen of queens,
born for the rightful ME,
born of a fate-laden body,
you are even greater than your own mother,
full of wisdom, foresight, queen over all lands,
who allows existence to many,
I now strike up your fate-determining song!
All powerful divinity, suitable for the ME,
that which you have said magnificently

is the most powerful!
Of unfathomable heart, oh highly driven woman,
of radiant heart, your ME, I will list for you now!
Into my fate-determining Gipar,
I had entered for you.
I, the en-priestess, I, En-hedu-Ana.
While I carried the basket,
I struck up the song of jubilation,
as though I had not lived there,
they offered the death sacrifice.
I came close to the light,
there the light became scorching to me.
I came close to the shadow,
there it was veiled by a storm.
My sweet mouth became venomous.
That with which I gave delight, turned to dust.

. . . . .

The Queen, the strong one,
the ruler over the gathering of the 'en',
she did accept her prayer and sacrifice.
The heart of fate-determining Inanna
has turned to its place.
The light was sweet for her,
delight was spread over her,
full of abundant beauty was she.
As the light of the rising moon,
she too was clothed in enchantment.
Nanna came out to rightfully gaze (at her) in awe,
(he and) her mother Ningal blessed her,
and then the gate post said unto her "Be hailed!"
What each said to the nugig is exalted.

Destroyer of enemy lands,
endowed with the ME from An,
My Queen, draped in enchantment,
to you, Inanna, be glory!

Enheduana received her name when ordained as a priestess of the Moon (from *en*, high priestess, *hedu*, ornament, *ana* of the sky-god). Her primal poem, her jubilant song, was to Inanna. It's hard to believe these are words from 4,300 years ago, when the pyramids were being built. The hundred or so tablets recording her incantations date from a period five centuries later, but are reckoned to be copies of earlier material. The arrival of decent English translations is recent, maybe just a few years ago - but, no-one seems to be discussing the matter. Here for comparison is a hymn to Ishtar, in the later Babylonian culture of c.1600 BC:

She is clothed with pleasure and love.
She is laden with vitality, charm and voluptuousness.
Ishtar is clothed with pleasure and love.
She is laden with vitality, charm and voluptuousness.
In lips she is sweet; life is in her mouth.
At her appearance rejoicing becomes full.
She is glorious; veils are thrown over her head.
Her figure is beautiful; her eyes are brilliant.
The goddess - with her there is counsel.
The fate of everything she holds in her hand.
At her glance there is created joy,

Appendix 2

The Connecting Link

There is one interconnecting equation which is very useful, and not difficult. Let's start off with the Moon: its two primary cycles are its 27.3 - day orbit-period, in which time it travels round once against the stars, and the 29.5 - day synodic cycle. These two cycles are linked via the length of the year:

$$1/27.3 - 1/365.24 = 1/29.5 \text{ days}$$

Picture these reciprocal functions as rates of movement: the orbit speed of the Moon, less that of the 'Sun' (Earth's period going round the Sun), equals the relative speed of motion between the Sun and Moon.

Next, let's ask: how often does Venus grow into the bright Evening Star? That interval will be its 'synodic' period. The approximate years of Venus and Earth are put into it, and then out comes the rough answer:

$$1/224 - 1/365 = 1/584 \text{ days}$$

Moving onto Mercury, how long is the Mercury day? To find that, its spin period ('axial rotation'), together with its year (its 'orbit period') are put into this same equation, and then we find:

Spin period	Year	Day
1/59.6 –	1/88.0 =	1/176 days

i.e., its 'day' lasts a whole 176 earth-days. Asimov's robots on their visit to Mercury would have seen the 'terminator,' i.e. the day-night boundary, return to the same spot on the ground over this period. The length of Venus' day is vital to the harmonies we have examined, and we derive this likewise from its orbit-period (i.e., year) plus spin-period:

Spin period	Year	Day
1/243 +	1/225 =	1/117 days

See! It's really much easier than you think!

Quiz Question: which has the longer day, Mercury or Venus?

Answer: Mercury — Its day is twice its year – while Venus' day is, roughly, half its year.